I0019822

Xinyu Zhou

Testing and Verifying Web Services

Xinyu Zhou

Testing and Verifying Web Services

From the Researcher's Perspective

VDM Verlag Dr. Müller

Impressum/Imprint (nur für Deutschland/ only for Germany)

Bibliografische Information der Deutschen Nationalbibliothek: Die Deutsche Nationalbibliothek verzeichnet diese Publikation in der Deutschen Nationalbibliografie; detaillierte bibliografische Daten sind im Internet über http://dnb.d-nb.de abrufbar.

Alle in diesem Buch genannten Marken und Produktnamen unterliegen warenzeichen-, marken- oder patentrechtlichem Schutz bzw. sind Warenzeichen oder eingetragene Warenzeichen der jeweiligen Inhaber. Die Wiedergabe von Marken, Produktnamen, Gebrauchsnamen, Handelsnamen, Warenbezeichnungen u.s.w. in diesem Werk berechtigt auch ohne besondere Kennzeichnung nicht zu der Annahme, dass solche Namen im Sinne der Warenzeichen- und Markenschutzgesetzgebung als frei zu betrachten wären und daher von jedermann benutzt werden dürften.

Coverbild: www.purestockx.com

Verlag: VDM Verlag Dr. Müller Aktiengesellschaft & Co. KG
Dudweiler Landstr. 125 a, 66123 Saarbrücken, Deutschland
Telefon +49 681 9100-698, Telefax +49 681 9100-988, Email: info@vdm-verlag.de
Zugl.: Tempe, Arizona State University, Diss., 2008

Herstellung in Deutschland:
Schaltungsdienst Lange o.H.G., Zehrensdorfer Str. 11, D-12277 Berlin
Books on Demand GmbH, Gutenbergring 53, D-22848 Norderstedt
Reha GmbH, Dudweiler Landstr. 99, D- 66123 Saarbrücken
ISBN: 978-3-639-07788-9

Imprint (only for USA, GB)

Bibliographic information published by the Deutsche Nationalbibliothek: The Deutsche Nationalbibliothek lists this publication in the Deutsche Nationalbibliografie; detailed bibliographic data are available in the Internet at http://dnb.d-nb.de.

Any brand names and product names mentioned in this book are subject to trademark, brand or patent protection and are trademarks or registered trademarks of their respective holders. The use of brand names, product names, common names, trade names, product descriptions etc. even without
a particular marking in this works is in no way to be construed to mean that such names may be regarded as unrestricted in respect of trademark and brand protection legislation and could thus be used by anyone.

Cover image: www.purestockx.com

Publisher:
VDM Verlag Dr. Müller Aktiengesellschaft & Co. KG
Dudweiler Landstr. 125 a, 66123 Saarbrücken, Germany
Phone +49 681 9100-698, Fax +49 681 9100-988, Email: info@vdm-verlag.de

Copyright © 2008 VDM Verlag Dr. Müller Aktiengesellschaft & Co. KG and licensors
All rights reserved. Saarbrücken 2008

Produced in USA and UK by:
Lightning Source Inc., 1246 Heil Quaker Blvd., La Vergne, TN 37086, USA
Lightning Source UK Ltd., Chapter House, Pitfield, Kiln Farm, Milton Keynes, MK11 3LW, GB
BookSurge, 7290 B. Investment Drive, North Charleston, SC 29418, USA
ISBN: 978-3-639-07788-9

To my mother Xianghua Chen, and to my father Hongjun Zhou.
To my wife Bo Liang.

ACKNOWLEDGMENTS

I first would like to thank my advisor, Professor Wei-Tek Tsai, for mentoring me during the past 4 years. Without his inspirations and guidance, I could not finish my PhD.

Many thanks to my PhD committee members: Professor Charles Colbourn, Professor Hessam Sarjoughian, and Professor Guoliang Xue, for their insightful advices and kindly guidance. Thanks to Dr. Yinong Chen and Professor Yann-Hang Lee for all the discussion we had through my studies.

Thanks to my colleagues and friends, for the friendship and their contributions to this book. They are Chun Fan, Bingnan Xiao, Weiwei Song, Xiao Wei, Dawei Zhang, Jingjing Xu, Zhibin Cao, Qian Huang, and Xin Sun.

Last, and foremost, I want to thank my family members: my mother Xianghua Chen, my father Hongjun Zhou, and my wife Bo Liang, for their deepest love, understanding, and confidence in me.

TABLE OF CONTENTS

LIST OF FIGURES

LIST OF TABLES

CHAPTER 1
INTRODUCTION AND MOTIVATION

1.1 Motivation

Service-Oriented Architecture (SOA) and its implementation Web Services (WS) received significant attention as major computer companies, such as IBM, Microsoft, Oracle, SAP, Sun Microsystems, and etc., are adopting this new approach to develop software and systems. SOA advocates run-time system integration of loosely coupled services across heterogeneous platforms in a distributed environment [200]. SOA improves the flexibility of system development. However, trustworthiness becomes a serious problem and appropriate tradeoffs have to be paid [45][111].

Traditionally, a software system is developed within a single organization. Requirements are centrally managed and quality-control policies are uniformly enforced. Different teams working on different subsystems trust each other and their deliveries are consistent and can be easily integrated. In SOA approach, systems are generated by integrating services from different providers published on the Internet. In most cases, services are self-contained and distributed components that are maintained by independent vendors [200]. System developers look up services through third-party service brokers who maintain the directory of registration information of the available services. It is hard for different parties to trust each other unless certain agreement has been achieved regarding system quality and security. Therefore, trustworthiness has been a major problem that hampers WS from wide applications in industry. Trustworthiness is an important issue in SOA, because SOA and services

- are based on *unreliable* and *unsecured* open Internet infrastructure, yet they are expected to be trustworthy.
- have a loosely coupled architecture, yet they are expected to interoperate and collaborate closely and seamlessly with other UDDI registries.
- involve runtime discovery, dynamic binding with multi-parties including middleware and other WS, and runtime composition using existing WS. Thus, WS must support dynamic and runtime behaviors.
- dynamic composition and re-composition to cope with the changing environment and changing requirements. Current technology did not address the dynamic feature of service registries. For example, the physical address of service registries may keep

changing.

- can be invoked by unknown parties with unpredictable or malicious requests.
- may go down from time to time. SOA must support dynamic configuration and reconfiguration to support fault-tolerant computing.
- are distributed and heterogeneous.

To address the challenge, some verification mechanisms are proposed to establish the trustworthiness among different parties [45][111][24][176][181][172][182][210][212]. However, SOA differs from traditional software architecture in various ways and imposes new challenges to traditional testing techniques. These new problems include:

- Collaborative Testing: Cooperation and collaboration among different verification activities and stakeholders including service provider, service requestors, and service brokers.
- Specification-Based Testing: SOA proposes a fully specification-based process. WS define a XML-based protocol stack to facilitate service inter-communication and inter-operation. Specifications in, such as WSDL, OWL-S, WSFL, etc., describe the basic information of service features. Hence, test cases have to be automatically generated based on the specifications.
- Run-time verification: All activities regarding service publishing, discovering, matching, composition, binding, execution, verification, and monitoring are implemented at run-time. To fit into the dynamic process, a dynamic verification is necessary to verify the dynamic changing attributes of SOA.
- Different implementations of the same specification: For the same specification of a service requirement, many alternative implementations could be available online. Effective algorithms are needed to rank and select the best WS.

Web services and service-oriented architecture are emerging technologies that are changing the way we develop and use computer software. As software structure is shifting from Object-Oriented architecture to Service-Oriented architecture (SOA), the verification technologies are required to improve to support the verification of SOA accordingly. However, the lack of SOA-friendly verification mechanisms hindered the advance of SOA considerably. The distributed and dynamic features add other difficulties of SOA verification.

This research tries to provide two types of verification mechanism to ensure the trustworthiness of SOA: static verification and dynamic verification. Static verification refers to the mechanisms that verify the SOA while the involved services are in standby status for invocation, while dynamic verification refers to verification mechanisms that support verification during service invocation.

1.2 Introduction

1.2.1 SOA and Service Registries

Service-Oriented Architecture (SOA) and the associated Web Services (WS) are emerging technologies that are changing the way computer software is designed and used. An application in typical SOA is comprised of three parties: *service provider*, *service consumer* and *service registry*. Among the three parties, service registry is pivotal, because it is responsible for the collaboration between services providers and service consumers. Many industrial standards have been defined for service registries. UDDI specification developed by OASIS is one such a standard. Many UDDI specification compliant service registries (UDDI registries) exists today, such as AUDDI [12], jUDDI [84], WebLogic Server UDDI Registry [17], WebSphere UDDI Registry [79], Microsoft Enterprise UDDI Services [109], Novell Nsure UDDI Server [122], OracleAS UDDI Registry [127], SAP UDDI Public Registry [149] and Sun Java WSDP Registry Server [162].

A typical UDDI registry consists of UDDI Entities and a set of *UDDI Interfaces* for external parties to access its entities. External parties can not access UDDI entities directly. They can access the internal UDDI entities through the *UDDI Interfaces*. The interfaces are designed for the operation of three types of interfaces:

- Discover and subscribe Interfaces for service consumers to find appropriate services and use them.
- Registration Interfaces for services providers to register their services into the UDDI Registry.
- Management Interfaces for UDDI operators to manage the UDDI Registry, and for service providers to customize their own services. The management Interfaces can be further classified into the following categories.

1.2.2 Roadmap of Service Registries

To be trustworthy, SOA must assured for security, reliability, and interoperability. Interoperability is particular important issue, because WS can be discovered automatically and invoked remotely, and SOA applications can be dynamically composed using WS discovered at runtime. Currently, WS are mainly assured by their providers. An independent assurance mechanism is needed to verify, validate, and evaluate WS objectively, so that WS users (application builders) can make runtime decisions based on an intelligent and unbiased evaluation.

This section presents comparison among the recent UDDI version 2, version 3, and the proposed federated UDDI, as summarized in Table 1. The comparison is based on the interface and entity criteria. In a federated UDDI Registry, entities may be organized in an ontology manner. In addition to the existing management services, policy management services should also be included as another management tool to enable policy-based management on federated UDDI.

Table 1 UDDI Version 2, Version 3 and the Proposed Federated UDDI Registry

Category	Details	UDDI V2	UDDI V3	Dynamic & Federated UDDI
UDDI Entities	Ontology-based	×	×	possible
	Ontology update	×	×	Uniform/incremental update/replication
Topological Characteristics	Distributed	×	×	√
	Federated	×	×	√
	Hierarchical	×	×	√
	Distributed	×	×	√
Interfaces for Service Providers	Service Publish	√	√	√
	Service Check in/out	×	×	√
UDDI Management Interfaces	Multi-language support	×	√	√
	Interoperability	×	×	√
	Dynamic	×	×	√
	Federation between registries	×	for Publisher key management Only	√
	Entries version update	×	×	Uniform/incremental update/replication
	Validation of services	×	limited	Various approaches
	Test Scripts Publish	×	×	√
	Ontology Management	×	×	√
Interfaces for Service Consumers	Service Subscribe	preliminary	Many	More
	Inter-Registry Query	×	×	√
	Application Template Publish	×	×	√
	Collaboration Template Publish	×	×	√
	Test Scripts Publish	×	×	√
Policy-based Security	Support for digital signature	×	√	√

Mechanism	Policy support	×	Only for Key Management	√
	Policy Specification	×	×	√
	Policy enforcement	×	×	√
	Simulation support	×	×	√
	Monitor	×	×	√
	Visualization	×	×	√

1.2.3 Static Verification and CV&V

Static verification can be performed during the whole service development lifecycle, including the requirement phase, design phase, deploy phase and testing phase. However, in this study, static verification is referred to as the testing after the services are deployed and ready for invocation request (i.e., service standby status).

Many testing approaches were proposed to address the static verification of SOA. The work proposed in [43] categorized several testing techniques for WS including: proof-of-concept testing, functional testing, regression testing, load/stress testing, and monitoring. [114] suggested that WS testing should include: basic WS functionality; SOAP messages; WSDL files; publishing, finding, binding capabilities of an SOA; asynchronous capabilities of WS; the SOAP intermediary capability; the quality of service of WS; dynamic runtime capabilities; SOAP and WS interoperability; and WS performance and load testing. [100] discussed that all three parties of WS including clients, providers, and brokers, should be involved in WS testing. In the meantime, some commercial tools were developed for WS testing [53][55][208][131].

Service-Oriented Architecture (SOA) and its implementation Web Services (WS) received significant attention as major computer companies, such as IBM, Microsoft, Oracle, SAP, Sun Microsystems, and etc., are adopting this new approach to develop software and systems. SOA advocates run-time system integration of loosely coupled services across heterogeneous platforms in a distributed environment [200]. SOA improves the flexibility of system development. However, trustworthiness becomes a serious problem and appropriate tradeoffs have to be paid during WS testing [45][111].

Traditionally, a software system is developed a single organization. Requirements are centrally managed and quality-control policies are uniformly enforced. Different teams working on different subsystems trust each other and their deliveries are consistent and can be easily integrated. In SOA approach, systems are generated by integrating services from different providers published on the Internet. In most cases, services are self-contained and distributed components that are maintained by independent vendors [200]. System developers look up services through third-party service brokers who maintain the directory of registration information of the available services. It is hard for different parties to trust each other unless certain agreement has been achieved regarding system quality and security. Therefore, trustworthiness has been a major problem that hampers WS from wide applications in industry.

Traditional software is tested using IV&V (Independent Verification and Validation) model, in which testing is done by an independent team different from the development team. This is a good practice. However it is not sufficient for WS testing because WS can be composed of constituent WS developed by different vendors and thus need to be tested collaboratively by multiple parties: service clients, brokers, providers including competing service providers, and other independent organizations. Thus, WS verification needs a new model: CV&V (Collaborative Verification and Validation). Under this model, the service providers can still perform IV&V during the development of WS, but when a service registers at a service broker, the service provider must provide a set of sample test cases. Then all the parties including clients, service brokers, and service providers collaborate to perform CV&V. All parties can submit test scripts. A test script defines a sequence of test cases to be used to test the WS. The infrastructure can also generate its own test scripts based on formal methods such as model checking or from extended WSDL, OWL-S. The provided test scripts must be validated before they can be applied to test WS. The validated test scripts will be added into the test script database. The table below compares and contrasts the IV&V and CV&V techniques.

1.2.4 Policy-based Dynamic Verification

Policy-based computing has been extensively studied and applied in many domains, such as in telecommunication [40] and management [46]. Policy could be viewed as an assertion, predicate, or constraint, to specify the system requirement. In the ebSOA (Electronic Business Service Oriented Architecture) [51] proposed by OASIS, policy is defined as "the governing directives and regulations that guide the processes and business of the entity and its transactions with other entities." According to Pleeger [135] and Burns [30], a policy is a statement of the intent of policy makers or administrators of a computing system, specifying how the system should be used. In the WS-Policy recommendation [201] submitted to the W3C Consortium, a policy is defined as a collection of assertions, and each of these policy assertions represent an individual requirement, capability, or other property of a behavior. XACML-Based Web Services Policy Constraint Language (WS-PolicyConstraints) [202] gives the definition of policy as "a set of rules that describe some aspect of the behavior of an entity". More concretely, and as used in this specification, policy is an expression describing all the acceptable sets of constraints on items in a given vocabulary.

Policy could be viewed as an assertion, predicate, or constraint, to specify the system requirement. However, policy is different from assertion in many different aspects.

- Assertion poses constraints on the programming language level, while policy is a model-driven approach of specifying expected system behaviors.

- Assertion is enforced by programming language, while policy specification is delivered along with executable code.

- Assertion does not support monitoring mechanism. In a policy-based system, the system behavior is monitored. The monitor will notify the policy enforcement component when triggering event is detected.

- Assertion is manually placed where the system is error prone. This method relies heavily on programmer's experience. While policy enforcement can be enforced all through the system execution. The level of abstraction of policies facilitates their expression in user-friendly languages such as controlled natural language.

- Policies are more concise and easier to understand, share and maintain, especially in a global open environment such as the web, where self-documenting specifications are one of the current approaches to enabling interoperability.

- Policy can be used only to enforce a security policy, but also to enable negotiations and explanations. For example, in the emerging area of service oriented computing, the word "policy" is sometimes used to refer to the orchestration of elementary and compound services.

A policy-based system has the advantage of flexibility. Traditionally, policies are considered to be requirements and are hard-coded into the system implementation. For instance, if a policy states that "passwords must be at least 6-character long", there must exist a snippet of code in the system implementation that checks the length of passwords. Hard-coded policies can cause major problems such as:

It is difficult and expensive to change. Whenever a policy needs to be changed (e.g. the system administrator wants to increase the minimum length of valid passwords from 6-character long to 8-character long), the whole system has to be shut down. The code needs to be inspected, modified, recompiled, and redeployed. The process is lengthy and error prone. It significantly increases an organization's operating expenses and risk. Shutting down a mission-critical system, in most cases, is prohibitive and may cause disastrous consequences to the mission.

It is difficult to manage. Hard-coded policies do not separate the policy specification from the system implementation. Policies spread over everywhere in the system implementation. If a policy maker wants to know "How many policies are there in the system" or "What are the policies that are defined on the role of Supporting Arms Coordinator", there is no easy way to find out the answers.

Here we give an example of policy:

- Drivers are not allowed to disarm the Car Alarm System after 11:00pm
- No kids are allowed to go out before finish his homework.

Policies are ubiquitous in most, if not all, computing systems. However, one might not be aware of their existence, because most policies are coded into a system's implementation by functional requirements, language features, and design decisions. For example, if a policy says, "passwords must be at least 8 characters long", there must exist a segment of code in the system that checks the length of passwords. This traditional approach to implementing a policy-handling system has some limitations:

- It does not separate policy specification from policy implementation.
- Policies are difficult and expensive to change. Adding new policies or updating / removing existing policies requires modifying the policies, recompiling and redeploying these policies into the system.

If policy specifications and implementations are separated, any change of policies can be easily implemented without changing the architecture of the system, and this significantly simplifies the entire process. *Policy specification languages* are an attempt to meet the above requirements. A policy specification language defines entities (including subjects and objects) and their attributes as well as the actions that can be given. A policy is thus a binding of entities and their attributes to specified actions. What entities, attributes and actions can be represented depends on the concrete system in which policies are to be specified.

Some of benefits of employing policy specification languages to implement a policy-handling system are:

- Policy specification languages enable policies to be defined, independent from a concrete system implementation.
- Policy specification languages are to be interpreted by a policy engine at runtime, which makes dynamical policy changes possible.
- Policy specification languages formalize the intent of the controller into a form that can

be read and interpreted by systems.

- Policy specification languages are high-level languages, which makes it easy to learn and use by policy makers who are normally non-programmers.

Policy management consists of many large-scale problems, including policy specification, policy deployment, policy maintenance, and policy enforcement. New research direction in Policy literature is how to build dynamic, distributed, adaptive, and intelligent policy management systems.

CHAPTER 2
TESTING SOA APPLICATIONS: REVIEW AND PERSPECTIVES

2.1 Introduction

Service-Oriented Architecture (SOA) and Web services have received significant attention recently. SOA is used in the Web 2.0 [1], which facilitates collaborative sharing and communication for all participants. One reason that prevents services to be widely used, particular those services developed by third parties, is whether these services are reliable enough to be trusted in mission-critical applications. As reported in CBDi Forum in November 2002:

"Web services are not yet widely used because of reliability concern. The concern is 'Will the service work correctly every time when I need it?' As yet few are thinking about the issues of testing and certification. We suggest that testing and certification of Web services is not business as usual and that new solutions are needed to provide assurance that services can really be trusted."

While the security issues of services have been studied and produced many standards such as WS-Security, WS-SecureConversation, WS-Privacy, WS-Trust, XACML and SAML, The intensive study on Internet security has produced the level of security that customers are confident with. For example, people are now doing their banking, billing, and shopping through Internet. However, despite progress in SOA, service verification and testing techniques are not mature enough to support dependable and trustworthy computing. The current web service and SOA research is largely focused on protocols, functionality, transactions, ontology, composition, semantic web, and interoperability. Little research has been done on dependability and trustworthiness of services developed by different service providers.

In software development in SOA, application builders can search and discover services from service brokers and use services provided by different services providers. Who is responsible for the overall dependability of a system that consists of many services developed by different service providers? At what layers should reliability and security mechanisms be deployed? These are new challenges. To address these new problems, efforts from all the involved parties are necessary, including policy makers such as government agencies that may propose reliability criteria, standard making consortiums to establish the means to evaluate those criteria, industries such as service providers and brokers to follow the agreed criteria, service consumers to use only those certified services, and research institutions to provide technology for reliability modeling and evaluation.

Current web services are based on UDDI or ebXML server that provides directory and brokerage services similar to the telephone yellow book. A service broker is not responsible for the quality of services it refers to. Thus, the trustworthiness of service presents a concern for users. Traditional dependability techniques such as correctness proof, fault-tolerant computing, model checking, testing, and evaluation, can be used to improve the trustworthiness of individual service. However, these techniques need to be redesigned to handle the dynamic applications composed of service at runtime.

Verification can be enforced through the entire SOA development lifecycle, including modeling phase, development phase, composition phase, deployment phase, and even at runtime. A traditional approach to verify an SOA application via the IV&V (Independent Verification and Validation) is to have all the service code available, and let an independent team to test each code, and then test the application exhaustively using all the combinations of services. In this way, a SOA application can be composed without dynamic testing, because all the combinations have been tested earlier. However, this approach can be too expensive to implement, because the number of services available as well as their combinations can be huge. Another serious issue of this approach is that service providers may not be willing to share the source code, and thus making this approach infeasible.

A number of studies have been done to address the testing problems of SOA applications. In [34], Canfora and Di Penta presented the opportunities and challenges in SOA testing. In general, testing SOA software needs to address the following:

- SOA protocol testing: Testing functionality and performance of SOA protocols, e.g., testing SOAP, testing service publishing, testing discovery, evaluate protocol performance, evaluate asynchronous nature of SOA operations;
- Test and evaluate individual services: Test, evaluate and rank services with source code (both white-box and black-box testing can be used) and those without source code (black-box testing only);
- Test an integrated application or composite services: multi-level integration testing and evaluation with or without all the source code.
- Quality of services evaluation: performance evaluation;
- Interoperability testing: conformance testing to ensure SOA protocol compliance;
- Regression testing: Modification compliance;

- Load/stress testing: Examine system behavior at different loads;
- Monitoring: Tracking runtime behaviors and evaluation;
- Security testing: Ensure the enforcement of security properties;
- Testing service brokers: ensure service brokers such as a UDDI broker to perform registration and discovery properly, and also enhance a service broker to act as an independent verification agent to verify and rank services submitted for publication.
- SOA test and evaluation framework: Various integrated frameworks with processes and tools to test and evaluate services and applications.

2.2 Categorization of SOA Testing Techniques

Current SOA applications are not dependable. Testing and other verification mechanisms are highly needed. This section reviews existing SOA testing technologies from two dimensions: the SOA lifecycle, and the integration level, as shown in Figure 1.

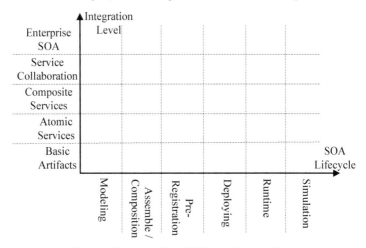

Figure 1 Categorization of SOA testing techniques

2.3 SOA Integration Level

Figure 2 illustrates the SOA integration levels and lifecycles. Different from traditional applications, SOA is a multi-level architecture and each level consists of various SOA artifacts.

- System specification level: artifacts on this level are the specifications of the SOA applications. Two major artifacts on this level are the workflow specification and the policy specification. Workflow specification specifies the process and behavior of the SOA application, while policy specification specifies the constraints of the SOA system.

- Workflow instances level: artifacts on this level are the implementations of the SOA system.   Each workflow specification may have multiple implementations, published by different SOA application providers.

- Service specification level: SOA applications bind its services with suitable service specifications rather than service instance. Service specifications specify the required information about the service, such as the input/output interfaces of the services. A number of service instances may implement the same service specification.

- Service instances level: this level contains the atomic/composite services. An atomic service is a service that does not depend on other services. An composite service is a service that uses other services.

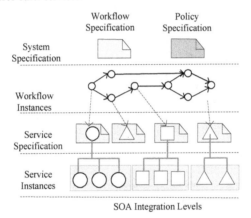

Figure 2 SOA integration levels

2.4 SOA Application Development Lifecycles

Another dimension to categorize the SOA testing techniques is by the SOA application development lifecycles. In Wikipedia [199], SOA lifecycle is defined as "a model that is intended to illustrate relationships and dependencies between various independent lifecycles that comprise a mature, enterprise SOA program." SOA lifecycle is a multi-phase model, including planning, development, and deployment. This section reviews the related works on the SOA lifecycle model.

2.4.1 OO Lifecycles and SOA Lifecycles

Object-Oriented (OO) software lifecycle are different from SOA software lifecycle as shown in. Table 2.

Table 2 OO lifecycles and SOA lifecycles

Lifecycle	Tasks in OO Computing	Tasks in SOA Computing	Difference
Analysis	System specification document	Both System specifications document and XML-based document, including BPEL, WSDL etc	Models are different. SOA has BPEL, PSML, workflow, UDDI etc. In addition, SOA has service-oriented modeling.
Design	Design software artifacts, such as objects, interfaces etc.	Design services only. External services should be included in the design.	OO design can use UML and model-driven approach. UML does not fit SOA very well. SOA can use external services without service code.
Development	Coding, programming all the artifacts.	Can use external services using service assemble/composition techniques	OOP can use extreme/agile programming. SOA paradigm cannot fully adopt extreme/agile programming.
Testing	Unit test, integration test, system test, etc	Can apply the same test techniques for own code. Do not have code for external services.	SOA can not perform whitebox testing for external services.
Deploy	Deliver the executable application.	Publish/registration into the service registry.	Services are deployed on the owners' server. Information about the service, such as interface information, are published on a service registry.
Runtime	Dynamic binding on methods by polymorphism	Service binding	SOA is more dynamic than OO. OO has dynamic binding on methods only by polymorphism, while SOA has dynamic binding on services.

2.4.2 IBM's SOA lifecycle

IBM has been developing and enhancing an SOA Foundation Architecture [71][82] to outline an integrated SOA application development and operation processes: model and assemble (development), deploy and manage (operation) as illustrated in Figure 3.

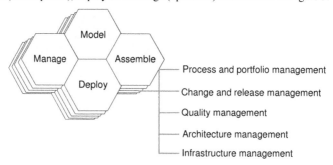

Figure 3 IBM SOA Foundation Architecture

Following the process, SOA application developers build their SOA application by first modeling the application after gathering requirements and designing business processes. After processes are optimized, they implement them by assembling new and existing services to form these business processes. They then deploy these assets into a highly secure and integrated service environment. After the business processes are deployed, SOA builders manage and monitor these processes. Information gathered during the manage phase is fed back into the life cycle to enable continuous process improvement. During all these stages, governance and processes are performed to provide guidance and oversight for the target SOA application [82].

IBM SOA foundation model is not only a cyclic process, but also a linear process, which means there are no branches. Furthermore, the entire process is driven by the same model. The entire process will be controlled and orchestrated through the governance policies. IBM SOA foundation architecture is based on a model-driven process. This looping back process along with the governance and other processes can be delivered together with the target SOA application to the user. When there is a need of changing the application architecture, the user can re-specify the system model, and the application can be re-assembled and re-deployed.

In [54], Endrei and his colleagues introduce the process of selecting and applying business, application and runtime patterns and discuss the guidelines for applying the patterns and service-oriented architecture approach to a sample business scenario and for selecting services technologies. It also provides detailed design, development, and runtime guidelines for several scenarios, including synchronous and asynchronous service buses, UDDI service directory, and theWeb Services Gateway.

In [11], Arsanjani lists the key activities that are needed for the analysis and design required to build a SOA, as illustrated in Table 6.

Based on the IBM SOA Foundation Architecture, IBM proposed service-oriented analysis and design (SOAD) [23], which adds innovations for service repositories, service orchestration, and the ESB.

2.4.3 SAP's SOA lifecycle

In [145] and [146], SAP proposed the SOA lifecycle that is supported by the business processes management (BPM) [147], as illustrated in Figure 4. The lifecycle includes five phases: scoping, business modeling, service modeling, implementation design, verification & justification.

- Scoping: in the scoping phase, the requirements are documented in the specification.

Objectives of the SOA application are defined.

- Business modeling: in this phase, business models are defined, analyzed, and refined.
- Service modeling: in this phase, service model is defined, designed, analyzed.
- Implementation design: the SOA application is designed and implemented.
- Verification & justification: in this phase, various verification and justification techniques are applied to the SOA application, such as sanity check, and cost estimation.

Figure 4 SOA lifecycle supported by BPM

In [148], the SOA development cycle is further discussed in detail, as shown in Figure 5. In this development cycle, the business requirements are collected and modeled. Then, service is defined and its proxy is generated. After that, service is implemented and registered into the service broker, and then service can be discovered and composed by service consumers into their enterprise SOA applications.

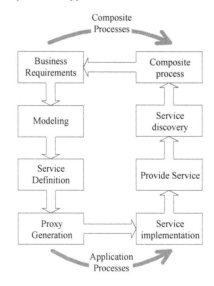

Figure 5 SOA development cycle

2.4.4 ASU's Model-Driven SOA Lifecycle

We have proposed a model-driven SOA development process with V&V activities as shown in Figure 6. The proposed SOA lifecycle is a recursive process. The SOA lifecycle emphasizes verification and pre-verification for services. Before each phase in the lifecycle, the services should be pre-verified.

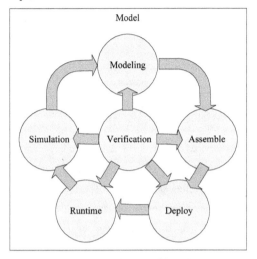

Figure 6 ASU's SOA lifecycle

- The SOA lifecycle supports online mode and offline mode for services, as shown in Figure 7. The services can be in two modes: online mode and offline mode. In offline mode, various verification mechanisms can be applied to test the service, including unit testing, integration, workflow testing, simulation and check-in testing. In online mode, three technologies can be used, including policy enforcement, performance testing and monitoring.

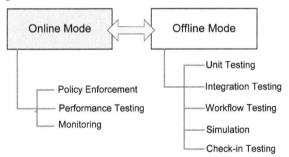

Figure 7 Testing services at online/offline mode

- The proposed lifecycle supports pre-registration testing for services, as shown in Figure 8. SOA applications are composed by workflow and services, and each service specification may have a group of candidate services. If the service provider wants to register their services into the service broker, the submitted services must pass the unit testing first. For all selected services, they must pass the integration testing as well.

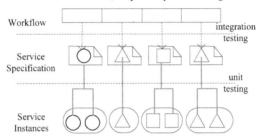

Figure 8 Services must pass unit testing and integration testing

- The proposed lifecycle also supports verification for simulation. Figure 9 illustrates the simulation-based verification mechanism. The verification has four concurrent processes: System execution, simulation and evaluation, policy enforcement and controller. When the system is execution, the simulation and evaluation process can simulate and evaluate the system behaviors. Meanwhile, policy can be enforced by policy engines. All the three processes are controlled by controller. This verification mechanism is especially helpful for mission critical SOA systems.

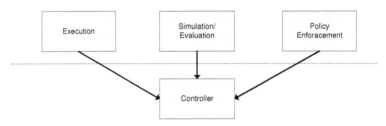

Figure 9 Testing by simulation

- This lifecycle model also supports Completeness and consistency (C&C) analysis. Web service requirements are often incomplete, inconsistent, and ambiguous. Faults introduced in this stage of development have been shown to be difficult and more expensive to correct than faults introduced later in the lifecycle. Completeness and consistency (C&C) analysis on requirements aims at eliminating requirement-related faults. Specification-Based Test Case Selection is the topology-based rapid systematic positive and negative testing approach that assures the trustworthiness of WS by completeness and consistency (C&C) analysis, pattern identification technique, rigorous positive and negative test case generation. These techniques not only perform positive testing that verify the required functionality but also perform negative testing that investigates the robustness of WS under irregular inputs. Negative testing is particular important for WS, because a WS can be composed of WS from different service providers without the availability of the source codes.

- The model-driven SOA lifecycle is based on the single model multiple analyses (SMMA) approach. The idea is that a core model is used to derive other models for analysis, simulation, and code generation. In this way, SOA system development can be rapidly performed. Some models are suitable for certain analyses, while others are more suitable for other kinds of analyses. For example, the state model is suitable for reachability analysis, simulation, and data flow analysis, but it is not the most suitable model for analyzing data security, reliability, and integrity, and it may be difficult to derive the state model from other models. The SMMA simply says that once the core model is updated, rest of the models needed for analyses are automatically generated from the core model, and other models may include the state model, code model, policy, and architecture-based reliability model. The core model also need to be consistent with SOA, specifically the core model should support service specification, workflow specification, ontology, and possibly even architecture.

2.4.5 Summary of SOA Application Development Lifecycles

Model-driven approach implies that model must be correct. Otherwise model-driven approach will fail as the model is the root. All the lifecycle models are model-driven. However, there is no consensus about best modeling language for SOA application modeling yet. There are several schools of thoughts:

- Use UML-- UML is indeed the industrial de factor standard language for modeling OO applications. However, OO software architecture is often different from SOA software architecture because OO architecture often has classes, inheritance, design patterns, and architecture patterns. But SOA application architecture has workflows and services, and SOA architecture. Another issue is the UML models often are not in synchronized with the corresponding code, and furthermore, test case generation from UML is another issue. While test case generation from UML has been studied, but application of these model-driven testing has not been fully investigated for SOA software.

- Use BPEL or other SOA standards to model applications. There are distinct advantages of taking this approach because a BPEL model can be used to generate executable code, and also the model can be in synchronized with the code because the code is automatically generated. However, this approach requires engineers to use BPEL or SOA standards to model the applications, and as most of engineers today are trained with OO modeling, it will take some times for engineers to be familiar with modeling applications using SOA standards. Our experiences certainly validated this. In a senior/graduate class at Arizona State University, students first receive instructions about SOA, and then asked to develop an SOA application. Unfortunately, most of students actually turned in OO designs rather than SOA designs. And when asked why they turned in an OO design, students often replied this way, "We have been trained to develop software in the OO manner for years, and then suddenly we were asked to develop an SOA applications, it is really difficult to change our mindset".

- Use an integrated model where a set of core model is used to develop other supporting models. This has been a research and experimental approach. One example of such modeling language is PSML, which includes a process language for services PSML-S [180], and an extended collaboration description language PSML-C [205]. Furthermore, PSML can generate various other models for analyses such as completeness and consistency checking, and execution thread generation. The PSML ontology is integrated with the process model and with various analysis tools. Any change in one sub-model such as the process model will not cause other sub-models to be updated.

Table 3 summarizes the three SOA lifecycles.

Table 3 SOA Lifecycles

Lifecycles	SAP	IBM	ASU
Modeling	Include four steps: business requirements, business modeling, service modeling and service definition	Requirement gathering. Data modeling.	Use SMMA. Model-driven. Simulation. Core model. Single model multiple analysis.
Development	Include proxy generation and service implementation.	Assemble services, components, and data.	Automatic code generation, code execution
Testing	Verification and justification	Quality management supports the whole lifecycle.	Model checking, runtime verification and validation, policy
Deployment	Include two steps: provide service, and service discovery.	Use WebSphere to deploy the components and services.	Automatic code deployment
Runtime		Use WebSphere Businesses Monitor to monitor the business process and services.	runtime verification and validation, policy, dynamic analysis, reliability analysis

Simulation			static simulation, and runtime simulation

2.5 Testing during SOA Lifecycles

2.5.1 SOA Testing Challenges

This section reviews the evaluation of SOA application models, and how to use these models for testing. Table 4 outlines testing techniques in SOA lifecycle and their issues.

Table 4 Challenges in SOA Testing

Testing Methods	Issues
Model-based Testing (Petri Net, UML, State Machine, Graph, Process Algebra)	The SOA models are heterogeneous and cannot describe the behavior of services comprehensively. Based on such incomplete models, the advantage of model checking is limited. Only interfaces model (e.g., WSDL) are published, while most SOA models are not published (e.g., BPEL). Usually need to transit from one model (BPEL) to a formal model (Petri Net, State Machine etc.)
Agent-based Testing	Each service must be equipped with an agent stub which contains intelligent behavior.
Policy	Need distributed policy enforcement supports. Trade-off between efficiency and reliability.
Monitoring	Need distributed monitoring mechanism supports. Trade-off between efficiency and reliability.
Fault Injection	Need to implement a trigger to inject faults into the message/system. Sometimes, code instrumentation is impossible.
Pre-registration	Need to extend current UDDI.
Simulation	Simulation cannot cover all real situations.
Perturbation	Test XML messages only.
Mutation Testing	Test WSDL only.
Unit testing	Test BPEL or atomic service only
Group Testing	Need a group of similar services. When the volume of services is larger, group testing is more efficient.

2.5.2 Testing Techniques in SOA Lifecycles

This section reviews the evaluation of SOA application models, and how to use these models for testing. Table 4 outlines testing techniques in SOA lifecycle.

Table 5 Testing in SOA lifecycle and the challenges

SOA Lifecycle	Testing Category	Testing Methods
Modeling/Design	Model-based Testing	Model Checking [56][58][215]
		Petri Net[119]
		UML [158]
		State Machine [59][157]
		Specification-based [177]
Development/Assemble/Composition		Model Checking[66][67][41][65]
		Fault Injection[61]
Registration	State Machine	Protocol State Machine[20][21]

	Agent-based Testing	"discovery services" [69]
		"testing services" [217]
	Contracts	Test cases as contracts [27]
	Pre-registration testing	Check-in/out [13][172][169]
Deployment	Stress testing	TTCN-3 based test case generation[151][206]
	Performance testing Tools	JMeter[120]
		WEbInject[196]
	Policy	WS-Policy[201]
		WS-PolicyConstraints[204]
		Pi4SOA[187]
Runtime	Monitoring	Agent-based testing and monitoring [50]
		Monitoring and testing [33]
	Other methods	Fault Injection[101]
		Runtime Model checking [193]
		Agent-based testing [168][170]
Simulation		Fault Injection [102][104]
		Model-driven simulation[188]
		Policy [190]

2.5.3 Testing/Verification in Modelling Phase

When the requirements of a system are determined, the next task is to build the model. A few most commonly used models are discussed in under [160][52], including: Finite State Machines, Grammars, Markov Chains (Markov process), Unified Modeling Language (UML), Statecharts, Decision Tables, Data Flow Diagram, and Decision Tree. This section reviews the evaluation of SOA application models, and how to use these models for testing.

In [56], Foster et al proposed a verification mechanism which can be applied at the modeling phase of SOA applications. First, the SOA application can be specified in a Message Sequence Chart (MSC) by a modeling tool called Labelled Transition System Analyzer (LTSA).Second, the SOA application is specified in a web service workflow specification such as BPEL4WS. Then the specification is translated into the Finite State Process (FSP). With all of this information, the LTSA model checker can detect unspecified or undefined scenarios, perform "safety check", and check trace results based on the FSP. Further, in [58], Foster et al argued that model checking approaches without the consideration of resource constrains are insufficient to verify the safety and liveness of service orchestrations. Therefore, they used a Finite State Process (FSP) notation, which is a resource aware process modeling language, to model the SOA applications. The FSP code can be automatically generated from the BPEL by using the provided tool WS-Engineer, which is an add-on of the existing LTSA tool suite. The proposed validation mechanism can detect and resolve deployment deadlocks.

In [215], Zheng et al proposed a model checking based test case generation framework to test whether the implementation of web services conforms to its BPEL and WSDL models. The SPIN and NuSMV model checkers are used as the test generation engine, to achieve state, transition and du-path coverage criteria for BPEL models.

In [119], Narayanan and McIlraith proposed a Petri Net (PN) based web service simulation, verification and validation. In their approach, web services are modeled by DAML-S, then translated to PN. Based on the Petri Net model of the web service, many existing Petri Net techniques can be applied to simulate, verify and validate the web service. Specifically, linear algebraic techniques can verify the properties of the web service; Coverability graph analysis, model checking and reduction techniques can analyze the dynamic behavior of the Petri Net; Simulation and Markov-chain analysis can evaluate the performance of the web service. The verification on the Petri Net can check the reachability, liveness and deadlocks of the web service.

In [158], Smythe proposed the model-driven interoperability testing technique that can test the conformance for a service. Test cases can be automatically generated from the UML model of the service by using a series of transformations of the XML Metadata Interchange (XMI).

In [157], Sinha and Paradkar proposed a model based test case generation technique that can generate functional conformance test cases for web services based on the Extended Finite State Machine (EFSM). Web services are first specified in a new standard named WSDL-S, and then translated into EFSM by a novel algorithm. Based on the EFSM model of the web service, existing test case generation techniques can be applied to generate test cases.

In [59], Frantzen et al proposed a model-based testing approach to test SOA applications. Their approach uses a special variant of state machine: Symbolic Transition System (STS) to formally specify the coordination protocols in SOA applications. Based on the STS, test cases can be generated by using such tools as TorX.

In [177], Tsai et al. proposed a novel specification-based test case generation technique named as Swiss Cheese (SC). The proposed SC is an approach to identify potent test cases based on the Boolean expressions extracted from the conditions and decisions in a software program. SC technique can generate both positive and negative test cases. Based on the SC technique, a framework was proposed to assure the trustworthiness of Web services. New assurance techniques are developed within the framework, including specification verification via completeness and consistency checking, test case generation, and automated

Web services testing.

Discussion: This section reviews existing verification technologies for the modeling phase of SOA applications. Since only models are available during the modeling phase, model-based testing is intensively used in this phase. The model-based testing can be classified into two categories: use SOA specific models, such as BPEL and WSFL; use models derived from the SOA specific models, such as Petri Net and State Machine. Both approaches have advantages and disadvantages. The former approach verifies SOA applications on the SOA models directly, thus it does not involve extra efforts. Since SOA models are usually simple so the verification methods are limited. The latter approach usually needs model translation, e.g., translate the BPEL model to another formal model, and then use those existing verification mechanisms that are specific to the formal model to SOA model. However, the translation process may incur information loss or inconsistence with the original SOA model.

2.5.4 Testing in Assemble/Composition Phase

In [112], Milanovic and Malek reviewed and compared existing approaches to service composition, including BPEL, OWL-S, Web Components, Algebraic Process, Petri Nets, Model checking and Finite State Machines.In [92], Koehler and Srivastava discuessed and compared two approaches to service composition: an industry solution which uses WSDL and BPEL4WS, and a semantic web solution which uses RDF/DAML-S and Golog/Planning.

In [61], Fu et al presents a coverage analysis approach for the exception handlers in Java web services. A coverage metric called e-c (exception-catch) links were defined to analyze the coverage, where exceptions are fault-sensitive operations, and catch blocks are uses of exceptions. During compile time, the possible e-c links in the web service are analyzed and calculated. In the meantime, the compiler instruments the web service code so that the faults can be injected by the fault injection engine called Mendosus during execution. At runtime, Mendosus injects faults into web services, and e-c links are observed and gathered. After execution of the web service, the def-catch coverage is calculated and analyzed by a test harness.

In [66] and [67], Garcia-Fanjul et al used SPIN model checker to automatically generate test suites for composite Web service specified in BPEL. In their approach, BPEL specification is first transformed into a PROMELA model, and then test case are generated and selected to provide transition coverage.

In [41], Dai et al presented a model checking framework to specify and verify service composition, as shown in Figure 10. The framework extends the BPEL4WS with constraints information by using one or more annotation layers to enable various analysis and increase the reliability of service composition. First, the BPEL is translated to an extended Timed Predicate Petri-net (TPPN), and then the verification properties and verification methods are applied to the TPPN.

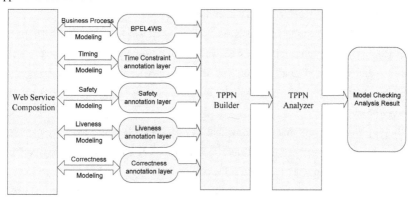

Figure 10 Service composition with model checking framework

In [65], Gao et al proposed a model checking approach to verify composite services during the assembling phase. The model checking tool, called WebJetChecker, is based on Pi-calculus, and is an add-on of the "dynamic assembling framework for business process" environment named as WebJet. In this approach, the BPEL4WS is first automatically translated into Pi-calculus, and then formal verification techniques can be applied on the Pi-calculus model. Three types of formal methods can be used to verify the Pi-calculus, including open bisimulation checking, property checking and compatibility checking.

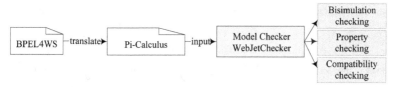

Figure 11 verify service composition with Pi-Calculus

Discussion: This section reviews existing verification technologies for development phase of SOA applications. The development of SOA includes programming atomic services, and assembling/composing of these atomic services. In this phase, both codes and models are available for the service providers. But since the services are not published yet, service consumers and the broker can not see the service.   Since the dependency among the services is decided in this phase, model checking approach is intensively used. The existing model checking approaches are similar: translate the SOA models, usually BPEL, into a formal model, and then the model checker can be applied to verify the properties of the BPEL.

2.5.5 Testing in Registration Phase

After service is tested and deployed by the service provider, it should be tested again by other parties before its registration on the service registry.

In [20] and [21], Bertolino et al presented a framework which extends the UDDI registry role and supports the validation of services before registration. The testing approach, which is called audition, is based on a Protocol State Machine (PSM) which is a behavior diagram of the UML 2.0. PSM is a state machine with the pre-conditions and post-conditions specified along with each state.

In [69], Heckel and Mariani proposed that services should be tested by automatic testing agents called "discovery services" before their registration. The "discovery services" uses Graph Transformation (GT) rules to test the compatibility between clients and services. The discovery service can automatically generates conformance test cases based on the service description and its GT rules, then execute the test cases on the Web Service.

In [217], Zhu proposed a service oriented testing framework which involves various parties in the testing of WS applications. When registering a service, a kind of auxiliary service called "testing services" should also be registered with the "functional service". The testing service can be provided by the same vendor or by a third party. One functional service can correspond to multiple testing services to perform various testing tasks. Ontology can be used to describe, publish and register testing services.

In [27], Bruno et al. proposed the use of test cases as contract between the service provider and the service consumer. The test cases are encoded into XML format and attached to the service.

In [169], Tsai et al proposed an adding verification mechanism to the UDDI servers. The key idea is that test scripts should be attached to WS, and these test scripts will be used by both WS providers and clients. Before accepting a new WS into the service directory, the new WS must be tested by the associated test scripts, and they will be accepted only if the test was successful. Before using a specific WS, a client can use the appropriate test scripts to test the WS and it will be used only if the test was successfully. While the code for WS may be not available, but the associated test scripts can be openly available. This paper also suggests test script specification techniques and distributed test execution techniques to perform testing with a UDDI server.

In [13] and [172], Tsai et al proposed a trustworthy service broker architecture and a dependence-based progressive group testing technique. The new service broker extends the traditional UDDI server by introducing the check-in and check-out interfaces. The trustworthy service broker performs testing and evaluation on Web services before their registration.

Discussion: This section reviews existing verification technologies for the registration of SOA applications. Many existing approaches share the same concept: verify the services before its registration. This concept can also be referred to as "pre-registration testing". To fulfill this concept, it is necessary to enhance the current service broker because current service broker such

2.5.6 Testing in Deployment Phase

In [151] and [206], a TTCN-3 based stress testing approach was proposed. The tests stored on the server side are in the form of Abstract Test Suite (ATS), which is a language and platform-independent format. The ATS test cases are publishable and discoverable. The TTCN-3 compiler can convert the ATS test cases into various language-dependent formats, such as test in java, test in c#, test in Perl and so on.

In [120], Nevedrov introduced a performance testing tool JMeter to check the performance of SOA applications. WebInject [196] is also a performance testing tool.

Discussion: This section reviews existing verification technologies for the deployment of SOA applications. After services are deployed, it is important to test the stress performance. Since the service invocation process is based on the standard html protocol, it is possible to use existing http stress testing tools to test the performance of services as well.

2.5.7 Testing in Runtime Phase by Policy and monitoring

Service-Oriented Computing (SOC) and Web Services (WS) provide a flexible computing platform for electronic business and commerce. In the service oriented development paradigm, a number of candidate services are composed rapidly to form a Service-Oriented Architecture (SOA). The verification of SOA applications is important. Among various verification mechanisms, policy is a promising method because it provides runtime verification and validation. In addition, policy can be used along with SOA simulation during simulation time.

A policy can be viewed as an assertion, predicate, or constraint, to specify the system requirement. In the ebSOA (Electronic Business Service Oriented Architecture) proposed by OASIS, a policy is defined as "the governing directives and regulations that guide the processes and business of the entity and its transactions with other entities." In the WS-Policy recommendation submitted to the W3C Consortium, a policy is defined as a collection of assertions, and each of these policy assertions represent an individual requirement, capability, or other property of a behavior. The Internet Engineering Task Force (IETF) defined a Common Information Model (CIM) [115] to tackle distributed policies. This CIM suggests that a policy infrastructure should include two key components: Policy Decision Points (PDP) and Policy Enforcement Points (PEP). PDP determines how a policy should be enforced, while PEP performs the policy enforcement task. Shafiq [153] et al proposed a two-step policy-based approach for verification of distributed workflows in a multi-domain environment. Agrawal et al [2] presented that policy could be leveraged to validate the storage area networks. In the SCA (Service Component Architecture) policy framework [150], two kinds of policies were given: interaction policies affect the contract between a service requestor and a service provider; implementation policies affect the contract between a component and its container.

Introducing policy-based computing to service-oriented business systems adds another dimension of flexibility and security. While service composition and re-composition in service-oriented business systems allow major system reconstruction, policy-based computing can better deal with the small and routine changes of business processing. Policies and policy enforcement mechanism should reside in all the three parties of a SOA: WS provider, WS consumer and WS broker.

- WS Provider Policy: Polices on the WS provider specify those requirements posed on WS consumers. WS consumers have to meet the requirement in order to invoke the WS. WS provider should publish its policies along with its WSDL file to all potential WS consumers. During WS invocation, the local policy engine on the WS provider enforces polices at runtime.

- WS Consumer Policy: WS consumer could also have the policy to negotiate with the policy from the WS provider. The WS consumer could put the constraints of establishing a connection into the policy file, and send the policy file along with the service request to the WS broker when binding service and then send to the WS provider to do further policy checking.

- WS Broker Policy: Polices on the WS broker are global policies since WS broker has the information about both WS consumer and WS provider. The policy engine on the WS broker is used to enforce global policies.

A policy infrastructure should support policy modeling, specification, enforcement, and management. Thus, a policy infrastructure should be a multi-layer architecture. This section presented three major policy-based verification framework for runtime SOA verification: WS-Policy, WS-PolicyConstraints and Pi4SOA.

The Web Services Policy Framework (WS-Policy) [201], developed by BEA, IBM, Microsoft, and SAP, provides a general-purpose model and corresponding syntax to describe and communicate the policies of a Web Service. WS-Policy defines a base set of constructs that can be used and extended by other Web Services specifications to describe a broad range of service requirements, preferences, and capabilities. WS-Policy provides a flexible and extensible grammar for expressing the capabilities, requirements, and general characteristics of entities in an XML Web Services-based system. WS-Policy defines a framework and a model for the expression of these properties as policies.

The following diagram shows the three layers of the WS-Policy framework. At the model layer, there are three elements, WSDL, External model and external attributes. External model refers to XML file, while attributes can refer to the tModel (technical interface model) stored in the UDDI server. The model layer is extensible because the model layer can access external resources through the external model element and the external attribute element. However, the model layer does not have its own modeling language. At the policy language layer, the policy is constructed by the vocabulary extracted from the model layer. The WS-Policy framework does not mention the policy enforcement layer.

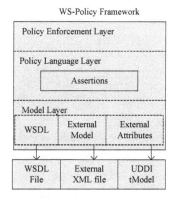

Figure 12 WS-Policy Framework

Web Service Policy Constraint Language (WS-PolicyConstraints) [204], evolved from Web Service Policy Language (WSPL), is a draft standard developed in OASIS. WS-PolicyConstraints can describe the following web service policies: Authentication, Authorization, Quality of protection, Quality of service, Privacy, Reliable messaging, and

Service-specific options. The syntax of WS-PolicyConstraints is a strict subset of the eXtensible Access Control Markup Language (XACML) standard of OASIS. Policies could be distributed as a source, and merged into one policy by a negotiation mechanism at run time. WS-PolicyConstraints is a language for expressing constraints for a web service policy (constraints are also known as predicates or assertions). With this language, constraints for any type of policy can be written without requiring changes to the policy processor. WS-PolicyConstraints is designed to complement higher level policy frameworks, as well as to facilitate policy intersection and direct verification of messages against policies

The following diagram shows the OASIS XACML based Policy infrastructure. The model layer is based on the eXtensible Access Control Markup Language (XACML), which is an access control language instead of a generic modeling language. Thus, the policy language layer can only refer to access control related vocabulary. This means that the XACML-based policy language is an access control domain specific policy language rather than a generic policy language. At the policy enforcement layer, it provides a conceptual PEP and PDP.

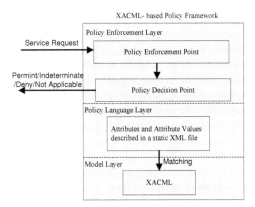

Figure 13 WS-PolicyConstraints Framework

Pi4SOA [187] is a policy enforcement framework that dynamically verify and control the collaboration process in Service-Oriented Architecture (SOA). Dynamic SOA collaboration is different from traditional service collaboration where the workflow is pre-defined at design time while the services used can be discovered at runtime. In dynamic collaboration, both the workflows and services can be determined at runtime. As they will be determined at runtime, thus many verification activities can be performed at runtime. Pi4SOA follows the dynamic SOA collaboration process to ensure that various system constraints can be enforced at runtime. The framework includes a policy specification language, a policy completeness and consistency checking, and distributed policy enforcement.

- Model Layer: this provides the vocabulary to specify and model policies.
- Policy language layer: this defines the syntax and semantics of the policy language.
- Policy enforcement layer: this defines the process of policy enforcement. The policy enforcement process involves monitoring, policy analysis, and policy coding.

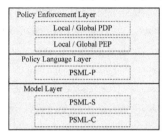

Figure 14 Pi4SOA Framework

The model layer of Pi4SOA is the foundation because policies are specified in the vocabulary defined in the model layer, thus the capability of a policy infrastructure primarily depends on the model layer. Pi4SOA uses PSML-S to specify workflows and services, and uses PSML-C (extended from PSML-S) to specify service collaboration. PSML-P can be applied to both PSML-S and PSML-C.

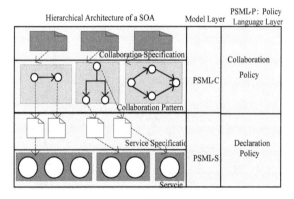

Figure 15 Pi4SOA for collaborative SOA

The system structure is modeled by model elements: actors, conditions, data, actions, attributes, and events. PSML-C is used to model collaborations among services. Service collaboration processes can be categorized into reusable collaboration patterns with service stubs. Each service stub is a placeholder in the collaboration pattern. Multiple candidate services can be linked to a service stub, but only one concrete service will be selected and bound to a service stub at runtime. After policies are specified in PSML-P, they can be enforced in the policy enforcement layer of Pi4SOA. Policy enforcement includes policy dissection, policy analysis, policy dispatching, policy checking, policy compensation, and policy profiling. Figure 3 shows the policy enforcement framework.

In [142] and [141], Robinson proposed a monitoring framework called ReqMon that supports formalization of high-level goals and requirements. ReqMon also supports the automation of monitor generation, deployment, and optimization. ReqMon is composed of five components: event capture, analyzer, repository, presenter and reactor. The event capture component receives runtime events and put the events into the evetn streams. The analyzer is used to update the status of monitors. The repository is a database for storing the events and monitor histories. The monitors are implemented by model checking, SQL sqeries and Event Condition Action (ECA) rules.

In [134], Pistore and Traverso presented the assumption-based automated synthesis and the runtime monitoring for web service compositions. In their approach, BPEL is used to specify the behavior of the composite web services. At runtime, the composite web services and the monitoring execute concurrently as shown in Figure 16. The monitoring environment consists of the following components: monitoring inventory, monitor instances, runtime monitor, admin console, mediator, BPEL engine and processes. Their framework also supports planning by using a formal model called state transition system.

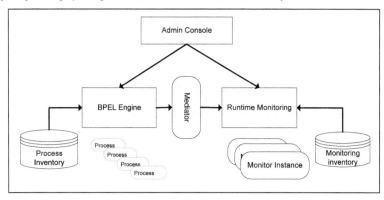

Figure 16 the runtime monitoring framework

In [15], Baresi et al proposed a monitoring framework to check the policies. They also proposed an assertion language WS-CoL to express non-functional constraints. In [14], two different implementations for the monitoring services are discussed. The first approach uses C# while the second uses Xlinkit, which is an assertion language processor.

In [106], Mahbub and Spanoudakis proposed an event calculus based framework for monitoring the compliance of SOA systems specified in BPEL4WS. The monitoring framework includes an event receiver, an event database, a monitor and a requirements editor. The requirements editor is used to specify the assumptions and behavioral properties to be monitored. The monitor is the consumer of the events. Based on the framework, five event calculus predicates are defined: Happen(). Initially(), Initiates(). Terminates(), and Holdsat().

In [137], Pudhota et al presented a conceptual framework for synchronizing and monitoring the collaborative workflow. In [96], Lazovik et al resented a framework that can associate business rules with workflows. The proposed framework includes planning and monitoring of the services.

In [33], Canfora and Di Penta discussed the roles of testing and run-time monitoring for SOA systems. The authors proposed that both testing and monitoring can be used: testing acts as a preventive activity, while monitoring is performed after the service has been executed.

In [50], Dustdar and Haslinger proposed an agent-based distributed monitoring and testing framework named SITT (Service Integration Test Tool) to test and monitor SOA applications at runtime. In SITT, each service has a "Test Agent" which parses the local log file and sends the message to the global "Master Agent". The Master agent then stores the message to a test database. A testing engine called "test daemon" analyzes the test database periodically to check if the current status of the SOA application is consistent with its predefined behavior.

In [101], Looker et al discussed fault injection for the verification of web services. The authors also proposed that fault injection technique can be applied at both compile-time and runtime of web services. Particularly, runtime injection techniques use a triggering mechanism to inject faults into a runtime system. The triggering mechanism can be implemented in various ways, such as time based triggers, tnterrupt based triggers, code insertion and so on.

In [193], Walton proposed a model checking based verification mechanism to verify the interaction protocols in the SOA applications. The approach models SOA applications as multi-agent systems (MAS), and each service is equipped with an agent stub which contains intelligent behavior. Further, the approach defined a lightweight protocol language called Multi-Agent Protocol (MAP) to express the interaction protocols between services. The MAP is translated into PROMELA and then input into the model checker SPIN to verify the SOA application. In [129], they applied model checking at runtime to verify the interaction protocol dynamically. In a MAS, the model checker can be invoked by agents at runtime.

In [168] and [170], Tsai et al proposed a Web Services Testing Framework (WSTF) to perform WS testing for WS participates. WSTF provides three main distributed components: test master, test agents and test monitor. Test master manages scenarios and generates test scripts. It initiates WS testing by sending test scripts to test agents. Test agents dynamically bind and invoke the WS. Test monitors capture synchronous/asynchronous messages sent and received, attach timestamp, and trace state change information. The benefit to use WSTF is that the user only needs to specify system scenarios based on the system requirements without needing to write test code.

Discussion: Testing service at runtime might be the most challenging task for the verification of SOA applications, and therefore, it attracts the most attentions from researchers. Dynamic verification mechanisms can address this problem. Existing approaches include monitoring, policy enforcement, and dynamic model checking. The monitoring approach itself cannot correct the behavior of service when the service malfunctions. Policy enforcement not only monitors the services, but can also compensate the application when the service malfunctions. Dynamic model checking is more powerful in terms of detecting errors, but it needs a model checker as backend and intelligent agent equipped with every service, which are not possible for most SOA applications at current stage.

2.5.8 Testing by Simulation

SOA simulation can play an important role in SOA software development as it can be used to verify the SOA application models and to demonstrate runtime and collaborative behaviors of the SOA applications. SOA simulation differs from traditional simulation as it emphasizes on reusability, collaborative behaviors, and its unique model-driven development. For example, SOA simulation is considered a key technique for business modeling and process management for IBM WebSphere training. Due to the dynamic nature of SOA, the behavior of the SOA, as well as most of the analyses on SOA applications, may occur in the runtime and may need to be changed / reconfigured in the runtime. Moreover, the workflows and the architectures of the SOA applications can be dynamically changed. For this reason, simulations are necessary to evaluate the runtime behaviors of the SOA application.

In [188], Tsai et al proposed a model-driven simulation, verification and validation framework to verify SOA applications. Simulations can also be applied on Consumer-Centric SOA (CCSOA) to evaluate the publishing, discovery, matching, and subscription of services, workflows and application collaboration specifications, as shown in [183]. Different from traditional SOA applications, each service and workflow in CCSOA may have multiple copies of implementations, published by different service providers. Therefore the hybrid simulations on CCSOA may involve simulations on different combinations of service and workflow implementations.

In [190], Tsai et al further proposed Event-driven Policy Enforcement (EDPE) verification framework to verify the simulation of SOA applications. In EDPE, a BPEL engine is used to simulate the SOA application by executing the BPEL process. During simulation, the EDPE collects the runtime events and verify the SOA application against the policies specified in PSML-P.

In [104], Looker et al. identified a number of failure modes in SOA applications. They addressed certain SOA failure mode by using an enhanced fault model, and implement the model in a fault injection tool WS-FIT. In [102], they further proposed a fault injection approach to simulate errors in web services. Various SOAP level errors are injected into the SOA applications, and their affects on the SOA applications are observed and analyzed.

Discussion: SOA simulation can play an important role in SOA software development as it can be used to verify the SOA application models and to demonstrate runtime and collaborative behaviors of the SOA applications. SOA simulation differs from traditional simulation as it emphasizes on reusability, collaborative behaviors, and its unique model-driven development. For example, SOA simulation is considered a key technique for business modeling and process management for IBM WebSphere training. Due to the dynamic nature of SOA, the behavior of the SOA, as well as most of the analyses on SOA applications, may occur in the runtime and may need to be changed/reconfigured in the runtime. Moreover, the workflows and the architectures of the SOA applications can be dynamically changed. For this reason, simulations are necessary to evaluate the runtime behaviors of the SOA application.

2.6 Testing SOA Artifacts

This section reviews existing research and works in testing SOA artifacts. Table 6 outlines testing techniques for SOA artifacts.

Table 6 Testing Integrated SOA

Integration Level	Testing Category	Testing Methods
Basic Artifacts	XML Validation	Perturbation[211][124]
Atomic Services	Unit Testing	Unit testing framework [107]
		Design by Contract[70]
	Unit Testing Tools	WSUnit [203]
		HP Service Test [74]
Composite Services	Formal method based	Structural-Based Workflow Framework[90]
		Two-level abstract model [164]
		Petri Nets [48] [38]

		model checking[99]
	Testing-based	Group testing [173][173]
Dynamic service collaboration		Petri Nets [213]
		finite state machine[57]
Enterprise SOA		Task Precedence Graph and Timed Labled Transition System[165]

2.6.1 Basic Artifacts (XML etc)

In [211] and [124], Perturbation technique was proposed to test the XML-based communication and data. A formal model for the XML is created to represent any XML tree. The XML tree is modeled as T= (N, D, X, E, n_r), where N is a finite set of elements and attribute nodes, D is a finite set of build-in and derived data types, X is a finite set of constraints, E is a finite set of edges, and n_r is the root node. Based on the formal model, four primitive perturbation operations (insertN, deleteN, insertND, deleteND) and three non-primitive perturbation operations (insert, deleteT, changeE) are introduced to modify the XML tree into a "perturbed tree". Three test coverage criteria: Delete Coverage(DC), Insert Coverage (IC) and Constraints Coverage (CC) are defined and test cases can be generated to satisfy the coverage requirement.

Discussion: XML is the basic artifact in SOA applications. XML testing includes two aspects: the semantic and the syntax. Perturbation and mutation testing were proposed to test XML-based communication and data. In these approaches, the original XML document is modified and then tested.

2.6.2 Atomic Services

In [107], Mayer et al proposed an open unit testing framework which supports automated test execution and offers test case management capabilities. Along with the framework, a BPEL-level testing specification language was proposed to specify the test case execution for a BPEL process.

In [70], Heckel and Lohmann applied the Design by Contract concept to web services testing. Two types of contracts are defined in web service testing: required contracts, and provided contracts. Provided contracts specify the behavior offered by a web service, while required contracts describe the behavior needed by a web service. The Graph Transformation (GT) rules are used to specify these contracts. Based on the contracts, test cases can be generated automatically by using the Parasoft's Jtest tool to perform unit testing on web services.

WSUnit [203] and HP Service Test [74] are two unit testing tools for SOA applications.

Discussion: Testing atomic services is like testing a component. However, in SOA, services should be tested in a Collaborative Verification and Validation (CV&V) manner. Different parties use different testing techniques and they focus on different aspects of the services: the service provider performs white box testing because they have the source code. Service consumers can only perform black box testing. Service broker may or may not have the source code so he may use either black box testing or white box testing technique.

2.6.3 Composite Services

The technique proposed in [48] is used to analyze and test BPEL-based web service composition using High-level Petri Nets (HPN), as shown in Figure 17. The translation between BPEL-based web service composition and HPNs are defined, and the generated HPNs are verified using existing techniques, such as testing coverage and reduction techniques. The verification process is a multi-phase process. First, components in BPEL are identified and translated into the corresponding elements in HPN. Then, the HPN can be verified by various techniques, including the operation checking, operation cluster checking, service checking, and service cluster checking.

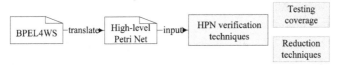

Figure 17 using High-level Petri Net to verify BPEL4WS

In [38], Chi et al. proposed a Petri Net based mechanism for the verification of composite services, as shown in Figure 18. In this approach, a BPEL4WS is first translated into a Petri Net Markup Language (PNML), which is XML-based format for Petri net model, and then three reliability issues are measured including safeness, reachability, and deadlock.

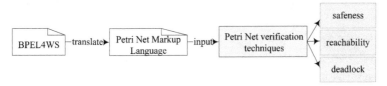

Figure 18 translate BPEL4WS to PNML

In [99], Lomuscio et al. proposed a model checking based approach to verify temporal and epistemic properties of composite web services, as shown in Figure 19. In their approach, a composite service is denoted in a specialized system description language (ISPL). After that, a symbolic model checker (MCMAS) can be used to verify the epistemic, correctness and cooperation modalities of the composite service.

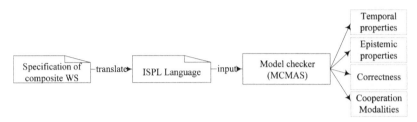

Figure 19 Verify composite services with MCMAS model checker

In [90], Karam et al defined Structural-Based Workflow Framework (SBWF) to test composite Web Services. In addition, a family of control-flow based test criteria was introduced.

In [164], Tarhini et al defined a two-level abstract model to specify composite web services. Based on the abstract model, a regression testing algorithm was proposed to test modified composite web services. The algorithm covers three kinds of modification on a composite web service: connecting to a newly established web service, adding/removing an operation, and modifying the specification of the web application.

In [173] and [173], Tsai et al proposed the group testing technique to test composite services. The group testing technique also has the ability to evaluate the test scripts, automatically establish the oracle of the each test script, and identify faulty WS in a failed composite WS. The group testing technique can be used by WS service providers, brokers, and clients. A WS provider or client can use the technique to find the best WS for composing new services or applications. For example, a WS provider can compose a digital imaging using the Fast Fourier Transformation service as a component service. A WS broker can use the technique to evaluate the quality of WS trying to be registered to make sure only WS with reasonable quality will be offered to the public. The group testing technique is not supposed to be used to rank different business logic or models. Instead, it is used to rank different WS implementations based on the same specification, the same business logic, and the same input and internal states.

Discussion: Existing testing techniques for composite services are similar to the model-based testing for SOA applications. That is, based on the BPEL specification, various formal models can be derived and then verified by formal methods. However, these testing approached can not suffice the need for the verification of dynamic composition of SOA applications, because at runtime, such a formal model might not be available. Therefore, dynamic verification mechanisms like group testing are preferable when dynamic composition is needed.

2.6.4 Dynamic Service Collaboration

In [213], Yi and Kochut proposed a Colored Petri Nets (CP-nets) based framework to specify and verify both the conversation protocols and process compositions in SOA applications. The framework can verify the SOA application at the design time. Particularly, protocol conformance, boundedness, liveness and reachability can be checked by existing CP-nets technologies.

In [57], Foster et al proposed a model-based approach to verifying the interaction and collaboration for web services composition. Their approach uses finite state machine (FSM) to specify web service orchestrations. Three kinds of compatibility: interface compatibility, safety compatibility and liveness compatibility can be verified by the FSM approach.

Discussion: Not too many testing mechanism are proposed to test dynamic service collaboration so far. Testing dynamic service collaboration will be an important research direction in the following years. This area requires runtime testing techniques which should cover the following aspects: conformance between services and workflow, collaboration correctness, collaboration protocols and so on.

2.6.5 Enterprise SOA Systems

In [165], Tarhini et al proposed a two-level abstract model to test web service-based applications. The two levels in this abstract model are: a Task Precedence Graph (TPG) level which is used to represent the web application, and a Timed Labled Transition System (TLTS) level which is used to represent the behavior of the composed components. The proposed test framework also supports test sequence generation, and test case execution.

Discussion: Like dynamic service collaboration, not too many testing mechanism are proposed to test enterprise SOA systems so far. Testing enterprise SOA systems will be an important research direction in the following years.

2.7 Testing SOA Protocols

It is necessary to test common SOA protocols such as UDDI, WSCI, BPEL and so on. This section reviews existing research and works in testing SOA protocols. Table 7 outlines testing techniques for SOA protocols.

Table 7 Testing SOA Protocols

SOA Protocol	Testing Category	Testing Methods
SOAP		Fault Injection [103][100]
		XMethods [207]
Service specification	Model Checking	Model checking OWL-S [76]
		Proof slicing [75]
	Other methods	mutation testing[154]

		extended WSDL[167]
	Tools	Web Service Tester[161]
		Websight [44]
Workflow Specification	Model checking	Bogor model checker[22]
		WSAT [62][63][64]
		Verbus[10]
		Model checking WSFL[117]
		UPPAAL model checker [136]
		Petri Net [152]
	Other methods	graph-search based test case generation[214]
		Unit testing [98]
		process algebra[94][95]
UDDI		IBM Unit Test (or private) UDDI Registry[80], private ebXML registry[60]

2.7.1 SOAP

In [103] and [100], Looker et al proposed a network level fault injection technology called Web Service-Fault Injection Technology (WS-FIT). WS-FIT is a fault injector that is used to assess SOAP messages.

XMethods [207] also provides a multi-round testbed named as SOAPBuilders for SOAP interoperability testing.

Discussion: SOAP (Simple Object Access Protocol) is at the lower level of the SOA protocol stack. SOAP is used for exchanging XML-based messages using HTTP/HTTPS. SOAP forms the foundation layer of the web services protocol stack and provides a basic messaging framework. SOAP messages and SOAP objects can be tested by fault injecting technique. The interoperability of SOAP exchange should be tested as well.

2.7.2 Service Specifications (WSDL/OWL-S)

In [76], Huang et al extended the BLAST model checker to handle the concurrency semantics in OWL-S. In the proposed approach, OWL-S process models are translated into a C-like specification language for BLAST. In [75], they further implemented the Proof Slicing techniques in the model checker named as Blade to enable the incremental verification for SOA applications.

In [154], Siblini and Mansour applied mutation testing technique to test WSDL documents. In their approach, nine mutant operators that are specific to WSDL documents are defined to detect interface errors and logical errors.

In [167], Tsai et al extended WSDL specification in four aspects: input-output dependency, invocation sequence, hierarchical functional description and concurrent sequence specifications. These four extensions is used to test web services as follows:

Input-Output Dependency: In numerous testing strategies such as regression testing and data flow testing, it is important to know the input and output dependency. The association between the inputs and outputs may help eliminate unnecessary test cases for carrying out the regression test. It also helps to produce expected outputs.

Invocation Sequences: A web service can have other web service to perform its tasks, and thus it is important to trace and state those calling relationship. By tracing this information among participating web services, it is possible to generate the complete calling sequence, and the calling sequence is useful in path testing and data flow testing.

Hierarchical Functional Description: In addition to providing structural information such as dependency and calling sequences. It is possible to incorporate functional descriptions into WSDL. Furthermore functional descriptions can be organized in a hierarchical manner and can be embedded into WSDL. By using this functional description, it is possible to provide analysis such as functional dependency analysis, and thus greatly improve the capability to perform various types of testing such as functional testing and regression testing.

Sequence Specifications: Sequence specifications have been found to be useful for testing OO programs as well as deriving test cases from formal specification languages such as Z.

IBM's Websight is a test and debugging tool under its WS framework [44]. Websight traces and visualizes the execution process of WS and thus helps the programmer to find syntax and semantic errors in WSDL. Web Service Tester [161] is a tool to test the WSDL file.

Discussion: Service specification, normally WSDL (Web Services Description Language), is used to specify the input/out information about a service. An important testing aspect about WSDL is the conformance between the specification and the actual behavior of the service. The following techniques are proposed to address this issue: mutation testing, model checking and WSDL enhancement.

2.7.3 Workflow Specifications (BPEL/WSFL)

In [214], Yuan et al proposed a graph-search based test case generation technique for the verification of BPEL model, as shown in Figure 20. BPEL Flow Graph (BFG), which is an extension of Control Flow Graph (CFG), is defined to specify the BPEL model. Concurrent test paths are generated by traversing the BFG, and test data for each test path are generated. With the generated test path and test data, test cases can be generated.

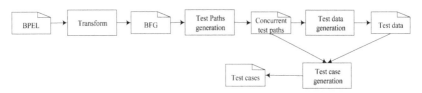

Figure 20 BPEL test case generation by BPEL Flow Graph

In [98], Li et al proposed a unit testing framework to verify BPEL4WS. The framework includes a BPEL4WS process composition model, a test architecture, a lifecycle management schema and a test design outline. The lifecycle management schema provides test interfaces such as beginTest and endTest.

Bianculli et al [22] proposed a model checking approach to verify workflows specified in BPEL4WS. The authors use a model checker Bogor to verify the deadlock freedom, properties and LTL temporal properties. The Bogor model checker supports the modeling of all BPEL4WS constructs. The tool BPEL2BIR translate the WSDL and BPEL4WS into BIR model, then the model checker Bogor takes the BIR model as input to verify the BPEL process.

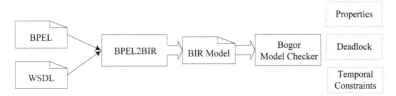

Figure 21 BPEL verification with Bogor model checker

In [62][63][64], Fu et al proposed a model checking tool, Web Service Analysis Tool (WSAT), to verify the composite web services specified in BPEL. The structure of WSAT is shown in Figure 22. First, the BPEL specification is translated into the Guarded Finite State Automata (GFSA) in a bottom-up manner, and the GFSA parser parses the conversation protocol in a top-down manner. Then, the analysis can be performed on the guarded automata. Two kinds of analysis were discussed by the authors: the synchronizability analysis, and the realizability analysis. Later, the GFSA is translated into Promela and fed into the model checker SPIN to check LTL properties.

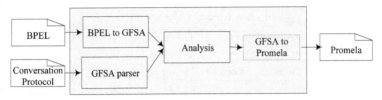

Figure 22 WSAT tool

In [10], Arias-Fisteus et al proposed a Verbus, which is a framework for the formal verification of BPEL business processes. The Verbus framework is a 3-layer architecture, as shown in Figure 23. The business process is designed by BPEL4WS or other languages. The Verbus then translated the business process into the Verbus. In the verification model, the model checking approaches, such as SPIN, can be used to verify the business process. A prototype of Berbus was implemented, and the prototype was mainly composed by two translation components: the first one translates BPEL into the Verbus formal model, and the second one translates the formal model into Promela, which is the input language of SPIN model checker. The prototype supports the verification of safety and liveness properties, such as invariants, goals, transition pre-condition and post-condition, activity reachability analysis, and LTL properties.

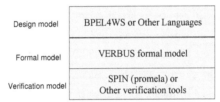

Figure 23 the VERBUS framework

In [117], Nakajima proposed a model checking based verification approach to test composite web services. The workflow of SOA application first is modeled by Web Service Flow Language (WSFL), and then translated into Promela which is the input specification language of SPIN. The properties of the SOA application are encoded into Linear Temporal Logic (LTL). With the LTL and Promela specifications, the model checker SPIN can identify fault in the workflow of the SOA application. In [118], Nakajima proposes a translation approach from BPEL to Extended Finite-state Automaton(EFA) for the formal verification of BPEL. The EFA is then translated into Promela and the model checker SPIN is used as a back-end engine to verify the Promela model. The proposed method can handle the Dead-Path Elimination (DPE) existing in the BPEL process.

Figure 24 Using EFA to verify BPEL

In [136], Pu et al proposed a formal model called u-BPEL model to represent business processes specified in BPEL, as shown in Figure 25. The BPEL4WS is first translated into u-BPEL, then the u-BPEL is translated into a extened Timed Automata (TA) network. Based on the TA network, various existing methods can be applied for the verification of the BPEL process. In the end, the model checker UPPAAL is used to further verify the BPEL process.

Figure 25 Using Timed Automata and UPPAAL to verify BPEL

In [152], Schlingloff et al formulated BPEL4WS to Petri net as shown in Figure 26. Several features of the Petri Net can be verified using stat space exploration techniques. An abstract correctness criterion called usability was defined and analyzed. A model checking tool called LoLA is used to validate the BPEL.

Figure 26 Petri Net approach using LoLA model checker

In [95] and [94], process algebra was proposed to verify the business processes specified in BPEL4WS, as shown in Figure 27. First, BPEL4WS is translated into a process algebra named BPE-calculus. Then, a process algebra compiler (PAC) takes the syntax and semantics defined in the BPE-calculus to produce a front-end for the verification tool named as concurrency workbench (CWB). The CWB can perform various verification techniques, such as equivalence checking, preorder checking, and model checking, on the BPE-calculus.

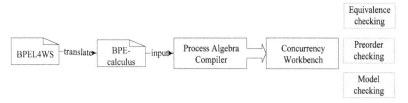

Figure 27 Using process algebra to verify BPEL

Discussion: Model checking is the major technique for the verification of workflow specifications. Existing model checking approaches are similar. Because existing model checker can not check SOA models directly, the translation from the SOA model to a formal model is necessary.

2.7.4 Web Service Choreography Interface

The Web Service Choreography Interface (WSCI) is W3C standard description language that specifies the interface and message flow exchanged in SOA applications. Similar to BPEL, WSCI can be used to specify web service orchestration [133]. To our best knowledge, there are no exiting tools that support WSCI testing. According to [133], "the SunONE WSCI Generator is the only product that supports WSCI, but there was no mechanism to test out the WSCI."

2.7.5 Service Registry (UDDI/ebXML)

Service-broker is an important mechanism in Service-Oriented Architecture (SOA), which facilitates service registration, publication, and discovery. UDDI and ebXML are two major standards that implement service brokerage by providing service registry and service repository. As SOA applications become pervasive, the need for more powerful service broker becomes a necessity.

Service broker is important because it enables service publication, discovery, evaluation, verification, and validation. A typical Service broker consists of a set of entities interfaces for external parties to access and retrieve the information about the services of interest. A service broker should support service publication, as well as other SOA entities, such as data, metadata, ontology, test scripts, policies, application templates, collaboration templates, and user interface, as shown in Figure 1. Furthermore, specific service broker may act as a COI (Communities of Interest) for specific application domains, also shown in Figure 28. External parties can access the internal service broker entities only through the service broker interfaces.

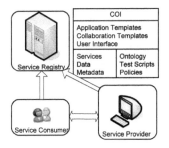

Figure 28 A service broker consists of various entities.

Different service broker may have different configurations for different usages. A service broker does not have to be configured to have all the functionalities when it is deployed. A

- 59 -

specific service broker can be composed of selected sub-services to provide partial functions for specific requirement. Numerous extensions to the current UDDI registries have been proposed. These extensions can be classified into four categories: the form of persistent entities it stores, the interfaces it supports, its architectural characteristics, and the organization structures.

Current UDDI server provides directory services similar to the telephone yellow book. But a UDDI server is not responsible for the quality of the services it refers. Thus, the dependability of WS presents a major concern for the users. Traditional dependability techniques such as correctness proof and model checking, fault-tolerant computing, testing, and evaluation techniques must be redesigned to handle the dynamic nature of WS. Testing these abundant features of service registries present a challenging. However, only a few research and works have been done in this field. As service registries is becoming powerful and complex, testing service registries might be an interesting domain in the future.

In [80], IBM implemented a Unit Test (or private) UDDI Registry. The Unit Test UDDI Registry serves as a testbed to test the UDDI registry before publish it. In [60], freebXML provides a similar private ebXML registry.

Discussion: Service broker, such as UDDI and ebXML, plays an important role in SOA. Service broker provides a set of interfaces to register and manage services. In addition, an enhanced service broker may provide testing and other interfaces as well. However, not too many tools are developed to test these interfaces. This field might be interesting for future research.

2.8 Summary and Perspectives

2.8.1 Summary

Table 8 summarizes available testing techniques in SOA lifecycle. Model-based testing needs model transition from SOA models to formal models, such as Petri Net, State Machine etc. Based on the formal models, model-based verification techniques can be applied. In particular, model checking techniques are used to verify these formal models. However, since model transition consume time, model-based testing is suitable to runtime testing.

Agent-based testing needs intelligent agents installed on each services. During runtime, these distributed agents collect runtime information, and send information to a test master. The test master analyzes the execution log at runtime. Agent-based testing can also be used during registration time.

Policy, monitoring, and fault injection can be used at runtime and simulation time. In addition, fault injection technique can be used in compiling time as well.

Perturbation and mutation testing can be used at modelling phase and service composition phase. The key concept of these two techniques is the same: change the system and check if the system behaves correctly.

Unit testing mechanism cannot be used by users and third parties after the service is registered into the service registry. This is because service code is not published. Group testing is a black box testing technique, thus group testing techniques can be used even if service code is not presented. Stress testing can be used to test if the server can handle a large amount of request. Contract concept can be used when registering the services into the service broker.

Table 8 Testing in SOA Lifecycle

Methods	SOA Lifecycle					
	Modeling	Composing	Registration	Deploy	Runtime	Simulation
Model-based	√	√	√	√	√	√
Agent-based			√		√	
Policy					√	√
Monitoring					√	
Fault Injection		√			√	√
Simulation						√
Perturbation	√	√				
Mutation Testing	√	√				
Unit testing	√	√				
Group Testing			√	√	√	
Stress Testing				√		
Contract			√			

Table 9 categorizes available testing techniques on various integration levels. Model-based testing can be used when the model is presented.

Agent-based testing, policy, and monitoring mechanism have the same concepts. Agent-based testing installs an intelligent agent on each service; policy mechanism installs a local policy engine on each service; monitoring mechanism installs a monitoring agent on each service. Therefore, all these three mechanisms can be used where services are presented.

Fault injection, mutation testing, and perturbation techniques verify the XML and WSDL.

Simulation can verify the correctness of composite service, service collaboration and enterprise SOA applications. In addition, it can verify the workflow specification, such as BPEL, is correct.

Unit testing can be used to verify atomic services and BPEL. Group testing can verify atomic service as well as composite services. In SOA applications, there are a large number of service requests/invocations. Therefore, stress testing is necessary to check the performance of the services. Design by Contracts can be used to check the conformance of each atomic service.

Table 9 Testing Categorization by Integration Level

Methods	SOA Integration Level					SOA Protocols
	Basics Artifacts	Atomic Services	Composite Services	Service Collaboration	Enterprise SOA	
Model-based			√	√	√	√
Agent-based		√	√	√	√	
Policy		√	√	√	√	
Monitoring		√	√	√	√	
Fault Injection	√					√
Perturbation	√					√
Mutation Testing	√					√
Simulation			√	√	√	√
Unit testing		√				√
Group Testing		√	√			
Stress Testing		√	√	√	√	
Contract		√				

2.8.2 Perspectives

Many efforts and works have been done to enhance the reliability of SOA. Nevertheless, the quality of services still presents a severe challenge to SOA paradigm. Based on the discussion in this chapter, we can safely conclude that not each individual testing technique can suffice the reliability requirements of SOA applications. This is due to the fact that SOA involves every aspects of SOA. SOA reliability should be ensured by a group of testing techniques to address all these aspects.

In the future, we envision that new techniques will emerge to address this issue. Two directions are promising to resolve this problem:

- Model based testing. SOA Standards and protocols will improve and the models will improve as well. Based on enhanced models, model based testing techniques can be more powerful to verify SOA applications. Model based testing can verify the static properties of SOA applications.
- Dynamic verification of SOA. Dynamic verification of SOA includes collaboration verification, composition verification, temporal verification, data verification etc. Dynamic verification presents a more challenging issue than static verification. Among

all dynamic verification techniques, model checking and policy might be promising to resolve this issue.

2.9 Introduction to the Proposed Verification Framework

2.9.1 Overview of the verification Framework

This research introduces a verification framework for SOA. An effective verification framework for SOA will greatly reduce the effort for rapid and adaptive service composition and evaluation of applications based on SOA. The proposed verification framework consists of two aspects: a testing infrastructure for static verification of services, and a policy-based dynamic verification mechanism for service collaboration and composition. The proposed verification framework provides the following advantages:

- The verification framework offers a CV&V mechanism to verify services. Traditionally, systems and software are verified using the IV&V (Independent Verification and Validation) approach, where independent teams are used to verify and validate the system during system development. The SOA challenges the IV&V approach as new services will be discovered after deployment, and thus it is necessary to have CV&V (Collaborative Verification and Validation) approach where service brokers, providers and consumers work in a collaborative manner, and some of testing need to be performed at runtime, e.g., when a new service is discovered and being incorporated into the application.

- The verification framework provides the function of integration testing and functional (black-box) testing. Service providers can have traditional coverage, and service brokers and clients may have black-box (such as WSDL) coverage only. As each service will have a partial view only, test coverage can be completed only when the actual collaboration is established.

- The verification framework provides the capability of test case profiling, test case ranking, service ranking, static service profiling, and dynamic service profiling.

- The verification framework has the capability of dynamic verification over services. To verify the SOA is more challenging than conventional applications because the collaboration between services might be determined at runtime. It is different to re-specify the workflow at runtime during the dynamic reconfiguration in SOA, where the actual collaboration is unknown until the participating services dynamically establish the protocol.

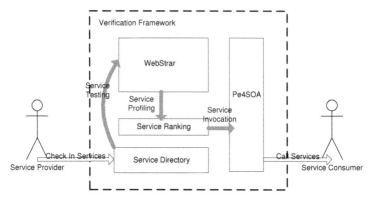

Figure 29 an Overview of the Verification Framework

Figure 29 presented the verification framework for SOA. The verification framework can reside in the service registry and can be seen as an extension of the service registry. The verification framework consists of three major components: the WebStrar (Web Services Testing, Ranking, and test case Ranking), and the Pi4SOA (Policy Enforcement for SOA). Figure 30 shows the inside of the verification framework.

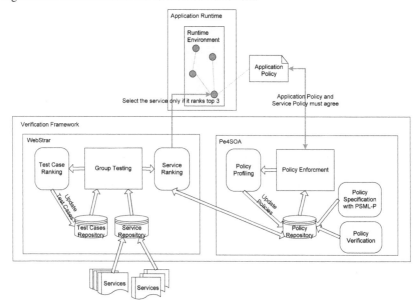

Figure 30 a Close Look at the Verification Framework

2.9.2 WebStrar: Web Services Testing, Ranking, and test case Ranking

WebStrar (Web Services Testing, Ranking, and test case Ranking) is the component in the verification framework to perform static verification. WebStrar assures the trustworthiness and reduces the vulnerability of WS by rigorous positive and negative testing, reliability assessing, and ranking.

In WebStrar, group testing algorithm was implemented, and the ranking of WS and test cases were studied. WebStrar not only performs positive testing that verify the required functionality but also perform negative testing that assures the robustness of WS under irregular inputs or attacks. Negative testing is particular important for WS, because a WS can be composed of WS from different service providers without the availability of the source codes.

This study proposes a technique to test large number of WS simultaneously, to determine the oracle and correctness of the WS under test by majority voting, and to provide quality ranking of WS and the test cases.

The proposed group testing technique can be used by WS service providers, brokers, and clients. A WS provider or client can use the technique to find the best WS for composing new services or applications. For example, a WS provider can compose a digital imaging using the Fast Fourier Transformation service as a component service. A WS broker can use the technique to evaluate the quality of WS trying to be registered to make sure only WS with reasonable quality will be offered to the public.

Following the Web 2.0 principles, where each user can also be an active contributor, an open verification framework for testing SOA software will be beneficial for all parties. The framework can provide an experimental testbed for regulators, service providers, service brokers, service consumers, and researchers:

- It allows regulators to decide the criteria to establish service quality criteria;
- It allows service providers to evaluate their services before and after publishing them, as well as to publish their evaluation data and mechanisms so that consumers can have more confidence;
- It offers ways for service brokers to provide value-added services by adding service verification as part of service discovery criteria.
- It allows service consumers to select services in an objective manner using quantitative data provided in the framework, and also allow them to submit their own test cases to the test case repository.
- It also provides researchers the data necessary for various research projects such as service performance and reliability assessments. Researchers are also allowed to

contribute various techniques into the framework.

Thus, in this open framework, the service repository, test case database, ranking data, test case generation mechanisms, and reliability models are all open to all the parties, and thus they can be all ranked.

The proposed group testing technique is not supposed to be used to rank different business logic or models. Instead, it is used to rank different WS implementations based on the *same* specification, the *same* business logic, and the *same* input and internal states. In other words, the WS under group testing should produce the same or close results if the same inputs are applied, e.g., various Fast Fourier Transformation WS should produce the same or close results based on the same input. .

WS testing is different from traditional software testing and requires distributed and coordinated testing. Within a few years, for each particular service, an enormous number of WS will be available over the Internet.

2.9.3 PSML-P and Pi4SOA

This study proposes a policy specification language PSML-P and a policy enforcement framework "Pi4SOA" (Policy Enforcement for Service-Oriented Architecture) to verify and control the collaboration process of SOA during service runtime.

PSML-P is based on the PSML-S (Process Specification & Modeling Language for Services) [190]. PSML-S is a modeling language to specify and model Service-Oriented Architectures. To obtain the PSML-S model (the process specification written in PSML-S language) from the informal specifications, users need to analyze the requirements, decompose the information into PSML-S model elements, and manually write the PSML-S specifications. PSML-C (Process Specification and Modeling Language for Collaboration) provides a service-oriented infrastructure for process collaboration specification, modeling, design, code generation, simulation, deployment, execution, and management. The overall modeling process in PSML-S is shown in Figure 31.

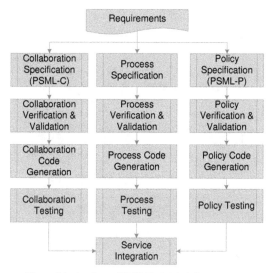

Figure 31: the Overall PSML-S Modeling Process

- Structure decomposition and specification: Decompose the system into components that can be described by the PSML-S ACDATE (actors, actions, attributes conditions, data, and events) building blocks. In order to perform automated execution, the atomic actors and actions must be able to map to existing services.

- Process (behavior) specification: Use the structural building blocks to compose processes (composite actors and actions). If alternative (redundant) actors and actions exist and fault-tolerant computing is necessary, compose reconfigurable or re-composable processes. The process specification includes internal (local) data and control flows and collaboration specification with external services.

- Policy specification: Constraint-related items in the requirements are specified as Policy elements which will be enforced by the policy engine.

PSML-P (Process Specification and Modeling Language for Policy) is the constraints defined on the system model as shown in Figure 32. PSML-P is independent of the development processes on functionality. In PSML-P specification phase, policies are extracted from the requirements and then specified in PSML-P. Similar to the functional specification, the policies are verified by C&C analysis to detect any incomplete and inconsistent policies. After the policies pass the verification, they are stored in a policy database. Test cases that dynamically drive the simulation can be generated based on the policies. During the simulation, a policy engine dynamically loads policies from the policy database, interprets them, and enforces them at runtime. The policy repository can be easily changed (added, removed, updated, and enabled / disenabled) on-the-fly at any time.

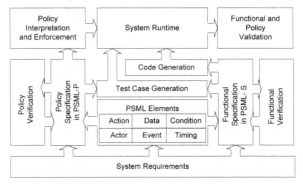

Figure 32 PSML-P is defined on the PSML-S elements

CHAPTER 3

WEB SERVICES TESTING, RANKING, AND TEST CASE RANKING

Web services and service-oriented architecture are emerging technologies that are changing the way we develop and use computer software. Due to the standardization of web services related description languages and protocols, as well as the open platforms, for the same web service specification, many different implementations can be offered from different service providers. This chapter presents an adaptive group testing technique that can test large number web services simultaneously and effectively.

Software development is shifting away from the product-oriented paradigm to the service-oriented paradigm. Due to the open and public nature of Internet and WS, the same service specification, e.g., tax return service, stock ranking service, and equations-solving service, can be offered by many service providers, based on the same theories but different implementations. How to effectively test this large volume of services is the focus of this chapter.

3.1 Problem Statement

In a SOA application, the service consumers or application builders may only concern about the functions (or interfaces, specification) of the services. They do not need to know the internal implementation of the services. In the meantime, due to the open platform of WS and free competition of offering WS over internet, for any given WS specification, there may exist thousands of WS designed according to the same specification as shown in Figure 33. Feeding hundreds of test cases to thousands of WS one after another is both time and resource consuming. For example, a composite WS is a supply-chain system and it is composed of six unit WS: ordering, retail, payment, transportation, lodging, and insurance. Assume there are 10 alternative WS for each unit service, the total number of possible composite WS is 10^6. It is extremely computationally expensive to test all the possible combinations.

It is a reasonable assumption that service consumers may only want to use trustworthy services with high quality. Therefore, how to efficiently test the services and rank the services in terms of their quality and trustworthiness is the issue that this chapter tries to address.

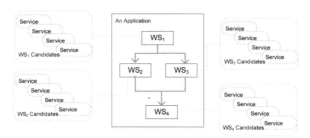

Figure 33 For a SOA, many services may implement the same specification

To solve these problems, the WebStrar framework is developed to comprehensively test and evaluate WS [176][181][172][182][197]. It includes the activities of group testing, oracle establishment, test case ranking, and WS ranking. To improve the efficiency, testing is divided into two phases: a training phase and a volume testing phase. This WebStrar framework has been found to be effectively in reducing the number of tests needed to evaluate a large number of WS rapidly. The larger the WS sample size, the more saving can be achieved.

3.2 Web Service Group Testing

The Service-Oriented Architecture (SOA) based WS broker allows WS developers and providers, based on published WS specifications, to freely register WS and compose complex WS from other WS dynamically and at runtime. As a result, for each WS specification, many alternative implementations may be available. The question is: how can a WS broker test large number of WS efficiently? A group testing technique originally developed for testing a large number of blood samples [49] and later for software regression testing [181][179][173][88][16] is an attractive solution to address this problem. However, blood group testing is different from WS group testing in many ways and may not be applied directly. Blood group testing has been applied in diverse areas, primarily to identify defectives in a homogeneous pool of items in a manner more efficient than individual testing (see [49], for example); WS group testing treats a pool of items differentiated by the service provided.

WS testing is different from traditional software testing and requires distributed and coordinated testing. It needs to handle a large number of WS at runtime and possibly in real time. The group testing technique was originally developed for testing a large number of blood samples. Blood group testing has been since applied in diverse areas primarily to identify defectives in a homogeneous pool of items in a manner more efficient than individual testing, including software regression testing. WS group testing is different from blood group testing in many ways. Table 10 compares and contrasts the two group testing techniques.

Table 10 Comparing and contrasting blood and WS group testing

Compared features	Blood Group Testing(BGT)	Web Services Group Testing (WSGT)
Testing goals	Find bad samples from a large pool of blood samples.	Rank WS in a large pool of WS with the same specification; Rank the fault detection capacity of test scripts; Determine the oracle of each test case; and fault identification.
Optimization objectives	Minimize the number of tests needed.	Minimize the number of tests and voting needed.
Sample mix	Arbitrary and physical mix.	Interoperability is constrained by WSDL, DAML-S, OWL-S, and composition semantics such as ontology.
Testing methods	Bio/chemical tests.	WS unit, integration, and interoperability testing using adaptive, progressive, and concurrent testing.
Testing location	Centralized testing	Distributed and remote testing by agents and voters.
Verification	Contamination analysis.	Oracle comparison and/or majority voting
Test coverage	One test for each mix.	Need many tests for each group of WS to verify a variety of aspects.
Reliability evaluation	Reliability of testing process	Reliability of WS under test and testing process
Reliability tests	Tests can be reliable or unreliable. Most BGT assumes tests are reliable.	The voting mechanism may be unreliable, and the number of faulty WS may be greater than the number correct WS to mislead the voter.

Group testing can be useful for both unit testing and integration testing on WS.

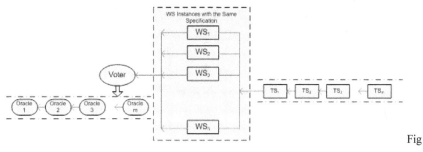

Figure 34 outlines the WSGT on one WS. For each test case, it has an oracle as the expected output of the test input. For all services implementing the same specification, they take the

input and generate the output. The voter uses the oracle to tell if the output is correct.

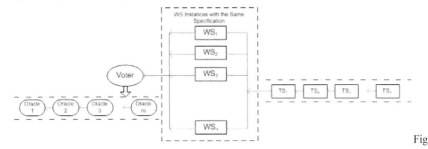

Figure 34 the Group Testing of Unite WS Testing

Testing each possible combination will be expensive or even impossible. Thank to ranking in WS unit testing, one can choose the best unit WS to construct the composite services. If five unit WS are chosen as the candidates for each participating service of the composite services, the total number of possible composite services is then limited to $5^6 = 15\ 625$, which is significantly smaller than 10^6. Then, WebStrar group testing technique can be applied to the composite WS by considering each composite as an individual WS in the group testing.

Now we present how WSGT is applied in integration testing of composite WS. Assume there are n sets of unit WS and Set_i have mi equivalent unit WS: $Set_1 = \{S_{11}, S_{12}... S_{1,m1}\}$, $Set_2 = \{S_{21}, S_{22}... S_{2,m2}\}$, ..., $Set_n = \{S_{n,1}, S_{n,2}, ..., S_{n,mn}\}$. A composite WS can be composed using one unit WS out of each set. Then, there are totally $m_1*m_2*... * m_n$ possible composite WS. For example, a composite WS is a supply-chain system and it is composed of six unit WS: ordering, retail, payment, transportation, lodging, and insurance. Assume there are 10 alternative WS for each unit service, and the total number of possible composite WS is 10^6. To reduce the testing cost, we can perform unit testing using WSGT on each unit WS, and only take the best 3 WS from each Set to join the integration testing. Therefore, the total testing runs would be 3^6, which is significantly smaller than 10^6. Then, WebStrar group testing technique can be applied to the composite WS by considering each composite as an individual WS in the group testing. Figure 35 illustrates how to use WSGT on WS integration testing.

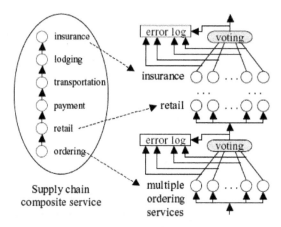

Figure 35 the Group Testing of Multiple Composite WS

3.3 The Architecture of WebStrar

This section research proposes a group testing-based WS verification architecture WebStrar (Web Services Testing, Ranking, and test case Ranking) to test a large number of WS efficiently. The architecture of WebStrar is shown in Figure 36. WebStrar can test a large number of WS at both the unit and integration levels. At each level, the testing process has two phases. WebStrar extends the progressive group testing technique into a comprehensive WS testing and evaluation framework. Essentially, WebStrar ranks test cases and applies the highly ranked test cases first. Thus, more failures can be detected in fewer test runs.

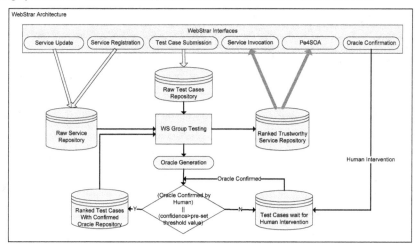

Figure 36 the Architecture of WebStrar

In WebStrar, test cases are ranked according to their *potency,* that is, the probability of detecting failures. Suppose during a test cycle, a test case is exercised on S WS under group test, and H of them failed, then the potency P of the test case is:

$$P = H/S$$

The higher the potency of a test case is, the higher its rank is. The purpose is to apply the test cases with the highest probability to detect failures first, and thus to reduce test cost by ruling out more failed WS earlier.

3.3.2 Oracle and its Confidence Level

One of the difficult problems in WS testing is to construct an oracle that can determine objectively and automatically if a failure has occurred. WebStrar automatically generate test oracles using the majority voting mechanism in group testing proposed in [181]. *Confidence level* is defined for each test oracle, i.e., the probability that the oracle is correct. Taking the formula above, the confident level can be defined to be the percentage of succeeded test runs:

$$C = (S- H)/S = 1-P$$

3.4 The Group Testing Process in WebStrar

In WebStrar, the group testing technique is further developed into a two-phase process, which significantly reduces the group testing overhead: the training phase and the volume testing phase.

- *Phase 1* (Training phase) is to establish the test oracle (the expected output of the test input) and the ranking of test cases.

- *Phase 2* (Volume testing phase) continues to test the remaining WS and any newly arrived WS, based on the profiles and history (test case potency, test oracle) obtained in the training phase. In this phase, it will first create the test hierarchy of group testing based on the potency of each test case obtained from the training phase. Then, the group testing technique is performed on all the remaining services layer-by-layer throughout the test hierarchy. At each layer, it will determine the correctness of a service output against the test oracle, eliminate the WS that have an unacceptable level of failure rate or reliability, update the confidence level of test oracles, and update the potency of test cases.

3.4.1 Phase 1: Training Phase

This phase is designed to test WS when the oracles (the expected output of the test input) and the effectiveness of the test cases are not available. The process assumes that a reasonably large number of test inputs or test cases are available to test the concerned WS before the start of this phase. This assumption is reasonable because the many techniques are available to generate test inputs from WS specifications [176][210]. In this phase, testing proceeds as follows:

1. Select a subset of WS randomly from the set of all WS to be tested. The size of the subset will be experimentally decided, as discussed in section 4.

2. Group testing: Apply each test case in the given set of test cases to test all the WS in the selected subset.

3. Voting: For each test input, the outputs from the WS under test are voted by a stochastic voting mechanism based on majority and deviation voting principles. The stochastic voting mechanism is studied in [181].

4. Failure detection and reliability computation: Compare the majority output with the individual output. A disagreement indicates a component failure. A dynamic reliability model is used to compute the reliability of each WS based on the failure rate and other factors [171].

5. Oracle establishment: If a clear majority output is found, the output is used to form the oracle of the test case that generates the output. A confident level is defined based on the extent of the majority. The confident level will be dynamically adjusted in the phase 2 as well.

6. Test case ranking: Test cases will be ranked according to their fault detection capacity, which is proportional to the number failures the test cases detect. In the phase 2, the higher ranked test cases will be applied first to eliminate the WS that failed to pass the test.

7. WS ranking: The stochastic voting mechanism will not only find a majority output, but also rank the WS under group testing according to their average deviation to the majority output.

By the end of training phase testing, we have tested the selected sample WS and we have the test cases ranked by their capability so far in detecting failures; the oracle for test cases established with respect to their confidence levels; the sample WS ranked;

3.4.2 Phase 2: Volume Testing Phase

This phase continues to test the remaining WS and any newly arrived WS, based on the profiles and history (test case effectiveness, oracle, and WS ranking) obtained in the training phase. Phase 2 continues to rank the WS, rank test cases, and update the oracles. The testing process is outlined as follows:

1. Test cases have been ranked by their capabilities in detecting failures/faults in Phase 1. Now they are divided into layers, with layer one having the highest capability.
2. Select layer one test cases and apply them in the next step;
3. For each layer of test cases, group-test all the WS;
4. If an oracle with acceptable confident level (e.g., greater than 50%) exists, no voting is necessary: Use the oracle to detect failure: Determine if each WS has produced a correct answer and then compute the failure rate and possibly the reliability of each WS using the given reliability model;
5. If no oracle with acceptable confident level exists, use voting mechanism to detect failure, as described in phase 1.
6. Update the confident level of the oracles: an agreement between the oracle and the current test output increases the confident level, otherwise, decreases the confident level accordingly;
7. Update the ranking of test cases by including the new number of failures detected;
8. Update the ranking of WS and eliminate the WS that have an unacceptable level of failure rate or reliability. The elimination of unnecessary testing in this step saves testing time
9. Select next layer of test cases, and return to step 3.

By the end of Phase 2 group testing: all the WS available are tested and a short list of WS is ranked; test cases are updated and ranked; oracles and their confidence levels are updated.

3.5 An Experiment

This section uses a real-time stock-buy-sell WS as an example to illustrate the application of WebStrar technique. In this example, the WS under development consist of a server WS and multiple client WS, residing in different locations. A client can send requests to the server and the server responses to the requests. All WS under group testing implement the same specification.

The simulation environment is shown in Figure 37. The database consists of objects of stock information, as defined in the Class Stock. Each stock object is set to an initial value at certain time point. The evaluation engine then uses randomly generated purchase and sale information, or uses replayed data from past stock dump, to decide the price dynamically once every minute. Once the price is changed, the other members (the percentages of changes in a minute, a day, a month, and a year) of each stock object are computed and updated.

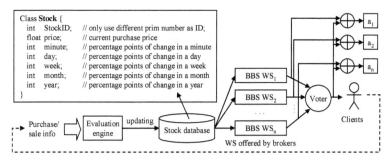

Figure 37 the WebStrar Simulation Environment

Table 11 lists the specification of the WS. The WS Server offers two functions and Client WS can access these two functions.

Table 11 Real-Time Stock-Buy-Sell WS

Event	Specification
A client queries a stock's price	Client can query any stock's price. If queried stock name is not empty and requested stock information is available, the server WS sends the requested stock price to the requesting client.
20 minutes have past since last stock price checking	The service automatically checks stock prices every 20 minutes. If the prices of some stocks increase >= 5% within the past 20 minutes, it will send messages to the all stock owners, reminding them to sell the stocks whose prices increase >= 5%, or buy the stocks to sell at a higher price.
	If the prices of some stocks decreases >= 10% within the past 20 minutes, the server WS will send messages to the stock owners, reminding them to buy the stocks whose prices decrease >= 10% or sell them to stop further losses.
	If the advancing volume or declining volume of some stocks increases >= 100% in the past 20 minutes compared to the same period of yesterday, it will send messages to alert the stock owners.

To explore the relationships among the training size, target size, and the test cost, we constructed 60 different WS implementations for the given specification in section 3, in which 12 WS are fault-free, 18 WS contains a single faults of different kinds, and the remaining 30 WS have multiple faults of different kinds. We have used the Swiss Cheese test case generation technique [176] to analyze the scenario specification and to generate test cases. Thirty-two test cases are generated that cover the fully functionality of the specification. Without using WebStrar processes, the total number of test runs need to be executed is 60*32 = 1920. Using the WebStrar process, only t WS will be tested by all 32 test cases, where t is the training size. Thus, 32*t tests will be executed in the phase 1. In phase 2, the oracle (majority output for each test case) found in phase 1 will be use to determine the correctness of WS output. Those WS that can no longer enter the best k WS, based on their performance so far, will be immediately eliminated, where k is the target size. Figure 38 plots the experiment results of the 60 WS under 32 test cases, indicating the impact of the training sizes and the target sizes on the total testing cost in two phases. The cost shown in the figure is the ratio of the test runs used to total number, 1920, of test runs if all 32 test cases are applied to test all 60 WS.

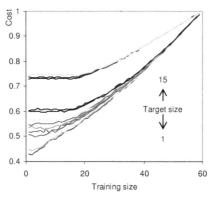

Figure 38 Impact of training sizes and target sizes

3.6 Experiment Result Analysis

3.6.1 Impacts of Target Size on Testing Cost

The 15 curves in Figure 38 correspond to 15 target sizes from 1 to 15. The lowest curve corresponds to size 1 and the highest curve corresponds to size 15. It can seen that

- The smaller the target size, the lower the cost. This is obvious because more WS can be eliminated sooner.
- The differences between the curves 1 to 12 are small, while a large gap exits between curves 12 and 13. The reason is that there are 12 fault-free WS under test. The number of failures detected from them is zero. If these fault-free WS are in the current target set, any WS will be eliminated if a single failure is detected.
- When the target size moves from 12 to 13 or higher, the testing cost increases sharply, because the algorithm must find a better WS among a set of imperfect WS.

3.6.2 Impacts of Training Size on Testing Cost

In the experiments, the training size is set to be 1, 2... 60. It can be seen from Figure 38:

- The smaller the training size, the lower the cost.
- When the training size is less than or equal to the target size, increasing the training size does not increase the cost (the initial part of the curves is flat). When the training size exceeds the target size, the cost increases as the training size increases. When the

training size equals the total number of WS under test, it becomes exhaustive testing and no test runs can be saved.

3.6.3 The Impacts of Training Size on Oracle

WebStrar technique divides testing into two phases. In phase 1 (training phase), a subset of WS is used to find the oracle (majority output) and to rank the fault detection capacity of the test cases. The size of the subset (training size) is critical. The smaller the size is, the cheaper (fewer test runs) the testing and ranking process will be. However, the smaller the size, the higher the probability that the training phase fails to find the correct oracle. An incorrect oracle will lead to incorrect ranking of the WS under test, while an incorrect ranking of test cases may result in more test runs in phase 2 of WebStrar process. Another factor that affects the testing cost is the target size, i.e., the number of WS to be ranked. For a given large number of WS to be tested, only a short list of best WS needs to be ranked.

Although Figure 38 suggests that a smaller training size leads to a lower cost, it does not take into account whether the correct oracle can be found in the training phase. An incorrect oracle can lead to incorrect test results or incorrect ranking of WS. Table 12 lists the experimental results on the probabilities that

1. a correct oracle is found in the training phase,
2. no oracle can be determined because insufficient data are available, and
3. an incorrect oracle is found, for training size = 1, 2, 3, 4, and 5. It can be seen that a small training size may lead to an incorrect oracle.

The probabilities of "no oracle" value in the table are evaluated when the number of agreements does not exceed 50%. An incorrect oracle is established when a false majority is found. For the training size 1, an oracle is always found because there could not be a disagreement if only one WS is tested in the training phase. However, the probability of finding an in correct oracle is high. Please notice that, although only 12 of the 60 WS are correct, the probability of finding a correct oracle for training = 1 is significantly higher than 12/60. The reason is that an incorrect WS does not always output an incorrect result.

Table 12 Probability of Establishing Correct Oracle

Training Size	Prob. of correct oracle	Prob. of no oracle	Prob. of incorrect oracle
1	76.9%	0.0%	23.1%
2	83.8%	16.3%	0.0%
3	98.1%	1.9%	0.0%
4	98.1%	0.6%	1.3%

5	98.1%	1.9%	0.0%

3.6.4 The Impacts of Training on Test Case Ranking

Data were also collected for evaluating the impact of training size on the probabilities of finding the most powerful test case in terms of the number of faults it can detect. The most powerful test cases are used first in phase 2 to eliminate incorrect WS faster and thus saving test runs. Table 13 shows the results for training sizes 1, 2, 3, 4, and 5. It can be seen that a small training size has a higher probability of resulting incorrect test case ranking.

Table 13 Impact of Training Size on Test Case Ranking

Training Size	Prob. of correct ranking	Prob. of no decision	Prob. of incorrect ranking
1	60.0%	0.0%	40.0%
2	35.6%	59.4%	5.0%
3	65.1%	21.5%	13.4%
4	71.5%	16.3%	12.2%
5	75.8%	15.2%	9.0%

3.7 Web Service Group Testing with Windowing Mechanisms

New WS may have been designed and test using the known test cases. We have defined an adaptive window to limit the age of test cases being used in group testing. Further research and experiments are being performed to explore the impact of the age of the test cases.

The basic WebStrar testing process may considerably reduce testing runs. However, several issues exist in the basic WebStrar testing process:

- First, the volume testing is still expensive if both of the number of test cases and the number of services are large.
- Second, in an open environment, the service providers can certainly improve the quality of their services using the published test cases. Thus, as new WS arrive, those early potent test cases may start to lose their potency because the new WS will have passed these known test cases before submission.
- Third, test case potency and test case's oracle confidence are conflict with each other.

A mechanism is necessary to balance the tradeoffs. To address these issues, the section proposes a windowing approach to further improve the test effectiveness of WebStrar process.

This section extends the basic WebStrar framework by introducing a windowing mechanism in the volume testing phase. The set of WS under test in this phase is divided into small groups called windows. At the end of each window, testing results are collected to re-calculate the ranking of test cases and the confidence levels of oracles. Different strategies can be incorporated to evaluate the potency of a test case, i.e., the probability of detecting a fault, such as based on all historical data (this corresponds to the basic algorithm without windowing), based on the current window only, or based on most recent n windows. Test cases are re-organized with new ranking before starting the next window. By constantly monitoring test results, the windowing mechanism enables dynamic adjustment of the test strategies, such as the group test hierarchy, service rule-out strategy, and window size. The basic WebStrar volume testing process is improved by the continuous learning process. By incorporating the windowing mechanism, the two-phase training and volume testing process becomes a continuous learning process and the basic group testing process becomes more adaptive to dynamically changing environment. A case study is performed to illustrate the approach and the impacts of window sizes on test cost.

This section extends the basic two-phase testing process and introduces the windowing mechanism to further improve testing efficiency. Rather than testing a large number of WS simultaneously, WS are divided into subsets called windows and testing is exercised window by window. Testing results are analyzed for different strategies such as

- using all of the historical data,
- using the most recent windows, and
- using the current window only.

3.7.1 Windowing Algorithm

While it is desirable that a test case has a high potency P, it is also necessary to have a high confidence level C of the oracle associated with the test case. However, the relation $P = 1-C$ makes these two factors conflict: higher test case potency implies a lower oracle confidence level. It is necessary to achieve a balance between these two factors. To achieve this balance between the test case potency and oracle confidence, a windowing mechanism is introduced into the WebStrar framework, which can further reduce the test cost. The windowing mechanism consists of following steps:

1. Break down the WS under test (called sample set) into equal-sized windows, which are simply sets of WS. The window size is the number of WS in the set. The last window may have a different size.
2. Apply group testing on each window.
3. Compute test case potency and oracle confidence level at the end of each window and use the statistic data to guide the selection of test case in the next window.

This process learns from the test results of the previous windows to optimize the new test strategies dynamically and hence can better balance the tradeoffs and improve the test effectiveness. Notice that the windowing mechanism is applied to the volume testing phase (phase 2) only without changing the initial training phase during which an initial set of WS is randomly selected, group tested, and the test cases are ranked at the end of the training phase. Although the training phase can be considered as the first window of the new process with windowing, it limits the training size to the window size.

The major difference between the basic WebStrar volume testing and this new windowing algorithm is that, in the former process, test case ranks and the confidence level are continuously updated after each test and it takes the entire history into consideration. In the latter scheme, the updates are done at the end of each window, resulting significant cost saving, and only the last window or last a few windows' test results are taking into consideration, giving a heavier weight to the latest testing results. This can prevent the WS developers to do "design-for-test-cases" work that make sure their WS pass the well-known test cases.

In fact, the basic WebStrar volume testing can be considered a special case of the process with windowing when

1. the window size = 1 and
2. all previous windows are taken into consideration in evaluating test case potency and oracle confidence.

3.7.2 Re-Evaluation of Test Case Potency

The windowing approach enables the re-evaluation of the test case potency at the end of the each window. Let

$H_{tc,i}$ be the number of failed services by test case *tci* in window *i*;

$S_{tc,i}$ be the total number of tested services by the test case *tci* in window *i*;

$P_{tc,i}$ be the potency of a test case *tci* in window *i*;

w_i be the weight of the window *i*, where $i \geq 1, w_{i+1} \geq w_i$; and

$PP_{tc,i}$ be the accumulated potency of a test case *tci* after window *i*.

We have:

$$P_{tc,i} = H_{tc,i} / S_{tc,i}, \text{ and } PP_{tc,n} = F(w_1 P_{tc,1}, w_2 P_{tc,2}, \dots w_n P_{tc,n}).$$

A simple definition of F is to use the weighted average:

$$PP_{tc,n} = \frac{\sum_{i=1,n} w_i P_{tc,i}}{\sum_{i=1,n} w_i}$$

Different strategies may be applied to select the weight. For example, we can simply take

$$w_i = i, \text{ and then we have } \quad PP_{tc,n} = \frac{\sum\limits_{i=1,n} iP_{tc,i}}{\sum\limits_{i=1,n} i} \qquad (1)$$

A more stringent strategy is to define F as the decay function since the influence of test case potency in previous windows on current test case ranking will decay over time. Hence, we have

$$w_i = e^{-(n-i)},$$

$$\text{and } \quad PP_{tc,n} = \frac{\sum\limits_{i=1,n}(P_{tc,i} * e^{-(n-i)})}{\sum\limits_{i=1,n} e^{-(n-i)}} \qquad (2)$$

Table 14 gives a simplified example of the dynamic adjustment process. Suppose 3 test cases tc_1, tc_2 and tc_3 are used to test 170 services which are divided into a training set of size 20 and three windows of size 50. The weight of the window is the sequence number of the window, that is, $w_i = i$. During the training phase, the potency of tc_1, tc_2 and tc_3 are tested 50%, 25% and 20%, and ranked 1, 2, 3 respectively. After each window test, the potencies of test cases are recalculated using the previous two functions: PP in (1) as the weighted average, and PP in (2) as the decay function. By constant adjustment after each window, the cost of each window test decreases. Compared with the basic WebStrar testing approach, the adjusted windowing approach can save test runs by $(370 - 320)/380 \approx 16\%$.

Table 14 Example test cases potency calculation

	Training			Window 1					Window 2					Window 3				
	H	S	P	H	S	P	PP(1)	PP(2)	H	S	P	PP(1)	PP(2)	H	S	P	PP(1)	PP(2)
tc1	10	20	50%	10	50	20%	20%	20%	5	20	25%	23%	24%	5	20	25%	24%	25%
tc2	4	20	20%	15	30	50%	50%	50%	20	50	40%	43%	43%	20	50	40%	42%	41%
tc3	5	20	25%	10	40	25%	25%	25%	10	30	33%	30%	31%	10	30	33%	32%	32%

In practice, the size of sample services and the number of test cases are much larger. The proposed mechanisms can greatly reduce test runs.

3.7.3 Fixed and Adaptive Window Size

In general, two approaches exist to address the sizing problem: the fixed window approach and the adaptive window approach. Fixed window is easier to implement and manage while adaptive window can be better reactive to the dynamically changing operational environment.

- If the window size is very small, the test cases can not rank sufficiently, which can lead to incorrect oracle, leading to incorrect WS ranking;

- On the contrary, if the window size is too large, then it goes back to the basic WebStrar volume testing without windowing.

Hence, the major issue for fixed window algorithm is to find an appropriate window size that could lead least testing runs. Different strategies exist to select a proper window size for the purpose of saving cost.

Rather than pre-defined window size, adaptive window size strategy is to dynamically determine the proper window size by monitoring run-time system behavior. A key issue of the adaptive approach is to decide when to adapt and how to adapt. One solution is based on the arrival rate of services, that is, based on TIME rather than the number of services. If the arriving rate is high, we can reduce the window size; otherwise, we can enlarge the window size.

Another solution is based on the change of the potency of test cases. A Ranking Difference (RD) is introduced as follows to show the fluctuation of potency changes.

$$RD_{i,i-1} = \sqrt{\frac{1}{n}\sum_{j=1,n}(PP_{tc_j,i} - PP_{tc_j,i-1})^2}$$

where,

$RD_{i,i-1}$ is the ranking difference of two successive windows i and i-1.

$RP_{tc_j,i}$ and $RP_{tc_j,i-1}$ are the accumulated potency of a test case tc_j at two successive windows i and i-1.

Figure 39 shows that the test cases Ranking Difference decreases when testing is exercised within a window.

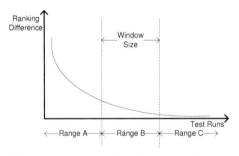

Figure 39 RD decreases when performing testing within the window

In range A, the RD is large, and test cases ranking changes dramatically, indicating that test case ranking are not solid enough to sufficiently decide the correctness of test cases potency. Window size could not be set into this range. In range C, the Ranking Difference decreases to 0, which means the test case ranking would not change even if more testing runs are exercised. Testing runs in this range are useless and wasteful so the window has to be closed before landing into range C. Hence, the window size should be set into range B. Two thresholds are set: the upper bound and the lower bound. The adjustment of the window size will be triggered once the RD drops outside the boundaries. When the RD is greater than the upper bound, the window size should be decreased; and if the RD is less than the lower bound, the window size should be increased.

3.7.4 Reliable Oracle Establishment

Though a smaller training size can lower the testing cost, a small training size can lead to incorrect oracle, leading to incorrect WS ranking. A small training size can also lead to incorrect test case ranking, resulting in a higher test cost in the second phase. Therefore, it is critical to select a reasonable training size in the first phase.

In the WebStrar training phase where group testing is performed, an oracle is established using the majority voting mechanism. Due to the limited size of the training set, an incorrect oracle may be established. The windowing approach allows for the re-examination of a test oracle after each window of test and the re-calculation of its confidence level based on the latest test results. A log is created for each test case which records its oracles and the associated confidence level after each window test as well as accumulated reliability based on the entire testing history. Continue the definition in section 3.2, let

$C_{tc,i}$ be the confidence level of an oracle of test case tc in window i test; and

$CC_{tc,i}$ be the accumulated confidence of test case tci after window i test.

We have:

$$C_{tc,i} = (S_{tc,i} - H_{tc,i}) / S_{tc,i} , \text{ and } CC_{tc,n} = F(C_{tc,1}, C_{tc,2}, ... C_{tc,n}).$$

Different functions can be used to calculate C based on historical data, such as taking the minimum, maximum or average value of historical data. The confidence level of an oracle should not be lower than 50% since it is defined by the majority principle. To ensure the reliability of the oracle, a threshold can be set to monitor the change of oracle confidence level during each window test, and policies can be defined to specify the conditions that an oracle needs to be revalidated. For example, we take the average function to calculate the accumulated confidence level of a test case, that is,

$$CC_{tc,n} = \frac{\sum_{i=1,n} C_{tc,i}}{n}$$

Taking the example in Table 15, Table 15 gives the confidence levels $C_{tc,i}$ and accumulated confidence levels $CC_{tc,i}$ of the oracle of each test case at each window test. Suppose the threshold, t, is set to 70% and the policy says: "for a test case tc, if the accumulated confidence level of its oracle drops below the threshold for continuous 3 windows, that is, the majority voting mechanism should be triggered to re-calculate the oracle."

$$\exists i, i \geq 1, \ CC_{tc,i} \leq t, CC_{tc,i+1} \leq t, \text{and } CC_{tc,i+2} \leq t,$$

According to the policy, the oracle of tc_2 needs to be re-calculated after the three window tests, and hence, tc_2 will go through the majority voting process to re-establish its oracle.

Table 15 Example Confidence Level

	tc_1		tc_2		tc_3	
	$C_{tc_1,i}$	$CC_{tc_1,i}$	$C_{tc_2,i}$	$CC_{tc_2,i}$	$C_{tc_3,i}$	$CC_{tc_3,i}$
Training	50%	50%	80%	80%	75%	75%
Window 1	80%	80%	50%	50%	75%	75%
Window 2	75%	72.5%	60%	55%	67%	71%
Window 3	75%	76.7%	60%	56.7%	67%	69.7%

3.7.5 Case Study and Experiment Results

To comparatively study the improvement based on windowing schemes, we use the same BBS (Best Buy Stock) example as defined in the basic WebStrar algorithm. For the same specification (on making decision of what stock is the best-buy stock) 60 different BBS WS were implemented. Some of the implementations contain faults. Thirty-two test cases were generated. In this case study, we will compare the test cost of basic WebStrar approach, fixed windowing approach, and adaptive windowing approach.

A decay function is used to compute the potency of test cases. To simplify the process, we compute the most recent three windows, i.e.,

$$PP_{tc,n} = \frac{P_{tc,n-2} * e^{-2} + P_{tc,n-1} * e^{-1} + P_{tc,n}}{e^{-2} + e^{-1} + 1},$$

In the adaptive windowing approach, the upper threshold is set to 1 and the lower is 0.5, that is, to keep $0.5 < RD < 1$. In this experiment, we set the training set size to 10. Table 16 shows the cost (in total test runs) of the three approaches. It can be observed from the statistical results that the adaptive windowing approach is the most efficient one in terms of cost saving.

Table 16 BBS experiment results

	Basic	Fixed Window	Adaptive

	WEBSTRAR							Window
Cost	1125	Size	1	2	3	4	5	1051
		Cost	1073	1089	1107	1118	1139	
		Size	10	15	20	30	40	
		Cost	1167	1191	1195	1198	1194	

Figure 40 shows the cost saving efficiency for different approaches: the upper line denotes the basic WebStrar algorithm, the middle curve denotes the fixed window scheme, and the bottom line denotes the adaptive windowing scheme.

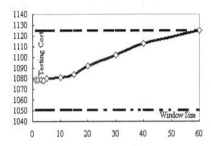

Figure 40 the Cost Comparison of the Three Schemes

CHAPTER 4
CRM: A COVERAGE RELATIONSHIP MODEL FOR TEST CASE SELECTION AND RANKING

Testing a group of software artifacts that implement the same specification might be time consuming, especially when the test case repository is large. In the meantime, some of test cases may cover the same aspects in the software, thus it is not necessary to apply all the test cases. This study proposes a Model-based Adaptive Test (MAT) case selection and ranking technique to eliminate duplicate test cases, i.e., test cases with the similar coverage, and rank the test cases according to their potency and coverage. This technique can be applied in various domains where multiple versions of applications are available to test, such as web service testing group testing, n-version applications, regression testing, and specification-based application testing. The MAT is based a statistical model based on earlier testing results, and the model can accurate determine the next sets of test cases to minimize the testing effort. The MAT is then applied to testing of multi-versioned web services and the results shows that the MAT can reduce testing effort while still maintain the effectiveness of testing.

4.1 Introduction

Statistics has been shown to be promising for software testing. Whittaker proposed a statistical software testing model and applied Markov chain to that model [198]. Statistical testing follows black-box testing with two extensions: the input sequence must be stochastically generated and the test history must be analyzed from a statistical point of view. The statistical testing model can be modeled as a Markov chain and a testing Markov chain. The usage Markov chain is used to model the state diagram of the software, while the testing Markov chain is used to collect the testing profiles. Software cybernetics [32] leverages controlled Markov chain (CMC) technique for software testing. The software under test serves as a controlled object and the software testing strategy serves as the controller and optimizer. In this way the software and the testing strategy forms a CMC, and control theory of Markov chains can be used to tackle software testing. However, CMC is currently limited to those software testing processes that can be modeled as Markov chains. The minimal test case selection algorithms were studied by Bryce and Colbourn [29].

This section proposes a Model-based Adaptive Testing (MAT) for multi-versioned software based a model called Coverage Relationship Model (CRM). The CRM can be used to select and rank test cases, and can identify and eliminate those duplicate test cases or those test cases that cover the same aspects. The MAT also can be used to rank the test cases according to their potency in an adaptive manner. In this way, software can be efficiently tested using the most potent test cases and with minimized effort. Furthermore, as more data will be collected, the model can automatically re-rank test cases based on the new testing results.

The proposed technique can be applied to various domains where multiple versions of applications are available such as:

- N-version programming [37]: N-version programming is used to fault-tolerance approach to ensure the reliability of systems. In an N-version programming model, multiple versions of system are used to implement the same function, and versions can be used as software recovery blocks as backup.

- Regression Testing: In a system development lifecycle, multiple versions of software will be developed, and in modern software development processes such as agile process, a new version of software can be created on a daily basis. Furthermore, in the Web. 2.0 paradigm [194], not only a new version will be created on a hourly basis, but also end users will be involved as co-developers while using the delivered products. Thus, during the entire development processes, numerous versions of software will be available.

- Standard-based testing: Standard-based applications are the systems that implement the functionality and interfaces specified in a published standard. For example, OASIS and W3C have published numerous standards, and vendors may develop their own software to implement those standards, and thus standard making organization often need to publish test cases to ensure that they meet the standard requirements. .

- Web Service Testing. Group Testing technique was originally developed for blood testing, and later for to software regression testing and web service testing. Group testing can be used when detecting faults in multiple versions of the same specification.

4.2 Coverage Relationship Model (CRM)

4.2.1 Motivation

For a sample set of applications S, after applying two test cases (TC) A and B respectively, A generates two output sets A_C and A_I. A_C denotes the correct output set, while A_I denotes the incorrect output set. Likewise, B generates a correct output set B_C and an incorrect output set B_I. Each set of artifacts is defined as a state. For example, if the software artifact generates the output A_C for a given test case, then the artifact is in state A_C.

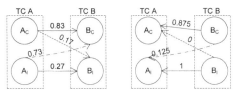

Figure 41 an example of overlap probability

For the artifacts in set A_C, they may be in set B_C or B_I when B is applied. The number on the arch from denotes the *Coverage Probability* $\vec{P}_{s1 \to s2}$ from set s1 to set s2. For example, from set A_C to B_C, the coverage probability $\vec{P}_{Ac \to Bc}$ is 0.83, which denotes that 83% artifacts in A_C will be in B_C when TC B is applied. The left part of Figure 41 shows the coverage probability from TC A to TC B. Similarly, from TC B to TC A, the coverage probability can also be calculated as shown in the right part of Figure 41.

Note that the coverage probability from one state S1 to another state S2 $\vec{P}_{s1 \to s2}$ does not necessarily be equal to $\vec{P}_{s2 \to s1}$. For example, if the size of A_C is 10, the size of B_C is 5, and the size of the intersection set between A_C and B_C is 4, then $\vec{P}_{Ac \to Bc}$ =4/10=0.6, while $\vec{P}_{Bc \to Ac}$= 4/5=0.8.

4.2.2 Coverage Relationship Model

Consider a more complex situation, where multiple TC exists and each TC has one correct set and multiple incorrect sets, as shown in Figure 42.

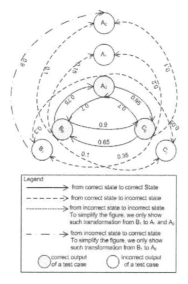

Figure 42.an example of test case Markov chain model

In the CRM, let

- $C= \{c_1, c_2,....c_m\}$ be the set of software artifacts that implement the same specification, where m is the size of the artifacts set.

- $T= \{t_1, t_2,....t_n\}$ be the set of test cases, where n is the size of the test case set.

- For each t_i, let

$$V_i = \{v_{i,0}, v_{i,1}, ..., v_{i,k}\},$$

be the different output values after applying t_i to C, where $(k+1)$ is the number of different output values.

- Let $s_{i,j}$ denotes the subset of C that generates the same output value $v_{i,j}$ for t_i, thus C can be represented as S_i after t_i is applied

$$S_i = \{\{s_{i,0}\}, \{s_{i,1}\}, ..., \{s_{i,k}\}\},$$

Because for a given input, there is one correct output (or a range of correct answers) and multiple incorrect outputs (or multiple ranges of incorrect answers), let $v_{i,0}$ be the correct output value, and $v_{i,1}, v_{i,2},...,v_{i,k}$ denote various incorrect output values. Thus, $s_{i,0}$ denotes the correct output set of C that generates the correct output value $v_{i,0}$, and $s_{i,1},s_{i,2},...,s_{i,k}$ denotes the incorrect output sets that generate those incorrect values $v_{i,1}, v_{i,2},...,v_{i,k}$, respectively.

- let $q_{i,j}$ be the size of the set $s_{i,j}$, thus Si has a corresponding Qi

$$Q_i = \{q_{i,0}, q_{i,1}, \ldots, q_{i,k}\},$$

- let $p_{i,j}$ denotes the probability that c generates the $s_{i,j}$,

$$p_{i,j} = \frac{q_{i,j}}{m}$$

4.2.3 Potency

The potency of a test case is that probability that the test case can detect a fault [182]. For example, if a test case has a potency of 0.5, it will fail half of the versions. Thus, a potency of test case ti can be defined as

$$Pot_i = 1 - p_{i,0} = 1 - \frac{q_{i,0}}{\sum_{0}^{k} q_{i,k}} = \frac{\sum_{1}^{k} q_{i,k}}{\sum_{0}^{k} q_{i,k}}$$

- For any two set of output $s_{i,\alpha}$ and sj,β, where $i \neq j$, the *Coverage Probability* $\vec{P}$ from $s_{i,\alpha}$ to sj,β is defined as:

$$\vec{P} s_{i,\alpha \to} sj,\beta = sizeof(s_{i,\alpha} \cap sj,\beta)/q_{i,\alpha}$$

The value on the edges of the CRM represents the Coverage Probability.

- use $\Delta(t_1, t_2)$ to denote if the testing domain of test case t_1 covers that of t_2, or simply say t_1 covers t_2; and use $\cancel{\Delta}(t_1, t_2)$ to denote if t_1 does not cover t_2;
- use the notation "+" to denote the overall testing domain of multiple test cases. For example, $\Delta(t_1 + t_2 + t_3 + \ldots + t_n, t_{n+1})$ means that the overall testing domain of $t_1, t_2, t_3 \ldots$ and t_n covers that of t_{n+1};

Lemma 1: For any two set $s_{i,\alpha}$ and sj,β, if $i = j$ then $s_{i,\alpha} \cap si,\beta = \emptyset$.

Proof: Because for any artifact, it cannot generate the correct output and incorrect output for a given TC at the same time.

Lemma 1 indicates that there is no coverage probability between two sets that belong to the same test case.

4.2.4 An Example

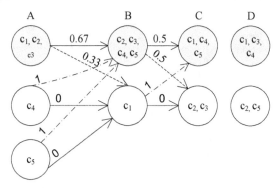

Figure 43 an Example of CRM consisting of 4 test cases and 5 versions

Figure 41 shows an example CRM consisting of four test cases and five versions, and shows the $\vec{P}$ from test case A to B, and the $\vec{P}$ from test case B to C. As can been seen from Figure 43, for test case A, there is:

$$S_A=\{\{c_1, c_2, c_3\}, \{c_4\}, \{c_5\}\},$$

and the potency of test case A is:

$$Pot_A=3/5=0.6$$

For test case B, there is

$$S_B=\{\{c_2, c_3, c_4, c_5\}, \{c_1\}\},$$

Thus, from the correct set of test case A to that of test case B, the transition probability is

$$\vec{P}= sizeof(\{c_1, c_2, c_3\} \cap \{c_2, c_3, c_4, c_5\})/sizeof\{c_1, c_2, c_3\}=2/3\approx0.67$$

4.3 CRM Construction

Table 17 shows an algorithm of construction the CRM. This algorithm uses a table data structure "CoverageProbalitilyMap" to store the coverage probability from one set to another set. Note that the arch in the map is bidirectional because the coverage relationship is bidirectional as shown in Figure 41.

Table 17 the Algorithm of Constructing the CRM

```
Input: C={c₁,c₂...,cₘ};
        T={t₁,t₂...,tₙ};
// 1st Step: Create all sets
foreach (tᵢ in T)
begin
        Vₗ←{vi,0};
        Sₗ←{Ø};
        foreach (cⱼ in C)
begin
                Output=apply tᵢ to cⱼ;
                if (output is NOT in Vᵢ)
                begin
                        Vₗ.addNewValue(Ouput);
                                Sₗ.addNewSet(cⱼ);
                end
                else Si.addComponentToSet(cᵢ);
        end
end

//2ⁿᵈ Calculate Coverage Probability
foreach (Sⱼ)
begin
        foreach (sᵢ,α in Sᵢ)
                foreach(sⱼ,β in Sⱼ)
        Begin
                P⃗ sᵢ,α→sⱼ,β ← sizeof(sᵢ,α∩sⱼ,β)/ sizeof(sᵢ,ⱼ)
                CoverageProbalitilyMap.addEdge(sᵢ,α, sⱼ,β, P⃗ );
        end
end
```

4.4 Simplified Coverage Relationship Model Analysis

It is expensive to construct the full CRM. Suppose on average each test case has k different outputs, the computational effort of calculating the coverage probability consisting of n test cases is $n*(n-1)*k^2$. Most times may only concerns about two sets: correct set and incorrect set, unless further study is needed to analyze the coverage relationship between different incorrect sets. Thus, this study proposes the Simplified Coverage Relationship Model (S-CRM) to reduce the computational complexity of constructing the full CRM. In S-CRM, each t_i has only two sets, a correct set $s_{i,C}$ and an incorrect set $s_{i,I}$, the incorrect set $s_{i,I}$ combines all the incorrect sets from the full CRM into one incorrect set by simply using the union operation, i.e.,

$$S_i=\{\{ s_{i,C}\}, \{ s_{i,I} \}\},$$

where $s_{i,I} = \bigcup_{j=1}^{k} s_{i,j}$

S-CRM can reduce the computational effort from $n*(n-1)*k^2$ to $n*(n-1)*4$. Hereinafter, the discussion will be based on the S-CRM.

4.4.1 S-CRM Analysis Preparation

In S-CRM, for two test cases, four types of coverage probability exist: from correct set to correct set (C→C), from correct set to incorrect set (C→I), from incorrect set to correct set

(I→C), and from incorrect set to incorrect set (I→I), as shown in

Figure 44:

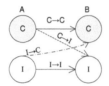

Figure 44 S-CRM example

For simplicity purpose, in the following analysis we will always calculate $\vec{P}$ from test case A to test case B, so in the subscript of $\vec{P}$ we will omit A and B. For example, $\vec{P}_{A,I\rightarrow B,I}$ is referred to as $\vec{P}_{I\rightarrow I}$.

The coverage probability from the any set is 1, thus we can have equation (1) and (2):

$$\vec{P}_{C\rightarrow C} + \vec{P}_{C\rightarrow I} = 1 \qquad (1)$$

$$\vec{P}_{I\rightarrow C} + \vec{P}_{I\rightarrow I} = 1 \qquad (2)$$

Since p is the potency of test cases, thus we can have equation (3) and (4)

$$1\text{-Pot}_B = (1\text{-Pot}_A) * \vec{P}_{C\rightarrow C} + \text{Pot}_A * \vec{P}_{I\rightarrow C} \qquad (3)$$

$$\text{Pot}_B = (1\text{-Pot}_A) * \vec{P}_{C\rightarrow I} + \text{Pot}_A * \vec{P}_{I\rightarrow I} \qquad (4)$$

Let $\vec{P}_H$ be the pre-defined high bound threshold on coverage probability, e.g., $\vec{P}_H = 0.99$.

Let $\vec{P}_L$ be the pre-defined low bound threshold on coverage probability, e.g., $\vec{P}_L = 0.01$.

Let Pot_H be the pre-defined high bound threshold on potency, e.g., $\text{Pot}_H = 0.98$.

Let Pot_L be the pre-defined low bound threshold on potency, e.g., $\text{Pot}_L = 0.02$.

Rule 1: Coverage relationship is not symmetric and in fact, for any two test cases t_a and t_b, if $\Delta(t_a, t_b)$, then $\not\Delta(t_b, t_a)$

Lemma 2: If $\text{Pot}_b < \text{Pot}_a$, then $\not\Delta(t_b, t_a)$; if $\Delta(t_a, t_b)$, then $\text{Pot}_b < \text{Pot}_a$.

Proof:

Let

A_C and B_C be the correct set of t_a and t_b respectively, and

The $\vec{P}\, t_{b,C\to}\, t_{a,C} = $ sizeof($A_C \cap B_C$)/sizeof(B_C)

The $\vec{P}\, t_{a,C\to}\, t_{b,\,C} = $ sizeof($A_C \cap B_C$)/sizeof(A_C)

$Pot_b < Pot_a => q_a < q_b$

$\qquad => \vec{P}\, t_{a,C} \to t_{b,\,C} > \vec{P}\, t_{b,C \to}\, t_{a,C}$

If $\vec{P}\, t_{b,C} \to t_{a,C} > \vec{P}_H$, then also $\vec{P}\, t_{a,C} \to t_{b,\,C} > \vec{P}_H$. In this case, $\Delta(t_a, t_b)$ instead of $\Delta(t_b, t_a)$, because the coverage relationship is not mutual according to rule 1.

Lemma 2 indicates that less potent test cases never cover more potent test cases. If a coverage relationship exists between any two test cases, it must be that the more potent test case covers the less potent test case.

Lemma 2 implies an optimization method to further reduce the effort of constructing the S-CRM. If all test cases are ranked in terms of their potencies, then those test cases in low rank do not cover the highly ranked test case. For example, if test case t_a ranks higher than test case t_b, one only needs to determine if t_a cover t_b by using $\vec{P}_{C \to C}$ or $\vec{P}_{C \to I}$ from t_a to t_b, or using $\vec{P}_{I \to C}$ or $\vec{P}_{I \to I}$ from t_b to t_a. Therefore, one only needs to calculate the coverage probability from the current test case to all test cases after it. Thus, the computational effort of construing the S-CRM can be further reduced from $n*(n-1)$ to $n*(n-1)/2$.

Lemma 3: for any two test cases t_a and t_b, and any test case set T, if $\Delta(t_a, t_b)$, then $\Delta(T+ t_a, T+t_b)$

Proof:

Because $\Delta(ta, tb) => \vec{P}_{t_a,C \to t_b,C} = $ sizeof($A_C \cap B_C$)/sizeof(A_C) $\geq \vec{P}_H$

$\vec{P}_{(T+t_a),C \to (T+t_b),C} = $ sizeof($T_C \cup (A_C \cap B_C)$)/sizeof($T_C \cup A_C$)

$\qquad\qquad \geq$ sizeof($A_C \cap B_C$)/sizeof(A_C)

$\qquad\qquad = \vec{P}_{t_a,C \to t_b,C} \geq \vec{P}_H$

When $T_C \subseteq A_C \cap B_C$,

sizeof($T_C \cup (A_C \cap B_C)$)/sizeof($T_C \cup A_C$) = sizeof($A_C \cap B_C$)/sizeof(A_C)

Otherwise,

sizeof($T_C \cup (A_C \cap B_C)$)/sizeof($T_C \cup A_C$) > sizeof($A_C \cap B_C$)/sizeof(A_C)

Thus, $\Delta(T + t_a, T + t_b)$

4.4.2 From Correct Set to Correct Set (C→C)

Two cases may happen to $\vec{P}_{C \to C}$:

$\vec{P}_{C \to C} > \vec{P}_H$

Analysis: According to equation (1), one can have

$$\vec{P}_{C \to I} < 1 - \vec{P}_H$$

This case indicates that for those versions that test case A cannot detect the fault, test case B is very unlikely to detect the fault as well. Therefore, test case A covers B, and applying test case B is almost in vain if test case A cannot detect the fault.

Conclusion: $\Delta(A,B)$

Recommendation: eliminate B and use A only

$$\vec{P}_{C \to C} < \vec{P}_L$$

Analysis: According to equation (1) and (4), one can have

$$\text{Pot}_B = (1-P_A)*(1-\vec{P}_{C \to C}) + p_A * \vec{P}_{I \to I} \approx 1 - p_A * \vec{P}_{I \to C} \quad (5)$$

This case indicates that, given a fixed $\vec{P}_{I \to C}$, the less possibly the test case A can detect the fault, the more possibly that test case B can detect the fault. Thus, test case A does not cover test case B, and one should calculate $\vec{P}_{C \to C}$ from B to A to see if $\Delta(B,A)$.

Conclusion: $\not\Delta(A,B)$

Recommendation: Calculate $\vec{P}_{C \to C}$ from B to A to see if $\Delta(B,A)$

4.4.3 From Correct Set to Incorrect Set (C→I)

This is the contrary case as C→C. Because according to equation (1), the larger the $\vec{P}_{C \to C}$ is, the smaller the $\vec{P}_{C \to I}$. Thus, the contrary rules in C→C can apply. Two cases may happen to $\vec{P}_{C \to I}$:

- $\vec{P}_{C \to I} > \vec{P}_H$
  - Analysis: This case indicates that $\vec{P}_{C \to C} < \vec{P}_L$
  - Conclusion: $\not\Delta(A,B)$
  - Recommendation: Calculate $\vec{P}_{C \to I}$ from B to A to see if $\Delta(B,A)$
- $\vec{P}_{C \to I} < \vec{P}_L$
  - Analysis: This case indicates $\vec{P}_{C \to C} > \vec{P}_H$
  - Conclusion: $\Delta(A,B)$
  - Recommendation: eliminate B and use A only

4.4.4 From Incorrect Set to Correct Set (I→C)

Two cases may happen to $\vec{P}_{I \to C}$:

- $\vec{P}_{I \to C} > \vec{P}_H$
  - This case indicates that for those versions that have been failed by test case A, it is very unlikely that test case can detect the fault. Thus, test case B does not cover test case A.

- o Conclusion: $\not\Delta$ (B,A)
- o Recommendation: Calculate $\vec{P}_{I\to C}$ from B to A to see if $\Delta(A,B)$
- $\vec{P}_{I\to C} < \vec{P}_L$
  - o This case indicates that if for those versions that have been failed by test case A, it is very likely that test case B can fail them as well. Thus, test case B covers test case A.
  - o Conclusion: $\Delta(B,A)$
  - o Recommendation: eliminate A, and use B only

4.4.5 From Incorrect Set to Incorrect Set (I→I)

This is the contrary case as I→C. Because according to equation (2), the larger the $\vec{P}_{I\to C}$ is, the smaller the $\vec{P}_{I\to I}$ is. Thus, the contrary rules in I→C can apply to I→I. Two cases may happen to $\vec{P}_{I\to I}$:

- $\vec{P}_{I\to I} > \vec{P}_H$
  - o Analysis: This case indicates that $\vec{P}_{I\to C} < \vec{P}_L$
  - o Conclusion: $\Delta(B,A)$
  - o Recommendation: eliminate A, and use B only
- $\vec{P}_{I\to I} < \vec{P}_L$
  - o Analysis: This case indicates $\vec{P}_{I\to C} > \vec{P}_H$
  - o Conclusion: $\not\Delta$ (B,A)
  - o Recommendation: Calculate $\vec{P}_{I\to I}$ from B to A to see if $\Delta(A,B)$

4.4.6 Summary Table

Table 17 summarizes the four ways to analyze the coverage relationship for S-CRM: $\vec{P}_{C\to C}, \vec{P}_{C\to I}, \vec{P}_{I\to C},$ and $\vec{P}_{I\to I}$. According to equation (1) and (2): $\vec{P}_{C\to C}$ and $\vec{P}_{C\to I}$ are interchangeable, and $\vec{P}_{I\to C}$ and $\vec{P}_{I\to I}$ are also interchangeable, thus these four parameters can be categorized into two groups in terms of their source sets: the source set $\vec{P}$ is correct set ($\vec{P}_{C\to C}$ and $\vec{P}_{C\to I}$), and the source set of $\vec{P}$ is incorrect set ($\vec{P}_{I\to C}$ and $\vec{P}_{I\to I}$). This study uses $\vec{P}_{C\to C}$ and $\vec{P}_{I\to C}$ to delegate each group respectively to explain the difference.

Table 18 Summary of the Coverage Probability Analysis

From Test Cases A to B	$\vec{P} < \vec{P}_L$	$\vec{P}_L < \vec{P} < \vec{P}_H$	$\vec{P}_H < \vec{P}$
C→C	Conclusion: Δ (A,B) Recommendation: Calculate $\vec{P}_{C\to C}$ from B to A to see if $\Delta(B,A)$	Conclusion: A covers B to some extent, Recommendation: Calculate $\vec{P}_{C\to C}$ from B to A to see if	Conclusion: $\Delta(A,B)$ Recommendation: eliminate B and use A only

		Δ(B,A).	
C→I	Conclusion: Δ(A,B) Recommendation: eliminate B and use A only	Conclusion: A covers B to some extent, Recommendation: Calculate $\vec{P}_{C \to I}$ from B to A to see if Δ(B,A)	Conclusion: Δ (A,B) Recommendation: Calculate $\vec{P}_{C \to I}$ from B to A to see if Δ(B,A)
I→C	Conclusion: Δ(B,A) Recommendation: eliminate A, and use B only	B covers A to some extent, Recommendation: Calculate $\vec{P}_{I \to C}$ from B to A to see if Δ(A,B)	Conclusion: Δ (B,A) Recommendation: Calculate $\vec{P}_{I \to C}$ from B to A to see if Δ(A,B)
I→I	Conclusion: Δ (B,A) Recommendation: Calculate $\vec{P}_{I \to I}$ from B to A to see if Δ(A,B)	B covers A to some extent, Recommendation: Calculate $\vec{P}_{I \to I}$ from B to A to see if Δ(A,B)	Conclusion: Δ(B,A) Recommendation: eliminate A and use B only

In most cases, both $\vec{P}_{C \to C}$ and $\vec{P}_{I \to C}$ can find the coverage relationship between two test cases. However, in the following cases, choosing $\vec{P}_{C \to C}$ or $\vec{P}_{I \to C}$ to calculate the coverage probability from test cases t_A to t_B is a tradeoff between accuracy and efficiency.

- When the potency of both test cases is very small, e.g., $Pot_A < Pot_L$ and $Pot_B < Pot_L$

For example, for a set C consisting of one hundred and two components, if t_A fails 101th application only, and t_B fails 100th application only, then from t_A to t_B: $\vec{P}_{C \to C} = 99\% >= \vec{P}_H$, which indicates t_A covers t_B, and t_B should be eliminated. However, the reason that $\vec{P}_{C \to C}$ reaches a large value is because the correct sets of both test cases are large, thus it does not necessarily indicate t_A cover t_B. On the contrary, from $\vec{P}_{I \to C} = 100\%$ one can conclude Δ (t_B, t_A), and both t_A and t_B should be kept for further testing. Thus, in this case $\vec{P}_{I \to C}$ is more accurate than $\vec{P}_{C \to C}$. On the other hand, compared to $\vec{P}_{I \to C}$, $\vec{P}_{C \to C}$ is more efficient in terms of test cases selection, because $\vec{P}_{C \to C}$ will eliminate ineffective test cases even if they are not covered by other test cases(e.g., t_B).

- Conclusion: In this case, $\vec{P}_{C \to C}$ misses some ineffective test cases if they are not covered by other test cases, which can lead to a compact but potent test case set; On the contrary, $\vec{P}_{I \to C}$ keeps any ineffective test cases even if they only add a little new coverage to the existing test case set T, which may lead an accurate but large test cases set. $\vec{P}_{C \to C}$ trades accuracy for efficiency, while $\vec{P}_{I \to C}$ trades efficiency for accuracy.
- Countermeasure: If accuracy is more important than efficiency, two alternative countermeasures can be used to increase the accuracy:
  - Use $\vec{P}_{I \to C}$ instead of $\vec{P}_{C \to C}$
  - If still use $\vec{P}_{C \to C}$, increase the threshold $\vec{P}_H$, make $\vec{P}_H > 1 - Pot_L$.

- When the potency of both test cases is very large, e.g., $Pot_A > Pot_H$ and $Pot_B > Pot_H$
  - Analysis:

    For example, for a set C consisting of one hundred and two components, if t_A fails all components except the 101th, and t_B fails all components except the 100th, then from t_A to t_B: $\vec{P}_{I \rightarrow C} = 1\%$, which indicates $\Delta(t_B, t_A)$, and t_A should be eliminated. However, the reason that $\vec{P}_{I \rightarrow C}$ reaches a large value is because the incorrect sets of both test cases are large, thus it does not necessarily indicate t_B cover t_A. On the contrary, from $\vec{P}_{C \rightarrow C} = 0\% < \vec{P}_L$ one can conclude Δ (t_A, t_B), and both t_A and t_B should be kept for further testing. Thus, in this case $\vec{P}_{C \rightarrow C}$ is more accurate than $\vec{P}_{I \rightarrow C}$. On the other hand, compared to $\vec{P}_{C \rightarrow C}, \vec{P}_{I \rightarrow C}$ is more efficient in terms of test cases selection, because $\vec{P}_{I \rightarrow C}$ will eliminate the test cases if they are cannot detect much more fault than other test cases. (e.g., t_A).
  - Conclusion: In this case, $\vec{P}_{I \rightarrow C}$ misses those test cases that only add a little new coverage than the existing test case set T, which can lead to a compact but still potent test case set; On the contrary, $\vec{P}_{C \rightarrow C}$ keeps any test cases as long as if they can add new coverage than the existing test case set T, which may lead an accurate but large test cases set. $\vec{P}_{I \rightarrow C}$ trades accuracy for efficiency, while $\vec{P}_{C \rightarrow C}$ trades efficiency for accuracy.
  - Countermeasure: If accuracy is more important than efficiency, two alternative countermeasures can be used to increase the accuracy:
    - Use $\vec{P}_{C \rightarrow C}$ instead of $\vec{P}_{I \rightarrow C}$
    - If still use $\vec{P}_{I \rightarrow C}$, decrease the threshold $\vec{P}_L$, make $\vec{P}_L < 1 - Pot_H$.

Since any of the four types of coverage probability ($\vec{P}_{C \rightarrow C}, \vec{P}_{C \rightarrow I}, \vec{P}_{I \rightarrow C}, \vec{P}_{I \rightarrow I}$) can be used to analyze the coverage relationship, one can use only one to construct the S-CRM. Thus, the computational effort of constructing the S-CRM can be further reduced from n*(n-1)*4 to n*(n-1).

4.5 Adaptive Test Cases Ranking

4.5.1 Test Case Ranking Criteria

This section proposes two adaptive test case ranking algorithms. Both algorithms rank test cases according to their potency and CRM. The higher the potency of a test case is, the higher its rank is. The purpose is to apply the test cases with the highest probability to detect failures first to reduce test cost by ruling out failed versions as soon as possible. However, ranking by potency alone is not an optimal way of test case selection, as two potent test cases may cover the same aspects of the software. Thus, ranking by potency may subject the software to be penalized by the same mistakes multiple times.

One way to address the problem is to analyze how test cases are developed. Specifically, if two test cases were developed to evaluate the same aspects of software, e.g., control flow or data flow, and on the same segments of software, then these two test cases have almost identical coverage. This section takes a new approach. Instead of evaluating how test cases are derived, it evaluates the test case coverage by the earlier results obtained. If TC A and B fail the same set of versions, their coverage is highly correlated. If they fail completely different set of versions, they may have no coverage overlap.

While analyzing how test cases are derived may yield accurate results, assigning coverage relationship by examining test results have several distinct advantages:

- The entire coverage identification process can be automated to eliminate human errors;
- There is no need to track and record the derivation or rational of test cases; and
- An identical testing process applied to the same code segments may still produce test cases that may have inconsistent results. For example, they may detect different bugs, or only one of them detects a bug. For example, one of two control flow test cases may detect an incorrect action within a path, while the other may detect a fault in a decision in the same path, or not at all. However, the CRM approach is completely results driven based on data collected.

As CRM is totally based on test results, thus two test cases derived from two different testing techniques and address two completely different code segments may still have identical coverage in the CRM. This does not imply that the two test cases address the same segment and/or aspects of the code. Instead, it implies only that the people who made the first mistake also made the second mistake in another part of the code by accident. This situation is rare, but it can happen. As more data will be collected during the process, test cases developed using different techniques will eventually detect different sets of versions. Statistically, test cases derived from different testing techniques should have different test coverage even though some coincidence may happen.

The proposed test case selection is based on

a) test case potency;

b) the CRM obtained.

The CRM overwrites the potency criterion, i.e..,, for a set of existing test case T, and two new test cases $t_a \notin T$ and $t_b \notin T$, even if $p_{a,I} > p_{b,I}$, but if $\Delta(T+ t_b, T+ t_a)$, then t_b should rank higher than t_a.

4.5.2 Test Case Ranking Algorithm

Two ranking algorithms are given in Table 19 and Table 20 respectively. Table 19 describes a C→C algorithm for adaptive test cases ranking by using $\vec{P}_{C \to C}$. Table 20 presents an I→I algorithm for test case ranking by using $\vec{P}_{I \to I}$.

Table 19 C→C Algorithm

Initialize component set $C=\{c_1,c_2...,c_m\}$;
Initialize test case ranking $T=\{t_1,t_2...,t_n\}$ according to their potency;

TestCase* $t=t_1$; $\vec{P}_{C \to C}=0$;
While (t!=null)
Begin
    foreach(t_i that t_i.rank<t.rank)
    Begin
        $\vec{P}_{C \to C}$←calculate the coverage probability from t to t_i;
        if ($\vec{P}_{C \to C} >= \vec{P}_H$)　// t covers t_i
            then delete (t_i);
        else if ($\vec{P}_{C \to C} <= \vec{P}_L$) // t does not covers t_i
            then calculate the coverage probability from ti　to t to see if t_i cover t;
            else moveToEnd(t_i); // t covers t_i partially, move t_i to the end of the rank
    End
    t.ranked=true;
    t=t→next;
End

Table 20 I→I Algorithm

Initialize component set $C=\{c1,c2...,cm\}$;
Initialize test case ranking $T=\{t_1,t_2...,t_n\}$ according to their potency;
TestCase* $t=t_1$; $\vec{P}_{I \to I}=0$;
While (t!=null)
begin
    foreach(t_i that t_i.rank<t.rank)
    begin
        $\vec{P}_{I \to I}$ ←calculate the coverage probability from ti to t;
        if ($\vec{P}_{I \to I} >= \vec{P}_H$)　// t covers t_i
            then delete (t_i);
        else if ($\vec{P}_{I \to I} <= \vec{P}_L$) // t does not covers t_i
            then calculate the coverage probability from t_i to t to see if t_i cover t;
            else moveToEnd(t_i); //t covers t_i partially, move t_i to the end of the rank
    end
    t.ranked=true;
    t=t→next;
end

4.5.3 An Adaptive Algorithm

These algorithms should keep adaptive because the test case can be re-ranked whenever new test cases are added. In this way, test cases are constantly being ranked as the test is being performed. Only the most potent test cases that has least coverage overlap with already applied test cases will be selected for test execution. A two-step adaptive algorithm is listed in Table 21.

Table 21 the adaptive algorithm

Initialize test case ranking $T=\{t_1,t_2...,t_n\}$ according to their potency;

Step1: $T' \leftarrow$ using the C→C algorithm or I→I algorithm to rank T.
Step2: Rank newly added test case t.

int index←0;
t.Pot←t.calculatePotency(C);

//two iterations: 1st iteration is to check if t is covered by more potent TC.
foreach(t_i in T')
begin
    if (t.Pot<= t_i.Pot)
    begin
        $\vec{P}_{t, I \rightarrow ti, I}$←calculate the $\vec{P}_{I \rightarrow I}$ from t to t_i;
        if ($\vec{P}_{I \rightarrow I} >= \vec{P}_H$) **then** exit; //$t_i$ covers t, just ignore t.
        index←i;
    end
end
//2st iteration is to check if t covers less potent TC.
foreach(t_i in T')
begin
    if (t.Pot> t_i.Pot)
    begin
        $\vec{P}_{ti, I \rightarrow t, I}$←calculate the $\vec{P}_{I \rightarrow I}$ from t_i to t;
        if ($\vec{P}_{I \rightarrow I} >= \vec{P}_H$) //t covers t_i, replace t_i with t.
        begin
            T'.delete(i);
            if (i<index) index←index-1;
        end
    end
end
T'.insert(t, index+1);

When a new test case t is added into the test case set, its potency is calculated and its result sets are established by performing testing on the component set C. For all test cases that are more potent than t, the coverage relationship is calculated to check if t is covered by these test cases; for all test cases that are less potent than t, the coverage relationship is calculated to check if t covers these test cases.

4.6 Test Case Generation by Swiss Cheese Approach

4.6.1 Swiss Cheese Approach Introduction

Swiss Cheese (SC) [177][176] is an approach to identify potent test cases based on the boolean expressions extracted from the conditions and decisions in the program. SC was developed from the modified condition/decision coverage (MC/DC) [39][36]. Different from MC/DC, SC generates a unique test case set for logically equivalent boolean expressions even if they may be in different format. MC/DC depends on how expression is formulated. SC is based on K-map. Because expressions that have the equivalent logic but different formats generate the same K-map, thus SC is independent of the topological structure of the expression. For example, as show in Figure 45, the following two boolean expressions have equivalent logic.

$$z = a\overline{c} + b$$
$$= bc + a\overline{c} + \overline{a}b\overline{c}$$

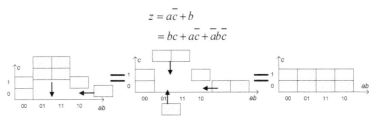

Figure 45. Two expressions are equivalent but in different expressions

MC/DC is also sensitive to user selection. Different minimal test set may be chosen by different users even for a same Boolean expression. A typical example is Boolean expression A xor B, whose pairs table is given in Table 22. Note that in this case, there are four minimal test sets, {1,2,3}, {1,2,4}, {1,3,4} or {2,3,4}. User can generate any of those four minimal tests while still satisfy MC/DC coverage criterion.

Table 22 Pairs Table of A xor B Using MC/DC

Number	AB	Result	A_1	B_1
1	TT	F	3	2
2	TF	T	4	1
3	FT	T	1	4
4	FF	F	2	3

4.6.2 Swiss Cheese Map

SC approach is named by the appearance of Swiss Cheese Map (SC-map). SC-map looks like a piece of bubbled Swiss cheese, as shown in Figure 46. In SC-map, each cell corresponds to a test case, and each cell contains a pair of Hamming distance (HD) and Boundary count (BC). The (HD, BD) pair indicates the potency of the test case.

Hamming distance, named after R.W. Hamming, is usually defined as the number of different bits between two strings. HD of two binary numbers or two min-terms in our study is defined as the number of bits between the two terms in which the two differ. For example, the HD between two min-terms "001111" and "010011" is three.

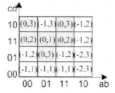

Figure 46. SC-map example

The HD of a cell is defined as following:

• The HD of a cell C is 0, if the cell is with non-white color and at least one of the neighboring cells has a white color. Cells with HD = 0 form the boundary of a Boolean expression.

• For positive test case generation, HD of a cell C is p+1, if at least one of the neighboring cells has a HD of p and there is no neighboring cells whose HD is less than p, where p $\geq$ 0.

• For negative test case generation, HD of a cell C is n-1, if at least one of the neighboring cells has a HD of n and there is no neighboring cells whose HD is greater than (or absolute value less than) n, where n$\leq$ 0. The purpose of defining negative HD is to emphasize the negative testing. If we consider the absolute value, the two cases are identical. Thus, we will imply the positive test generation unless explicitly mentioned.

Given a cell with HD = p, the BC is defined as:

• number of neighbor cells with HD = p – 1, if p >= 0

• number of neighbor cells with HD = p + 1, if p < 0

Figure 46 shows the SC-map corresponding to the Boolean expression: $\overline{abcd} + \overline{abc}\overline{d} + \overline{abcd} + \overline{abcd} + abcd + abc\overline{d}$. From the figure one can see that 6 cells correspond to *positive test cases* (HD = 0), marked in gray pattern. The remaining 10 cells correspond to *negative test cases* (HD < 0), in white color.

Three important lemmas about SC are listed as follows. The detailed proof can be found in [177].

1. the smaller the |HD| is, the more potent the TC is.

2. The larger the BC is, the more potent the TC is.

3. HD is the primary factor and BC is a secondary factor to decide the potency of test cases.

4.6.3 Specification-based Test Case Generation

SC approach can generate test cases based on the specification, for example, WS specification. A Web service is an instance or implementation of the Web service specification. Such a specification can be a Web Services Description Language (WSDL) file, or a Web Ontology Language for Service (OWL-S) file. WSDL file presents the required interface of a function. Web service client can invoke any external Web Services that implement the WSDL file. A number of Web service vendors may develop the same interface according to the WSDL or OWL-S but with different internal implementations. WSDL does not specify the algorithm to be used. Instead, it only specifies the input-output relationships. Thus, potentially different algorithms can be used if they achieve the same functionality. The OWL-S specifications are different as they may specify the high-level algorithms to be used. With the OWL-S, SC approach can generates test cases as shown in Figure 47.

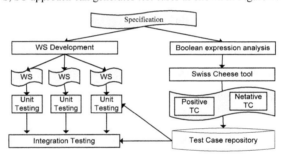

Figure 47 Specification-based TC generation

After obtaining the specification, boolean expression analysis method can be used to extract the full scenario coverage of boolean expressions. The Boolean expressions can be applied as the input to the Swiss Cheese Automated Test Case Generation tool. The Test Case Generation tool generates both positive and negative test cases and stores them into the test cases repository. Positive test cases are used to test if the WS output meets the specification for the legitimate inputs, while negative test cases are used to test the robustness, i.e., the behavior of the WS when unexpected inputs are applied. Negative test is particularly important for WS.

4.7 Experiment Design

4.7.1 Stock-buy-Sell experiment

This section uses a stock-buy-sell WS as an example to explain the test case generation process. In this example, 60 services are developed and then evaluated by 32 test cases. Each WS consists of a server application and multiple client application, residing in different locations. A client can send requests to the server and the server responses to the requests. All WS implement the same specification. Table 23 lists the specification of the WS. The WS Server offers two functions and Client WS can access these two functions.

Table 23 stock-buy-sell WS Specification

Requirement	Detailed Specification
(1) A client queries a stock's price	Client can query any stock's price. If queried stock name is not empty and requested stock information is available, the server WS sends the requested stock price to the requesting client.
(2) Every 20 minutes the system executes these functions:	If the prices of some stocks increase >= 5% within the past 20 minutes, it will send messages to the all stock owners, reminding them to sell the stocks whose prices increase >= 5%, or buy the stocks to sell at a higher price.
	If the prices of some stocks decreases >= 10% within the past 20 minutes, the server WS will send messages to the stock owners, reminding them to buy the stocks whose prices decrease >= 10% or sell them to stop further losses.
	If the advancing volume or declining volume of some stocks increases >= 100% in the past 20 minutes compared to the same period of yesterday, it will send messages to alert the stock owners.

The implementation of the experiment is shown in Figure 48. The database consists of objects of stock information, as defined in the Class Stock. Each stock object is set to an initial value at certain time point. The evaluation engine then uses randomly generated purchase and sale information, or uses replayed data from past stock dump, to decide the price dynamically once every minute. Once the price is changed, the other members (the percentages of changes in a minute, a day, a month, and a year) of each stock object are computed and updated.

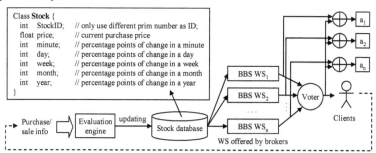

Figure 48 the stock-buy-sell experiment

4.7.2 Test Case Generation by Swiss Cheese Approach

After implementing the stock-buy-sell service, test cases are generated to test the services using Swiss Cheese approach. The requirements in Table 23 includes the following seven conditions

- c_1: Queried stock name is not empty
- c_2: Requested stock information is available
- c_3: The information of all stocks is complete
- c_4: The prices of some stocks increase >= 5% within the past 20 minutes
- c_5: The prices of some stocks decreases >= 10% within the past 20 minutes
- c_6: The advancing volume of certain stocks increases >= 100% in the past 20 minutes compared to the same period yesterday
- c_7: The declining volume of certain stocks increases >= 100% in the past 20 minutes compared to the same period yesterday.

For the second requirement in Table 23, the Boolean expression is:

$$S = c_3*c_4 + c_3*c_5 + c_3*c_6 + c_3*c_7$$

The SC-map of the above Boolean specification is 3-dimension, as shown in Figure 49.

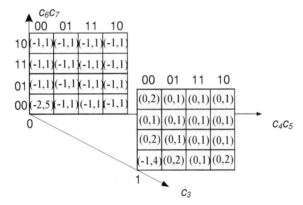

Figure 49 Swiss Cheese Diagram representing the test case set

In the SCmap, the cells that can satisfy expression S are defined to have HD = 0 and those cells that make the expression S be false are defined to have HD < 0. Each cell in the SC diagrams corresponds to a test case that checks if the scenario expression S is satisfied, and values in the cells are the (HD, BC) pair. Test cases with HD >= 0 are positive test cases, testing the specified functions of the Web service; and test cases with HD < 0 are negative test cases, testing the missing branches of the Web service specification. Table 24 classifies all 32 test by their (|HD|, BC). For example, the cell ($c_3 = 1$, $c_4 = 0$, $c_5 = 0$, $c_6 = 0$, $c_7 = 1$) in Figure 49 corresponds to the test case (10001) in Table 24. Among all the 32 candidate test

cases, four test cases with (|HD|, BC) = (0, 2) and one test case with (|HD|, BC) = (1, 4) are
identified as potent test cases.

1. 10001 (HD = 0 && BC = 2): small |HD| value, relatively large BC value.
2. 10010 (HD = 0 && BC = 2): small |HD| value, relatively large BC value.
3. 10100 (HD = 0 && BC = 2): small |HD| value, relatively large BC value.
4. 11000 (HD = 0 && BC = 2): small |HD| value, relatively large BC value.
5. 10000 (HD = -1 && BC = 4): large BC value, relatively small |HD| value.

Table 24 Test case set generated for the SC

(|HD|, BC)	Test Cases (TC)	# of TC
(0, 2)	10001, 10010, 10100, 11000	4
(0, 1)	10011, 10101, 10111, 10110, 11100, 11101, 11111, 11110, 11001, 11011, 11010	11
(1, 4)	10000	1
(1, 1)	00001, 00011, 00010, 00100, 00101, 00111, 00110, 01100, 01101, 01111, 01110, 01000, 01001, 01011, 01010	15
(2, 5)	00000	1

4.8 Experiment Analysis

4.8.1 Experiment Results

Table 25 shows the experiment result after the test cases are ranked by their potencies.
TC3 ranks first with the largest potency, while TC30 ranks last because it has the smallest
potency. As can be observed from Table 25, the potency values of all 32 test cases are smaller
than 50%. Thus, from the explanation in section 4.4.6, one can conclude that I→I algorithm
is better than C→C algorithm in this case because $\bar{P}_{I \to I}$ can lead to a more accurate test case
set.

Table 25 the test case ranking according to the potency

Rank	1	2	3	4	5	6	7	8	9	10	11	12	13	14	15	16
Test Case ID	3	4	2	1	10	11	9	12	16	6	7	13	14	15	8	5
No. of Failed WS	24	22	21	18	14	14	13	13	11	10	10	10	10	9	9	9
HD	0	0	0	0	0	0	0	0	-1	0	0	0	0	0	0	0
BC	2	2	2	2	1	1	1	1	4	1	1	1	1	1	1	1
Potency	0.40	0.37	0.35	0.30	0.23	0.23	0.22	0.22	0.18	0.17	0.17	0.17	0.17	0.15	0.15	0.15

Rank	17	18	19	20	21	22	23	24	25	26	27	28	29	30	31	32
Test Case ID	18	20	21	22	23	24	25	26	27	28	29	31	32	17	19	30
No. of Failed WS	3	3	3	3	3	3	3	3	3	3	3	3	3	2	2	2
HD	-1	-1	-1	-1	-1	-1	-1	-1	-1	-1	-1	-1	-2	-1	-1	-1
BC	1	1	1	1	1	1	1	1	1	1	1	1	5	1	1	1
Potency	0.05	0.05	0.05	0.05	0.05	0.05	0.05	0.05	0.05	0.05	0.05	0.05	0.05	0.03	0.03	0.03

Table 32 shows the test case rank after applying the I→I algorithm with $\bar{P}_H$=0.95. The
$\bar{P}_{I \to I}$ from TC3 to TC4 is 0.55. Table 27 shows the test case rank after applying the C→C

algorithm with $\vec{P}_H$=0.95. The $\vec{P}_{C\to C}$ from TC3 to TC4 is 0.72.

Table 26 select and rank the test cases by using the I→I algorithm

TC	3	4	2	1	10	11	9	12	16	6	7	13	14	8	15	18
$\vec{P}_{I\to I}$		0.55	0.33	0.72	0.79	0.93	0.92	0.92	0.64	0.8	0.9	0.8	0.9	0.89	0.89	0

Table 27 Select and rank TC using the C→C algorithm

TC	3	4	2	1	10	16	7	18
$\vec{P}_{C\to C}$		0.72	0.63	0.87	0.93	0.93	0.94	0.94

Compared with Table 26 and Table 27, one can find that all test cases retained by the C→C algorithm are retained by the I→I algorithm as well. This result supports Lemm4:

In this experiment, I→I algorithm eliminates 50% test cases (16/32), and C→C algorithm eliminates 75% test cases (24/32).

Compared Table 25 with Table 27, one can see the relationship between the number of eliminated test cases and the rank of the test cases. All top 10 test cases (in Table 25) are retained after applying the I→I algorithm (in Table 27). Only one test case from 11th to 15th (in Table 25) is eliminated, and the total number of eliminated test cases increases to 4, 9 and 16 for top 20, top 25 and all test cases respectively (in Table 25). Figure 50 shows the probability that a test case is eliminated increases if the test case ranks low in the test case set. This observation is interpreted as: if a potent test case is not potent, it is very likely that it is already covered by more potent test cases.

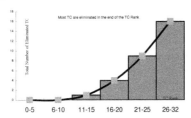

Figure 50 the possibility of elimination increases for less potent test cases.

4.8.2 Comparison Study between CRM approach and SC Approach

The coverage of all 32 test cases is shown in Figure 51. The most left column is the sixty web services, and the first show denotes the thirty-two test cases in the order of their potency. The test cases and web services are numbered by their ID. Each cell denotes the output of one TC and one WS. A white cell denotes a correct output, while a black cell denotes an incorrect output.

- The right three columns show the number of test cases in total thirty-two test cases, the sixteen test cases selected by the I→I algorithm, and the eight test cases selected by the C→C algorithm respectively, that fail a given web services. If the total thirty-two test cases set can detect the error for a given web services, the test case set selected by the I→I algorithm or C→C algorithm can detect the error as well. Therefore, in this experiment, the I→I algorithm and C→C algorithm do not lose any effective test cases.
- The 16 test cases (TC5, TC17, TC19~32) eliminates by both I→I algorithm (compared with Table 26) and C→C algorithm (compared with Table 27). As can be seen from Figure 51, TC18 can detect all those errors that are detected by TC17 and TC19~32. Similarly, TC5 is covered by TC1. Therefore, these 16 TC are eliminated by both algorithms.
- I→I algorithm retains 8 more TC than C→C algorithm (TC6, TC8, TC9, TC11~15). The difference of these 8 TC can be explained by Lemma4: When the potency of all test cases is small, C→C algorithm ignore tiny coverage difference between two test cases and eliminate one of them; while I→I algorithm eliminate test cases only if they have identical coverage with others. For example, as can be observed from Figure 51, TC1 covers TC9, TC11 and TC12 except for the error in WS53. C→C algorithm eliminate TC9, TC11 and TC12 because it trades accuracy for saving testing costs, while I→I algorithm retains all these test cases because it emphasize the accuracy of the final test case set.

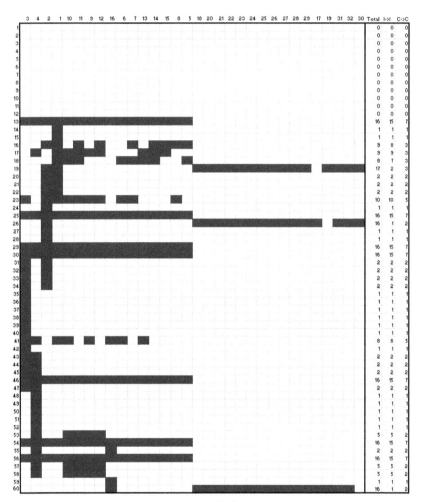

Figure 51 analysis of eliminated test cases

Comparing Table 25, Table 26 and Table 27, one can observe that those potent test cases (TC ID=3, 4, 2, 1, 16) identified by SC approach are retained by C→C algorithm and I→I algorithm as well. In addition, the rank order of these five test cases are consistent in Table 25, Table 26 and Table 27.Since SC approach was already proved in[177][176], this result justifies the effectiveness and correctness of CRM approach. This conclusion can contribute to the testing through the software development lifecycle. One can generate test cases by SC approach during the early phase of development lifecycle, and then optimize the test cases by CRM approach in the later.

4.8.3 Incremental Test Case Selection

When a new WS arrives, the test case set should re-rank and eliminate duplicate test cases according to the updated test outcome. If the WS sample set is small, and if most WS are correct, then I→I algorithm can have better accuracy than C→C algorithm. Otherwise, I→I is more accurate than C→C algorithm. For example, if the WS sample set has only one perfect WS, according to the C→C algorithm only one test case will be retained and all the other test cases will be eliminated. In this case, the C→C algorithm fails to retain all effective test cases. Therefore, in addition to the algorithms, the sample size is another criterion that can affect the effectives of the selected test cases. Figure 52 shows the relationship between sample size and the test case effectiveness. The X axis is the WS sample size. The Y axis denotes the difference between the test case set selected by I→I algorithm under current sample size and the 16 test cases set given in Figure 52. For example, when sample size=3, the candidate test case set is {TC3, TC4, TC2}. Since TC3, TC4 and TC2 are included in Table 26, the difference between the two test case sets is 13. According to Figure 52, nine WS is a reasonable sample size to retain all effective test cases.

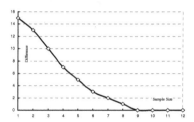

Figure 52 Test case set becomes more accurate as sample size increases

4.8.4 Test Case Selection by Potency Only

Another test case selection algorithm is based on potency only. The algorithm can select the n most potent test cases from the test case ranking list. However, there is no way to decide the minimal n to provide the full coverage in this algorithm. We did an experiment where n=8, and the cost is 8/32=25%. 2 errors out of 48 are missed. Therefore, the coverage= (48-2) /48≈96%.

4.8.5 Test Case Selection by Coverage only

To find the minimal test cases that provide the 100% coverage, an algorithm is given in Table 20. Note that step 3 is not time consuming, because only equally potent test cases may have identical coverage.

Table 28 Test case selection by coverage only

Step1: Rank test cases by potency only, and the result is $T=\{t_1, t_2, \dots, t_n\}$;
Step2: delete those perfect services;
Step3: If any two test cases detect the same error, then delete one of them;
Step4: rank services by the number of test cases that can detect the faults in it, and the result ranking is $S=\{s_1, s_2, \dots, s_m\}$;
Step5: The result test case set $R \leftarrow \varnothing$; MinimalSize=n;
    for (i=1; i<=m, i++)
    begin
      group all the test cases that fails s_i in the set R_i;
      if $(R_i \cap R == \varnothing)$ then
      for any test case t in R_i, generates a candidate result set $R \leftarrow R \cup \{t\}$.
          if $((\|R\|+1)<$MinimalSize) goto step5.
    end

The complexity of this algorithm is $O(n^m)$ where m is the number of services, and n is the number of test cases. However, in real situation, the algorithm maybe efficient. In this experiment, it takes only one iteration to identify the minimal test case set $\{t_1, t_2, t_3, t_4, t_{16}\}$ that provides the full coverage. The process is shown in Figure 10, Figure 54, Figure 55, Figure 56 and Figure 57 .

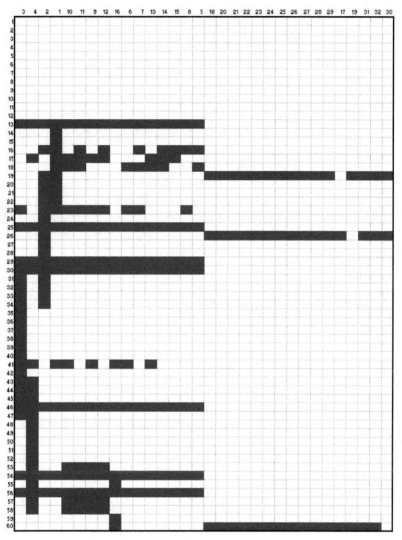

Figure 53 Step 1: Rank test cases by potency only

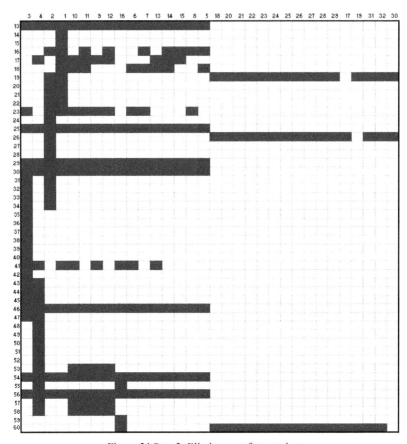

Figure 54 Step 2: Eliminate perfect services

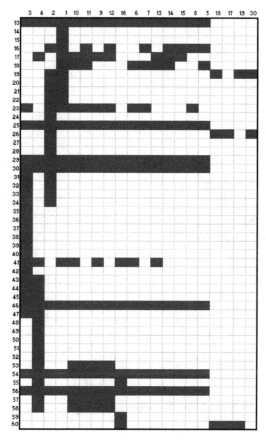

Figure 55 Step 3: Eliminate duplicate test cases

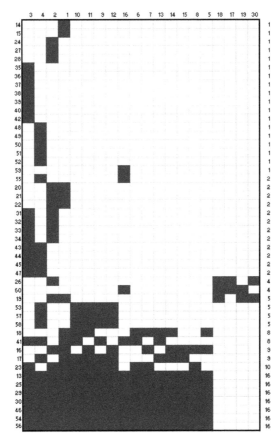

Figure 56 Step4: Rank services

The rightmost column shows the number of test cases that can detect the faults in it.

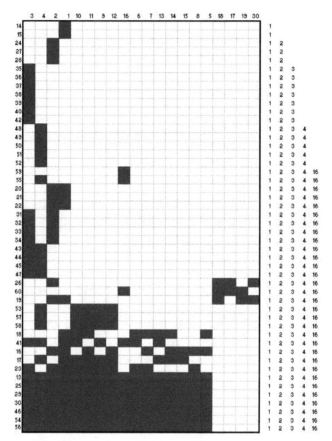

Figure 57 Step5: Find the minimal test case set.

4.8.6 Test Case Effectiveness Analysis

While the proposed CRM saves testing efforts by eliminating redundant test cases, it still keeps the effectiveness of the remained test cases. This section shows the effectiveness of CRM by experiment.

The test result is shown in Table 29. For the total 32 test case set, it can detect a total number of 262 failures in all 60 WS. For the test case set select by the I→I algorithm, the size of the test case set is 16, therefore the test effort can be reduced to 16/32=50%. All failures detected by the total test case set can be detected by the I→I test case set as well, therefore their coverage are the same: 100%. The I→I test case set can detect a total number of 208 failures for all 60 WS. The test case set selected by the C→C algorithm provides 100% effectiveness while reducing the test effort to 25% and can detect 123 failures. Two conclusions can be found according to Table 29:

- If the total thirty-two test cases set can detect the failure for a given web services, the test case set selected by the I→I algorithm or C→C algorithm can detect the failure as well in this experiment. Therefore, in this experiment, the I→I algorithm and C→C algorithm do not lose any effective test cases. However, this conclusion might no be true if one lower the threshold value $\bar{P}_H$.
- The test case set selected by the I→I algorithm usually can find more failures than that of C→C algorithm. This is because the latter test case set contains more test cases.
- Potency-based: Difficult to decide the size of the results test case set.
- Coverage-based: can save most test efforts while achieve the full coverage. The disadvantage is its complexity to identify the result test case set. However, in real situation, it maybe much less complex than it looks.

Table 29 Effectiveness and efforts comparison between the three test case sets

TC set	Effectiveness	Test effort	Complexity to identify the result test case set	Failures
total	100%	100%	$O(1)$	262
Potency-based	96%	25%	$O(1)$	139
Coverage-based	100%	16%	$O(n^m)$	96
I→I	100%	50%	$O(n^2)$	208
C→C	100%	25%	$O(n^2)$	123

4.8.7 Screening Testing

The screening testing experiment result is shown in Table 30. The coverage-based test case set consists of 5 test cases, the CRM-based test case set consists of 8 test cases, and the potency-based test case set consists of 8 most potent test cases. The result shows that the coverage-based test case set needs least test runs because it has fewest test cases while has full coverage.

Table 30 Screening testing result

Screen Testing	Coverage-based	CRM-based	Potency-based
Test Runs	153	191	195

4.8.8 Code Coverage Analysis

This section studies the service code to justify that CRM can truly reveal the coverage relationship among test cases. As can be observed from Figure 52, TC13 is totally covered by TC10. The full coverage sets of TC13 and TC10 are shown in Figure 58. TC10 can detect errors in more services, including WS53, WS57, and WS58 for incorrect service set 3, and WS23 for incorrect service set 4.

Figure 58 CRM between TC10 and TC13

The code is compared between a perfect service code and WS23 as shown in Figure 59. The fault can be identified in WS23. TC10 covers the decision1 so that it can detect the error. Similarly, the code of WS30 is also compared to that of the perfect service as shown in

Fig

ure 60, and another fault can be identified. The first decision is the same as the decision1 in WS23, and the second decision is covered by TC13, so both TC10 and TC13 can detect the fault in WS30. Thus, TC10 fails one more service WS23 in the incorrect service 4 than TC13 does. The comparison of code between WS23 and WS30 can disclose the reason as shown in Figure 61. TC10 covers the error code in both WS23 and WS30, while TC13 covers the error code in WS30 only.

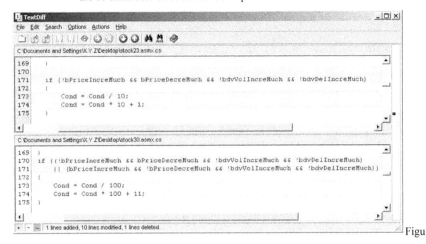

Figure 59 difference of code between a perfect service and WS23

Figure 60 difference of code between a perfect service and WS30

Figure 61 Differences between WS23 and WS30

Similar coverage relationship for TC10 and TC13 can be observed in the incorrect service set 2 as well. In addition, same code coverage can be found in the other redundant test cases.

Therefore, CRM implies the code coverage of test cases. The experiment results prove that CRM can identify coverage relationship among test cases.

4.9 Conclusion

This chapter presented a Model-based Adaptive Testing (MAT) for multi-version software based the CRM. The CRM can be used to select and rank test cases, and can identify and eliminate those duplicate test cases or those test cases that cover the same aspects. In addition, the adaptive test cases ranking algorithm is presented by using the coverage probability. Experiments are conducted using the proposed techniques, and experiment results are analyzed. The testing results of Swiss Cheese approach and CRM approach are compared and analyzed. The experiment results justify the CRM approach, and indicate that the CRM-based test case selection algorithm can eliminate redundant test cases while maintaining the effectiveness of testing.

CHAPTER 5
SURVEY ON POLICY SPECIFICATION AND ENFORCEMENT

In the past decade, a number of Policy Specification Languages (PSLs) have been proposed to solve the problems caused by hard-coded policies. Many PSLs provide a set of simple and easy-to-use syntax to specify policies which is separate from the system implementation. A user interface can provide how policy makers can specify and manage policies. A policy engine can load, interpret, and enforce policies, and allows policies to be dynamically added, removed, updated, and enabled or disabled.

Ontology-based policy specification, introduced in this chapter, provides a semi-formal method to specify policies and helps the users to analyze these policies by defining the relationship and concepts in the policy specification. Users can build the policies easily. And its analysis and enforce framework helps the end users to manage policies.

There are several Ontology-based policy specifications, such as KAoS and Rei. Both of them are presented by the Ontology specification language, such as Web Ontology Language (OWL). Moreover, both languages support the reasoning to detect the inconsistency among the policies.

5.1 Survey on PSL

5.1.1 Ponder

The Ponder language provides a generic language for specifying security policies that map onto various access control implementation mechanisms. It supports obligation policies that are event triggered condition rules for policy based management of networks and distributed systems. Ponder can also be used security management activities such as registration users or logging and auditing events for dealing access to critical resources or security violations. Ponder is declarative, strongly-typed and object-oriented which makes the language flexible, extensible and adaptable to a wide range of management requirements.

Like most policy specification languages, Ponder focuses on the security domain. Its specially designed syntaxes make it very difficult for future extensibility and limit its flexibility. Ponder doesn't have a forma model, doesn't support C&C checking. It also doesn't have an executable model, which makes dynamic verification and interaction with the system impossible. Ponder provides a flat syntactic architecture. With a compiler, Ponder can be used for interoperability.

Ponder defines a set of useful syntax to specify domain-independent obligation and authorization policies. Obligation policies in Ponder are also ECA rules that define actor's responsibilities. The syntax of Ponder obligation policies and an example are showed in Figure 62.

```
inst oblig policyName    "{"
     on                  event-specification ;
     subject    [<type>] domain-Scope-Expression ;
   [ target    [<type>] domain-Scope-Expression ; ]
     do                  obligation-action-list ;
   [ catch               exception-specification ; ]
   [ when                constraint-Expression ; ]   "}"
```

```
inst oblig loginFailure {
     on                  3*loginfail(userid) ;
     subject             s = /NRegion/SecAdmin ;
     target <userT>      t = /NRegion/users ^ (userid) ;
     do                  t.disable() -> s.log(userid) ;
}
```

Figure 62 Ponder Obligation Policy

The "On" keyword defines the event that triggers the policy enforcement. The "Subject" keyword defines the actor who takes the responsibility and the "Do" keyword defines the action list to be performed when an obligation policy is enforced. The optional "when" clause defines the conditions when an obligation policy is applicable. The example basically states "when three consecutive *loginfail* events occur, the security administrator (*SecAdmin*) must disable the *userid* and make a log".

Authorization policies in Ponder are explicitly defined on actors or domains. Figure 63 illustrates the syntax of Ponder authorization policies and an example.

```
inst ( auth+ | auth- ) policyName   "{"
     subject [<type>]   domain-Scope-Expression ;
     target  [<type>]   domain-Scope-Expression ;
     action             action-list ;
   [ when               constraint-Expression ; ]   "}"
```

```
inst auth+ switchPolicyOps {
     subject            /NetworkAdmin;
     target <PolicyT>   /NRegion/switches;
     action             load(), remove(), enable(), disable() ;
}
```

Figure 63 Ponder Authorization Policy

The "Subject" keyword and "Target" keyword define the subjects and objects of the action. The optional "When" clause specifies a condition when this authorization policy is applicable. In the example, the authorization policy gives network administrators (*NetworkAdmin*) the rights to perform *load*, *remove*, *enable* and *disable* actions on *switches*.

Ponder does not support system constraints. PSML-P supports two types of system constraints to be specified: system constraints on data and system constraints on actions.

Ponder supports delegation policies to temporarily transfer rights from an actor A to another actor B. After delegation, the actor B who obtains the delegation is able to perform all actions authorized to actor A. Figure 64 shows the syntax and an example of delegation policies in Ponder.

```
inst deleg+  "("associated-auth-policy  ")" policyName  "{"
    grantee    [<type>]   domain-Scope-Expression ;
    [ subject  [<type>]   domain-Scope-Expression ; ]
    [ target   [<type>]   domain-Scope-Expression ; ]
    [ action             action-list ; ]
    [ when               constraint-Expression ; ]
    [ valid              constraint-Expression ; ]   "}"
```

```
inst deleg+ (switchPolicyOps) delegSwitchOps  {
    grantee    /DomainAdmin ;
    target     /Nregion/switches/typeA ;
    action     enable(), disable();
    valid      time.duration(24) ;
}
```

Figure 64 Ponder Delegation Policy

The "Grantee" keyword defines the actor that obtains the delegation. The "Target" keyword and the "Action" keyword define the resources and the actions that are obtained through the delegation. The optional "When" clause and "Valid" clause are used to indicate when the delegation is valid. The above example states that "the Domain Administrator (*DomainAdmin*) obtains the *enable* and *disable* rights to switches of type A for 24 hours from the time of creation. PSML-P also has a role-based mechanism to specify delegation policies. Delegation in PSML-P is defined roles with allowing role A to temporarily transfer its rights to role B.

Ponder supports meta-policies that are used to specify application-specific constraints. Meta-policies are specified as a sequence of OCL expressions the last one of which must evaluate to true or false [42]. Figure 65 shows the syntax of Ponder meta-policy and the example of Separation of Duty.

```
inst meta metaPolName raises exception [ "(" parameters ")" ] "{"
    { OCL-expression }
    boolean-OCL-expression "}"
```

```
inst meta budgetDutyConflict raises conflictInBudget(z) {
    [z] = self.policies -> select (pa, pb |
        pa.subject -> intersection (pb.subject)->notEmpty      and
        pa.action -> exists (act | act.name = "submit")        and
        pb.action -> exists (act | act.name = "approve")       and
        pb.target -> intersection (pa.target)->oclIsKindOf (budget))
    z -> notEmpty ;
}
```

Figure 65 Ponder Meta-Policy

The "Raise" clause is followed by an action that is executed if the last OCL expression evaluates to true. Ponder employs OCL for meta-policy specification, which is powerful but complex. The syntax of specifying a meta-policy that satisfies the management requirements of policy-makes is difficult to learn and use. In PSML-P, we employed the role mechanism so that meta-policies can be specified on the top of roles. Several commonly used meta-policies are integrated into the PSML-P so that policy-makers can easily specify these meta-policies, such as Separation of Duties. In addition, we also support role hierarchy and cardinality constraints to be specified on roles.

Ponder provides two effective mechanisms to group policies in terms of the semantics: groups and roles. Groups are used to group relevant policies to a package for organization and future reuse. Roles are used to group policies defined on the same actors. However, neither groups nor roles are provided for role-based access control. They are designed so that we have a logical way to organize policies. In PSML-P, both obligation policies and authorization polices are defined on roles. Roles naturally organize a management position along with its associated obligations and rights. The syntax of defining a group and a role in Ponder is showed in Figure 66:

```
inst group groupName    "{"
    { basic-policy-definition }
    { group-definition }
    { meta-policy-definition } "}"
```
```
inst role roleName    "{"
    { basic-policy-definition }
    { group-definition }
    { meta-policy-definition }   "}" [ @ subject-domain ]
```

Figure 66 Ponder Group & Role

Ponder allows role hierarchy to be specified so that lower-level roles can inherit all policies specified on high-level roles. The syntax is showed in Figure 67:

```
type role roleTypeName "(" formalParameters ")"
    extends parentRoleType   "(" actualparameters ")"   "{"
    role-body   "}"
```

Figure 67 Ponder Role Hierarchy

5.1.2 PSML-P

PSML-P and the *ACDATE-Based Policy (ABP) Framework* to solve the problems addressed in Section 1.1. PSML-P is a policy specification language that provides a set of powerful syntax for policy specification, and ABP Framework provides an environment in which policy specified in PSML-P can be enforced and analyzed.

PSML-P supports *policy specification* of a broad range of domain-independent policies, including obligation policies, authorization policies, and various system constraints. Obligation policies [42], which are based on roles, specify a role's responsibilities in an organization. Authorization policies, also based on roles, specify a role's rights of performing actions. System constrains specify a variety of constraints on data and actions.

PSML-P supports *hierarchical policies*. Policy hierarchy organizes policies in a tree-like hierarchical structure such that high-level policies represent abstract goals to be refined by lower-level enforceable policies. An intermediate policy in the policy hierarchy involves two different views: its parent policy considers it as a plan to meet its goal, while its children policies consider it as a goal they must refine to meet. The motivation of policy hierarchy is to determine how to specify lower-level policies in order to refine the abstract goal of a high-level policy and whether lower-level policies completely meet the goal.

PSML-P supports *roles and role-based meta-policies*. Specifying policies on roles, rather than individual actors, significantly simplifies policy specification and management.

Role hierarchy [19] represents the superior / subordinate relationship among roles. If role A is a superior role to role B, role A will automatically obtain all permissions assigned to role B. The inheritance of permissions assigned to subordinate roles by a superior role significantly reduces assignment overhead, as the permissions need only be explicitly assigned to the subordinate roles. For instance, if role Fire Support Officer is superior to role Supporting Arms Coordinator, role Fire Support Officer automatically obtains the Issue Fire Order permission that is assigned to the role Supporting Arms Coordinator, as showed in the following screen shot.

Role delegation [85] allows a role to temporarily transfer its permissions to other roles. Separation of Duties (SOD) [42][26]prevents an actor from taking two mutual exclusive roles to avoid conflicts of interests. Cardinality constraints on roles specify constraints on user assignment.

ABP Framework provides *an integrated model* for both system modeling and policy modeling. Policies are part of system requirements and represent constraints on systems. The ACDATE is a model for system modeling. The system structure is modeled by ACDATEs that are the building blocks of a system, while system behaviors and constraints on system are modeled by scenarios and policies, respectively. Since both system modeling and policy modeling are based on the ACDATE model, it allows policies to be easily specified after the system modeling is done. Additionally, the system simulator / executor are able to drive the simulation / execution of system scenarios with policies enforced.

ABP Framework provides *policy enforcement*. Policy enforcement in the ABP Framework falls into three categories: policy checking, policy execution, and policy compensation. Policy checking verifies if there exist policy violations when actions are performed or data are changed. Policy execution executes the action defined in the policy when receiving the triggering events. Policy compensation executes the compensation action defined in the policy when policy checking detects policy violations, so that remedy measures can be taken.

ABP Framework provides various *policy analyses*. Policy C&C analysis is a process of identifying potential inconsistent or incomplete policies existing in a computing system. Inconsistent policies are identified by analyzing policy syntax and incomplete policies are identified by analyzing action hierarchy. ABP framework also provides an inconsistency resolution mechanism [85] that gives policy makers an alternative to deal with inconsistent policies through specifying precedence of modalities. When inconsistency arises, the policy with higher precedence of modalities will be enforced and the policy with lower precedence of modalities is ignored. Policy dependency analysis is a process of identifying all potential entities affected by policy changes. Policy access history analysis is a process of identifying vulnerable data after actors are downgraded and dangerous actors after data are upgraded. Authorization policies are intended to protect system resources from unauthorized access.

Most other policy specification languages only define a set of syntax to specify policies but mention nothing about how to model the system on which policies are to be enforced. Lacking of an integrated model makes policy enforcement and policy analyses hard to be achieved. Our work employs an integrated ACDATE model for both system modeling and policy modeling. System structure is decomposed and formally modeled by ACDATEs and system behaviors (represented by scenarios) and constraints on system behaviors and system status (represented by policies) are built on the top of ACDATEs. This integrated model allows agile modeling of a system, and system scenarios can be simulated / executed with policies enforced. System scenarios and policies can be changed on-the-fly without having to modify, recompile and redeploy the system. In addition, all kinds of analyses can be performed on the system to find out design bugs as early as possible.

Most other policy specification languages are either domain specific or do not have a broad coverage on policies. PSML-P covers a broad range of policies, including obligation policies, authorization policies, and various system constraints. Policy makers can use these three types of policies to specify almost all policies in a computing system. Since policies specification is integrated to the ACDATE model, the actions specified in policies can be linked to a handling scenario where complex logic can be employed to describe rich semantics behind complex policies. In addition, PSML-P provides a graphical interface and a policy editor for policy specification, through which policy makers can easily manage policies.

Few policy specification languages support policy hierarchy. For a large computing system, actors are usually organized in a hierarchical structure. Actors at different levels may have different views on the system. Policy hierarchy allows policy makers to specify policies at different levels, with each level representing different abstraction. High-level policies can not be enforced, but they objectively exist to represent the abstract goals of top-level policy makers, and need to be further refined by low-level enforceable policies. Through policy hierarchy, policy makers are able to specify both abstract goals with high-level policies and concrete plans with low-level enforceable policies.

ABP Framework provides an environment where system scenarios can be simulated / executed and policies can be enforced. Policy makers can easily change system scenarios and policies on-the-fly and updates take effect right in the next system simulation / execution without having to modify, compile and redeploy the system. Policy execution and policy compensation mechanism allow policies to change the paths of system simulation / execution. Policies are not any more a mechanism to verify system constraints in ABP Framework; they can be part of system behaviors, which makes policies an alternative to specify system behaviors.

Most policy specification languages proposed some mechanisms for policy analysis to guarantee policies in a computing system are correctly specified. However, all of them are focused on policy C&C analysis without mentioning other policy analysis methods. ABP Framework supports not only policy C&C analysis, but also policy dependency analysis and access history analysis. Policy analysis significantly reduces the workload of specifying policies for a large computing system. Policy makers can use this feature to easily detect mistakes they have made, and correct them in a minute. Policy analysis greatly minimizes the possibilities of existence of inconsistent and incomplete policies in a computing system, and makes the computing system behave as what policy makers expect.

Most policy specification languages introduce the roles to simplify policy specification and management. So does PSML-P. Roles allow policy makers to specify policies on roles rather than on individual actors, which significantly simplifies policy specification and management. However, most of them do not use the concept of roles for meta-policy specification. PSML-P makes use of roles to define meta-policies which significantly reduces the workload of policy makers. Role-based meta-policies allow policy makers to specify application-dependent constraints, such as separation of duties.

5.1.3 Java Policy Language

Java, through permission objects, provides a language-specific attempt to specify and enforce policies. The default file controlling Java policy (if a SecurityManager is invoked in the current JVM) is located in the JAVA_HOME/jre/lib/security/java.policy file, and has a series of "grant blocks" that allow a set of classes to have a predefined set of permissions (essentially an arbitrary collection of statements permitting the set of classes to invoke certain language functions). The Java policy file syntax is shown in Table 31:

Table 31 a Java Policy Example

```
grant SOME_CLASSES
{
    permission SOME_PERMISSION "args";
    permission ANOTHER_PERMISSION "args";
}
```

While the Java approach is a fairly good attempt, it suffers from two major weaknesses: difficulty of use and lack of a fine-grained approach. The file used to control the policy rules in the currently running JVM is often ignored because it is an additional layer of complexity in the design, construction, and testing of a system. In addition, the default policy mechanism is very course-grained and although it is easily extensible, does not lend itself to quick analysis of any given software. Even though there are a number of permissions to legislate, this set of permissions is not provably complete or precise enough for many complex applications.

Although Java policy doesn't have a forma model, Java policy is executable and allows dynamic verification since it can be interpreted by the Java virtual machine. Java policy focuses on the security domain, mainly controlling the accesses, and deal very little with other non-functional and functional policies. Java policy doesn't provide C&C checking or hierarchical architecture. Thanks to Java's excellent interoperability, Java policy is also highly interoperable, and can interact with the underlying system.

5.1.4 Structured Policy Command Language

The SPCL, designed to address policy specification, enforcement and revision, provides a domain-independent language for specifying policy requirements, principals, rules, and actions in a lightweight syntax with semantics as close to natural expression as possible.

SPCL's primary two features are an object-oriented-like command language (and compiler) and a PolicyEngine interpreter acting as an oracle to a number of other systems. A policy is specified in the SPCL syntax, parsed, and then translated to a form suitable for input to the PolicyEngine. The PolicyEngine should be thought of as a VM for policy. After parsing and construction, it then loads and interprets the policy. The PolicyEngine has a simple protocol for asking questions about the running policy (in SPCL) as well as loading new policies in, updating current policy, and retiring outdated policy. The following is a home policy specified with SPCL:

```
policy HomePolicy {
    default {
        DENY * { NOTIFY police; }
    }
    group parents {
        ALLOW * ON *;
    }
    principal Mom {
        public key = "ldap://192.168.4.240/mom/keys/pub.key";
        email = "mom@home.com";
        alias admin;
        groups parents;
    }
    principal Ken {
        ALLOW "play" ON outside WHEN (state = "sun shining" AND
        Ken.homework = true)
        {
            if( time > 1400 ) NOTIFY Police;
            else NOTIFY Mom;
        }
        GROUPS children;
    }
}
```

SPCL is powerful hierarchical language for policy specification, enforcement and revision. However, it does not sit on a formal model, although it can interact with the system after compiled and interpreted by a PolicyEngine. SPCL can be used in a variety of domains to specify a lot of functional policies, but it deals very little with non-functional policies, such as security, safety, performance and so forth. It is also fairly flexible and extensible thanks to its easily changeable syntactic constructs. SPCL doesn't deal with completeness and consistency (C&C) checking, but it allows dynamic verification. SPCL is executable after compiled and interoperable between systems.

5.1.5 LaSCO: Language for Security Constraints on Objects

As with Ponder, LaSCO is specially designed for specifying security policies. Policies in LaSCO consist of two parts: the domain (assumptions about the system) and the requirement (what is allowed assuming the domain is satisfied). Thus policies defined in LaSCO have the appearance of conditional access control statements. LaSCO policies are specified as expressions in logic and as directed graphs, giving a visual view of policy. A LaSCO specification can be automatically translated into executable code that checks an invocation of a program with respect to a policy. The implementation of LaSCO is in Java, and generates wrappers to check Java programs with respect to a policy. The following graph is a policy expressed in LaSCO, stating the Bell & LaPadula Model:

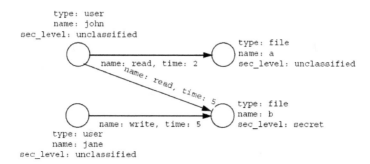

Figure 68 A LaSCO Policy Example

Specifying a security policy with a graph is a good attempt, since it simplifies the policy specification and makes policies easy to read. However, LaSCO doesn't support C&C checking.

5.1.6 Security: Policy-Based Cryptographic Key Management

Cryptography is now being used to protect information in multi-party information-sharing applications as well as two-party communications applications. The policy-controlled cryptographic Key Release Project (KRP) was initiated to define a new language for describing to whom and under what conditions access to a cryptographic key will be granted in a protective computer system. The design goals of KRP include: (1) developing a formal language for specifying policies indicating to whom and under what conditions a cryptographic key could be accessed; (2) implementing a prototype system for administering (i.e., enforcing) these policies; and (3) experimenting with automated verification tools which analyzed the policies for consistency and completeness. The following is an example policy in KRP:

Table 32 A KRP Example

create(((K1: key) :string), "K1's value",
policy(K1_policy, permit((Marty: user), read, (K1: key))
when ((project_status,Denny) = emergency), permit((Denny: user), {read,delete,modify},(K1:key)), permit((Jeff: user), {read,delete},(K1: key)), permit((David: user), read, (K1: key));

KRP is specially designed for key release, and its syntax limits its flexibility and extensibility. Key release is a sub-field in computing security; thereby KRP is another security policy specification language. KRP is building on a formal model, which makes completeness and consistency checking possible. It's also executable, and provides dynamic verification. KRP provides a hierarchical architecture for policy specification; however, its interoperability with other systems is relatively low. Since KRP is an inseparable framework, its interaction the system is guaranteed.

5.1.7 Generic Authorization and Access-Control (GAA)

The Generic Authorization and Access-Control (GAA) framework presents a new model for authorization that integrates both local and distributed access control policies and that is extensible across applications and administrative domains. With it policy language, GAA allows us to represent existing access control models (role-based access control, Clark-Wilson, ACLs, capabilities, and lattice-based access controls) in a uniform and consistent manner. Authorization restrictions allow the administrator to define which operations are allowed, and under what conditions. These restrictions may implement application-specific policies. The GAA policy language represents a sequence of tokens. Each token consists of:

- Token Type: Defines the type of the token. Tokens of the same type have the same authorization semantics.
- Defining Authority: Indicates the authority responsible for defining the value within the token type.
- Value: The value of the token. Its syntax and semantics are determined by the token type. The name space for the value is defined by the Defining Authority field.

The following policy expressed in GAA policy language states: "anyone authenticated by Kerberos.V5 has read access to the targeted resource":

Table 33 A GAA Example

Token Type: access_id_ANYBODY
Defining Authority: none
Value: none
Token Type: pos_access_rights
Defining Authority: local_manager
Value: FILE:read
Token Type: authentication_mechanism
Defining Authority: system_manager
Value: kerberos.V5

GAA policy language concentrates on authentication and authorization, which are in the security domain. Thanks to its ASCII representation form, it provides a good flexibility and extensibility. Because of lack of a formal model, C&C checking is provided. Since GAA policy language is embedded in an executable framework, it's executable and allows dynamic verification and interaction with the underlying system. Due to its flexible syntactic format, it's highly interoperable between systems. It doesn't offer a hierarchical architecture.

5.1.8 KeyNote System

The Keynote system is an engine that answers a query requested by an application. The answer is determined based on specified action attributes, the principal requesting the action and a set of assertions and credentials. The engine returns a policy compliance value for the aforementioned query. This value is one of an ordered set given to the system in the query. How the returned values are interpreted is left to the application requesting the determination.

One example is an email application that consults the Keynote engine to determine whether a user should be allowed to use a particular key to sign his message. Below is an example:

Table 34 KeyNote Example

Comment: This assertion is part of the policy, giving the RSA key "abcd1234" authority over application domain "email" Local-Constants: key = "RSA:abcd1234" Authorizer: "POLICY" Licensees: key Conditions: app_dom == "email" Comment: This assertion ties the user minzi to the key "minzi123" and the name "Minna Kangasluoma" Local-Constants: auth = "RSA:abcd1234" sign = "RSA:minzi123" Authorizer: auth Licensees: sign Conditions: app_dom == "email" && user == "minzi" && name == "M. Kangasluoma" Signature: "RSA-SHA1:dloi46h2"

Keynote is designed to be highly flexible and extensible to be used in various domains. Because of its executable engine, it allows dynamic verification. However, it doesn't have a formal model and doesn't provide C&C checking, neither. Policies specified with Keynote are interoperable and interactive between systems. It is a flat policy language, not proving hierarchical architecture.

5.1.9 The Common Intrusion Specification Language

The Common Intrusion Detection Framework (CIDF), a project supported by DARPA, has its main goal of the development of a means whereby independently developed intrusion detection, analysis, and response (IDAR) systems and components can share information and thereby interoperate. The main product of CIDF is the Common Intrusion Specification

Language (CISL), in which expressions about attacks, anomalies, and response prescriptions can be generated and encoded. CISL is essentially a standard reporting format with some imperative power. It consists of a group of S-Expressions each of which expresses a report. The following is a sample report, consisting of four S-Expressions, expressed with CISL:

Table 35 Example of the Common Intrusion Specification Language

(UserName 'joe')
(Action delete)
(FileName '/etc/passwd')
(Time '1997 May 10 0830')

The CISL also defined a macro rule, which allows the data for several S-expressions to be grouped into one. With this rule, the following declaration

(def OperateFile UserName Action FileName Time)

would allow one to write the expression

(OperateFile 'joe' delete '/etc/passwd' '1997 May 19 0830')

Since its main goal is to generate reports that can be shared by independently developed IDAR systems, CISL is essentially not a policy specification language. Since new attacks and response becomes available everyday, CISL is very flexible and extensible to deal with the new ones. CISL is not executable and focuses only on expressing security reports. It doesn't handle verification and C&C checking, neither. Since S-Expression can be nested and recursively defined, CISL has its hierarchical architecture. S-Expressions essentially are field-value pairs and in plain English, CISL is highly interoperable. CISL doesn't sit on a formal model and can't interact with the system.

5.1.10 REIN Policy

Rein policy [86][87] framework, with the same objective as Mindswap policy, aims at proposing a framework capable of encompassing different policy languages and supporting heterogeneous policy systems. Rein is grounded in Semantic Web technologies, and claims to own a distributed nature. Its principal goal is to provide ontologies for describing policy domains in a decentralized manner and provides a reasoning engine to reason over the policies.

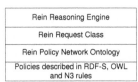

Figure 69 Rein Policy Framework

Rein Policy framework does not propose any policy languages. Instead, it claimed that users can still have their own policy languages. Rein connects all these heterogeneous policies by a policy network. The Rein policy network is described in the form of ontology. The Rein Request Class to provide an interface for querying a Rein policy network. The Rein Reasoning Engine reasons the Rein Policy Network Ontology through the Rein Request Class. Though Rein is a way of representing and reasoning over policies, it does not involve any policy enforcement.

5.1.11 RuleML-based Policy

Rule Markup Language (RuleML) [72] is a rule specification language which permitting both forward (bottom-up) and backward (top-down) rules in XML for deduction, rewriting, and further inferential-transformational tasks. Starting from version 0.91, the RuleML specification supports "Functional RuleML". For example, Figure 70 shows how to use RuleML to define the following equation.

$$home(mother\text{-}of(Jacob)) = Phoenix$$

```
<Equal oriented="yes">
   <lhs>
      <Expr>
            <Fun in="yes">home</Fun>
         <Expr>
            <Fun in="no">mother-of</Fun>
            <Ind>Jacob</Ind>
         </Expr>
      </Expr>
   </lhs>
   <rhs>
      <Ind>Phoenix</Ind>
   </rhs>
</Equal>
```

Figure 70 Using RuleML to express function

RuleML-based Policy [143] leverages RuleML as the policy language to implement semantic interoperation among heterogeneous policy languages, standards, protocols, and mechanisms. It will provide intermediate markup syntax, with associated deep knowledge representation semantics, for interchange between policy languages, standards and mechanisms.

The RuleML Technical Committee will develop tools to support translation and interchange between policy languages/standards/protocols/mechanisms that are already XML-based. They proposed that the translation between RuleML and other policy languages can be achieved by using XSL transformations (XSLT).

The initial plan of the RuleML Technical Committee is to use RuleML 0.85 to capture policies that can be encoded as derivation, constrained or reaction rules. The long-term plan is to extend RuleML towards incorporating deontic expressive features such as logics to capture rights, obligations and empowerments as aspects of policy rules. The RuleML Technical Committee gives some examples of deontic rules:

- Permission and Prohibition Rules. Example: Office clerks are prohibited to drive cars to the service station
- Duty Assignment Rules. Example: Customer service clerks have the duty to react to reservation requests
- Empowerment Rules. Example: A priest is empowered to marry a couple.

5.1.12 KAoS Policy

KAoS [192] is a set platform-independent service that lets people define policies ensuring adequate predictability and controllability of both agents and traditional distributed system. It represents the policies by using the OWL.

KPAT is the specification tools for KAoS policy specification. In this tool, the users can specify, manage, evaluate, and enforce the policies. The policy enforcement is manually. The execution environment of KAoS includes the Directory Service, Guard, and several factories. The Directory Service performs policy collecting and policy distributing, so the policies are translated from the OWL to another efficiently format. The necessary sub-assumptions on the concepts are cached into the policy packaged Guard so that the policy decision points can be located close to the running entities.

Table 36 Example of KAoS Specification

```
<owl:Class rdf:ID="FireMissleAuthAction">
<owl:intersectionOf rdf:parseType="owl:collection">
<owl:Class rdf:about="&action;AccessAction"/>
<owl:Restriction>
    <owl:onProperty rdf:resource="&action;#performedBy"/>
    <owl:toClass rdf:resource="&domains;MembersOfGeneral"/>
</owl:Restriction>
<owl:Restriction>
<owl:onProperty rdf:resource="&action;#performedOn"/>
<owl:toClass rdf:resource="&domains;MembersOfMissle"/>
</owl:Restriction>
</owl:intersectionOf>
</owl:Class>
<policy:PosAuthorizationPolicy rdf:ID="AccessAuthPolicy">
<policy:controls rdf:ID=" FireMissleAuthAction"/>
<policy:hasSiteOfEnforcement rdf:resource="#MissleSite"/>
<policy:hasPriority>1</policy:hasPriority>
</policy:PosAuthorizationPolicy>
```

5.1.13 REI

Rei uses the Prolog-like syntax and the customized Resource Description Framework (RDF). Rei provides an OWL-Lite based policy specification language. Rei support declarative policies for describing web service capabilities and constraints. Rei has a policy engine behind the scene. The policy engine could reason over Rei polices, domain information and the context to answer queries about the polices.

Not only Rei provides a set of useful syntax to specify obligation policies, authorization policies and some system constraints, it also provides a Policy Engine that parses and interprets policies in Rei syntax. Rei does not mention system model, and it has domain servers where the information of system modeling is stored. The policy engine talks to domain servers to obtain the system structure, behaviors and states.

The Rei policy engine provides a programmable interface to applications that need to enforce Rei policies. The policy engine is written in Java and has a command-line interface so that applications can load policies and speech acts, and submit queries about specific entities. During the system simulation / execution, applications can query the policy engine through the command-line interface to see if there are policy violations, and perform corresponding actions based on the query results.

Rei policy engine supports policy checking as well as policy execution. It is up to high-level applications to query the policy engine for results of policy enforcement and take corresponding measures when policy violations are detected. In other words, the failure semantics is hard-coded into the application implementation.

Rei also supports domain-independent policy specification using first-order logic. Four kinds of policy objects are supported in Rei: rights, prohibitions, obligations and dispensations. The core of Rei policy language is the constructs that describe the deontic concepts of rights, prohibitions, obligations, and dispensations [85]. These policy objects are represented as @ *(Action, Conditions)*. In order to associate a policy object with an agent, Rei uses the construct: *has (Subject, Policy Object)*. Since Rei supports policies to be specified on roles, the *Subject* can be a group of actors. *Policy object* is one of the four policy objects.

Rights are permissions that allow a subject to perform certain actions. Figure 71 shows the syntax of defining a right in Rei. In this example, an agent, *AgentA*, can perform an action, *ActionB* if and only if at least one of the following rights is defined. Rei rights are quite similar to authorization policies in Ponder, which gives actors the rights to perform actions. Similar to Ponder, rights in Rei are not based on an access control mode. Authorization policies have to be explicitly specified for each actor or role.

> *has(AgentA, right(ActionB, Conditions))* and *AgentA* satisfies *Conditions*
> *has(Variable , right(ActionB, Conditions))*, *AgentA* binds to *Variable* and satisfies *Conditions*

Figure 71 Rei Policy (Rights)

Prohibitions in Rei are actually negative obligation policies, which prevents a certain action from happening when conditions are held. Figure 72 shows the Rei syntax of defining a prohibition. In this example, an agent *AgentA* is prohibited from performing *ActionB* if and only if f at least one of the following policies is defined.

> *has(AgentA, prohibition(ActionB, Conditions))* and *AgentA* satisfies *Conditions*
> *has(Variable, prohibition(ActionB, Conditions))* and *AgentA* satisfies *Conditions*

Figure 72 Rei Policy (Prohibitions)

Obligations are actions that an agent MUST perform on receiving a triggering event. In PSML-P, positive obligation policies are used to express the same semantics. The Rei syntax of defining an obligation is showed in Figure 73. In this example, an agent AgentA is obligated to perform ActionB iff one of the following policies is defined.

> *has(AgentA, obligation(ActionB, Conditions))* and *AgentA* satisfies *Conditions*
> *has(Variable, obligation(ActionB, Conditions))* and *AgentA* satisfies *Conditions*

Figure 73 Rei Policy (Obligations)

Dispensations are an interesting mechanism in Rei to cancel the obligations on an agent.

After a dispensation is defined on an agent, it is no longer obligated to perform an action. In the following example showed in Figure 74, an agent *AgentA* is no longer obligated to perform an action *ActionB* iff the dispensation is defined.

> *has(AgentA, obligation(ActionB, OConditions))* and if *AgentA* satisfies *OConditions*
> *has(AgentA, dispensation(ActionB, DConditions))* and if *AgentA* satisfies *DConditions*.

Figure 74 Rei Policy (Dispensations)

Rei introduces the concept of action operators to specify several constraints on actions. The action operators are quite similar to the system constrains on actions in PSML-P. Currently, four types of action operators are supported in Rei: sequence, non-deterministic, iteration and once. For instance, seq (A, B) specifies that action B must be performed after action A. All of these four types of action operators can be covered by PSML-P.

To allow an agent to temporarily transfer its rights to another agent, Rei introduces the speech acts that provide the delegation between agents. With the delegation mechanism an agent can easily transfer its rights to other agents and delegated rights can be easily revoked. Four keywords in Rei are defined to implement the right transfer: delegation, request, revoke and cancel.

Rei uses meta-policies to resolve conflicting policies. The first mechanism is to use priorities to suppress conflicting policies. For instance, if policy p1 and policy p2 are conflicting, Rei can define p1 has the priority over p2 so that p1 is enforced and p2 is skipped. The second mechanism is to define modality precedence. For example, obligations can be defined to have precedence over rights. The meta-policies in Rei is totally different from the concept of meta-policies in Ponder and PSML-P. In Ponder and PSML-P, meta-policies are used to specify application-dependent constraints such as Separation of Duties. Both Ponder and PSML-P have other mechanisms to perform policy analysis and resolve conflicts.

Not also obligation policies and authorization policies can be specified in Rei, constraints on system behaviors can also be specified. However constraints on system status are not supported by Rei.

Rei supports policy deployment in distributed and heterogeneous environments. In its enforcement infrastructure, each client has a policy enforcer to enforce polices. And there is a global policy engine at the server site to coordinate all enforcers and the policy server. The policy engine uses Prolog as reasoning engine to check the policy library. The result of the reasoning process is either to grant an access or deny an access to the resource. If the request of the resource is verified, then a policy certificate will be issued to the resource requestor. The policy certificate will be periodically updated.

5.1.14 Mindswap

Mindswap is research group of University of Maryland. They developed a mapping relationship from WS-Policy to OWL-DL [93][132]. Based on the fact that most existing policy languages lack formal semantics, one can acquire a clear semantics for the policy languages by mapping them into logic language, such as some variant of first order logic. The following benefits can be accomplished if this method is applicable.

- *Policy Standardization:* Mapping policy languages into a standardized logic, one can use existing tools and general expertise to compare and contrast these policy languages.
- *Policy Interoperability:* The logic can acts as a bridge among different policy languages. By mapping two different policy languages into the same formalism, one is able to interoperate distinct policy languages in some extents.
- *Policy Reasoning:* Reasoning mechanism can be built upon the standardized logic to do reasoning.

Mindswap chose the Web Ontology Language (OWL) and the Resource Description Framework (RDF) as the logic language, because both RDF and OWL are strict subsets of first order logic.

Mindswap proposed a mapping algorithm which could translate WS-Policy to OWL. The translation consists of two processes. One process was translating WS-Policy grammar into OWL and the other was mapping the WS-Policy formalism directly in OWL.

After polices are mapped into OWL, the policy reasoner Pellet can be used to analyze policies. Pellet is an open-source Java based OWL DL reasoner. Pellet is capable of fulfill tasks like ontology analysis, repair and reasoning.

The core of the Pellet reasoner is the reasoner that checks the consistency of a knowledge base (KB). The policies, which are in the form of OWL ontology stored in the KB, are loaded to the reasoner after a step of species validation and ontology repair. The conceptual diagram of Mindswap policy specification and reasoning process is shown in Figure 75.

The Mindswap policy reasoner is a centralized component, and does not support policy enforcement. Since translating from one policy language to OWL-DL policy takes considerable overhead time during system execution, it does not support run-time policy analysis very well.

Figure 75 Mindswap Policy specification and reasoning

5.2 Survey on SOA Policy Enforcement

In the past decade, a number of Policy Specification Languages (PSLs) have been proposed to solve the problems caused by hard-coded policies. Many PSLs provide a set of simple and easy-to-use syntax to specify policies which is separate from the system implementation. A user interface can provide how policy makers can specify and manage policies. A policy engine can load, interpret, and enforce policies. This section will introduce several PSLs along with their enforcement mechanisms.

Service-Oriented Computing (SOC) and Web Services (WS) provide a flexible computing platform for electronic business and commerce. Introducing policy-based computing to service-oriented business systems adds another dimension of *flexibility* and *security*. While service composition and re-composition in service-oriented business systems allow major system reconstruction, policy-based computing can better deal with the small and routine changes of business processing. In this section we report the latest research on integrating policy-based computing into service-oriented business system and discuss its feasibility, benefits and cost.

Policies and policy enforcement mechanism should reside in all the three parties of a SOA: WS provider, WS consumer and WS broker.

WS Provider Policy: Polices on the WS provider specify those requirements posed on WS consumers. WS consumers have to meet the requirement in order to invoke the WS. WS provider should publish its policies along with its WSDL file to all potential WS consumers. During WS invocation, the local policy engine on the WS provider enforces polices at runtime.

WS Consumer Policy: WS consumer could also have the policy to negotiate with the policy from the WS provider. The WS consumer could put the constraints of establishing a connection into the policy file, and send the policy file along with the service request to the WS broker when binding service and then send to the WS provider to do further policy checking.

WS Broker Policy: Polices on the WS broker are global policies since WS broker has the information about both WS consumer and WS provider. The policy engine on the WS broker is used to enforce global policies.

A policy infrastructure should support policy modeling, specification, enforcement, and management. Thus, a policy infrastructure should be a multi-layer architecture. In [8], Anderson proposed that a SOA policy infrastructure consisting of five layers (bottom up): a vocabulary layer, an assertion or predicate layer, a policy layer, a domain binding layer, and a service interface binding layer. Currently, there are several existing policy enforcement architectures.

5.2.1 IETF Policy Information Model

The IETF Policy Core Information Model (CIM) is reported in [115]. IETF Policy model is not specifically devised to SOA. Instead, it tried to propose a generic policy framework for distributed systems, especially for management tasks in the context of internet. Several interesting points are presented in [115].

- The CIM is influenced by a declarative approach (like Prolog) for specifying policies. However, it still supports procedural policy specification languages (like C).

- This policy model suggests that a policy infrastructure should include two key components: Policy Decision Points (PDP) and Policy Enforcement Points (PEP). PDP determines how a policy should be enforced, while PEP performs the policy enforcement task.

- The CIM is capable of specifying timing related polices. It has a Class "PolicyTimePeriodCondition" which owns six properties: *TimePeriod, MonthOfYearMask, DayOfMonthMask, DayOfWeekMask, TimeOfDayMask and LocalOrUtcTime*. Date/times are expressed as substrings of yyyymmddThhmmss. For example, the *TimePeriod* property 20000101T060000/20000131T120000 designates the time from January 1, 2000, 06:00 to January 31, 2000, 12:00. The other five properties are used to extract corresponding time information from the data/time substring.

5.2.2 Web Services Policy Framework (WS-Policy)

The Web Services Policy Framework (WS-Policy), developed by BEA, IBM, Microsoft, and SAP, provides a general-purpose model and corresponding syntax to describe and communicate the policies of a Web Service. WS-Policy defines a base set of constructs that can be used and extended by other Web Services specifications to describe a broad range of service requirements, preferences, and capabilities.

WS-Policy provides a flexible and extensible grammar for expressing the capabilities, requirements, and general characteristics of entities in an XML Web Services-based system. WS-Policy defines a framework and a model for the expression of these properties as policies. Policy expressions allow for both simple declarative assertions as well as more sophisticated conditional assertions. WS-Policy defines a policy to be a collection of one or more policy assertions. Some assertions specify traditional requirements and capabilities that will ultimately manifest on the wire (e.g., authentication scheme, transport protocol selection). Some assertions specify requirements and capabilities that have no wire manifestation yet are critical to proper service selection and usage (e.g., privacy policy, QoS characteristics). WS-Policy provides a single policy grammar to allow both kinds of assertions to be reasoned about in a consistent manner. WS-Policy stops short of specifying how policies are discovered or attached to a Web service. Other specifications are free to define technology-specific mechanisms for associating policy with various entities and resources. Subsequent specifications will provide profiles on WS-Policy usage within other common Web service technologies. The following example illustrates how to specify an access control policy:

Table 37 an Access Control Policy Example

```
<wsp:Policy xmlns:wsse="..." xmlns:wsp="...">
<wsp:ExactlyOne>
<wsse:SecurityToken wsp:Usage="wsp:Required"
wsp:Preference="100">
<wsse:TokenType>wsse:Kerberosv5TGT</wsse:TokenType>
</wsse:SecurityToken>
<wsse:SecurityToken wsp:Usage="wsp:Required"
wsp:Preference="1">
<wsse:TokenType>wsse:X509v3</wsse:TokenType>
</wsse:SecurityToken>
</wsp:ExactlyOne>
</wsp:Policy>
```

WS-Policy is a domain-independent policy specification language that can be used in various domains, although its initial intention is focused on security issues. However, it doesn't provide a formal model, which makes C&C impossible. Thanks to its XML nature, WS-Policy is very flexible, extensible, and highly interoperable. WS-Policy itself is not executable, but it allows dynamic verification that is enforced by an application server. It doesn't have a hierarchical architecture, but it can interact with the system after interpreted by the application server.

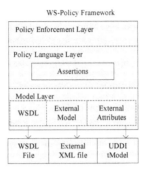

WS-Policy Framework

Policy Enforcement Layer		
Policy Language Layer		
	Assertions	
Model Layer		
WSDL	External Model	External Attributes

WSDL File	External XML file	UDDI tModel

Figure 76 the WS-Policy Framework

Figure 76 shows the three layers of the WS-Policy framework. At the model layer, there are three elements, WSDL, External model and external attributes. External model refers to XML file, while attributes can refer to the tModel (technical interface model) [191] stored in the UDDI server. The model layer is extensible because the model layer can access external resources through the external model element and the external attribute element. However, the model layer does not have its own modeling language. At the policy language layer, the policy is constructed by the vocabulary extracted from the model layer. The WS-Policy framework does not mention the policy enforcement layer.

5.2.3 WS-PolicyConstraints

Web Service Policy Constraint Language (WS-PolicyConstraints) , evolved from Web Service Policy Language (WSPL) [5], is a draft standard developed in OASIS. WS-PolicyConstraints can describe the following web service policies: Authentication, Authorization, Quality of protection, Quality of service, Privacy, Reliable messaging, and Service-specific options. The syntax of WS-PolicyConstraints is a strict subset of the eXtensible Access Control Markup Language (XACML) [123] standard of OASIS. Policies could be distributed as a source, and merged into one policy by a negotiation mechanism at run time.

WS-PolicyConstraints is a language for expressing constraints for a web service policy (constraints are also known as *predicates* or *assertions*). With this language, constraints for any type of policy can be written without requiring changes to the policy processor. WS-PolicyConstraints is designed to complement higher level policy frameworks, as well as to facilitate policy intersection and direct verification of messages against policies

WS-policyconstraints proposes seven-layer WS Policy architecture [7] as Figure 77 shows:

Vocabulary Specification
Vocabulary Translation
Vocabulary Semantics
Policy Constraints
Policy Sets
Policy Bindings
Service Metadata

Figure 77 Seven layers in WS-policyconstraints architecture

Vocabulary Specification Layer: This layer defines vocabulary items which are used to characterize a service or aspect of a service. A vocabulary item is defined as one independent technical feature or parameter in a vocabulary. One might think of this as a variable used in a policy. Vocabulary is defined as a set of attributes or as an XML schema. One might think of the vocabulary as the set of variables used in stating a policy. Some standards in this layer include WS-Security, WS-Reliability and so forth.

Vocabulary Translation Layer: This layer is used to translate existing vocabulary syntax to the syntax used by the policy constraints layer if necessary. Some standards in this layer include XSLT and XPath.

Vocabulary Semantics Layer: This layer defines domain-specific semantics of the vocabulary. OWL could be used in this layer to define the vocabulary semantics.

Policy Constraints Layer: This layer defines constraints (generic semantics) on individual vocabulary items and how to compute the intersection of such constraints. In this layer, WS-PolicyConstraints could define the policy constraints.

Policy Sets layer: This layer defines acceptable sets of policy constraints and how to compute intersection and composition of such sets. Note that constraints themselves are opaque to this layer. Policy set is defined as a set of simple constraints (predicates) on vocabulary items such that any set of vocabulary items that satisfies this set also satisfies the entire policy. WSDL Compositors and WS-Policy could be used in this layer.

Policy Bindings layer: This layer is used to bind policies to service descriptions. WSDL features & properties and WS-PolicyAttachmentsOWL could be used in this layer.

Service Metadata layer: This layer is used to make policies available to clients or other services. Some standards in this layer include WSDL, ebXML Reg/Rep, SOAP and

WS-MetadataExchange.

WS-policyconstraints uses standard data types and syntax extracted from the OASIS XACML. WS-policyconstraints supports intersection operation of multiple policies. The intersection of two policies is a single policy that will accept every set of vocabulary items that would be accepted by both of the original policies. The intersection of two policy constraints is a single constraint that will accept every vocabulary item value that would be accepted by both of the original constraints.

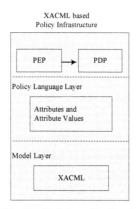

Figure 78 The XACML-based Policy Framework

Figure 78 shows the XACML-based Policy framework. The model layer is based on XACML which is an access control language instead of a generic modeling language. Thus, the policy language layer can only refer to access control related vocabulary. This means that the XACML-based policy language is an access control domain specific policy language rather than a generic policy language. At the policy enforcement layer, it provides a conceptual PEP and PDP.

In [8], Anderson proposed that a SOA policy infrastructure consisting of five layers (bottom up): a vocabulary layer, an assertion or predicate layer, a policy layer, a domain binding layer, and a service interface binding layer. The infrastructure does not consider policy enforcement.

5.2.4 Systinet Policy Manager

Systinet Policy Manager [163] is an enterprise-class governance application that simplifies the creation, management and enforcement of SOA policies and provides the basis for ensuring quality and consistency within an SOA.

Current SOA infrastructure does not support policy very well, if not policy-enabled at all.

Systinet Policy Manager has made the following efforts to incorporate policy into the SOA.

- Systinet has a prototype of WS-Policy implementation.

- Focused on implementing the infrastructure to support the policy-enabled SOA. Especially, tried to enhance the capability of the service broker (UDDI) so that the UDDI could function as the core of policy-enabled SOA.

- Developed some components to facilitate policy operation. These components include policy management, policy association, policy validation, and policy reporting component.

- For policy registration, Systinet believes service providers should register their services as well as policies into the service registry. So, Systinet believes service provider should author the policy. However, we believe that users should author policies as well. This is because service provider wishes more users to use their service, so they are reluctant to put very strict policies on their services. Thus, the validation, integrality, conformance of associated policies will be in doubt. If users can publish collaboration patterns and author policies, then policies are more detailed and dependable.

- For policy enforcement, Systinet believes each service developer should develop his own policy enforcement algorithm. This mechanism will put the whole SOA at stake, because the quality of policy enforcement can not be guaranteed. Nobody will know if the service obtains a policy enforcer or not. It might be worse if the service has a very bad policy enforcer. We argue that there should be a generic framework to specify how policy should be enforced.

CHAPTER 6
PI4SOA: VERIFICATION AND CONTROL OF SERVICE COLLABORATION

This chapter proposes a policy enforcement framework to dynamically verify and control the collaboration process in SOA. In this policy framework, policies are specified in the policy specification language PSML-P, and collaboration processes are specified in the language PSML-C. Collaboration processes can be controlled and verified by leveraging policy enforcement agents. A collaboration policy example is presented, and experiments are conducted to quantitatively analyze the impact of policy enforcement on collaboration process performance.

6.1 Introduction

In Service-Oriented Architecture (SOA), services can collaborate with each other, and the collaboration can be specified using a formal model. Current approach is that each service consumer develops a workflow including the specifications of services needed. The services can be discovered at runtime.

Service collaboration [113] needs to be compatible with service composition rules and constraints. Thus these rules and constraints can be used to verify and validate the service collaboration. One way is express these rules and constraints as policies and enforce these policies at runtime. A policy can be viewed as an assertion, predicate, or constraint, to specify the system requirement. In the ebSOA (Electronic Business Service Oriented Architecture) proposed by OASIS, a policy is defined as "the governing directives and regulations that guide the processes and business of the entity and its transactions with other entities." In the WS-Policy recommendation submitted to the W3C Consortium, a policy is defined as a collection of assertions, and each of these policy assertions represent an individual requirement, capability, or other property of a behavior. The Internet Engineering Task Force (IETF) defined a Common Information Model (CIM) [115] to tackle distributed policies. This CIM suggests that a policy infrastructure should include two key components: Policy Decision Points (PDP) and Policy Enforcement Points (PEP). PDP determines how a policy should be enforced, while PEP performs the policy enforcement task. Shafiq [153] et al proposed a two-step policy-based approach for verification of distributed workflows in a multi-domain environment. Agrawal et al [2] presented that policy could be leveraged to validate the storage area networks. In the SCA (Service Component Architecture) policy framework [150], two kinds of policies were given: interaction policies affect the contract between a service requestor and a service provider; implementation policies affect the contract between a component and its container.

In our previous work, we have proposed the policy language PSML-P [186] and the collaboration framework PSML-C [184]. PSML-C provides a service-oriented infrastructure for process collaboration specification, modeling, design, code generation, simulation, deployment, execution, and management. To provide the PSML-C with the ability of verification and control of collaboration process, in this chapter we propose a policy-based infrastructure Pi4SOA. Pi4SOA is a hierarchical infrastructure for collaboration policy specification, modeling and enforcement.

The rest of the chapter is organized as follows. Section 2 discusses existing policy specification languages and their enforcement. Section 3 presents the policy infrastructure Pi4SOA. On the model level of Pi4SOA, PSML-S and PSML-C are the two modeling languages. Section 4 presents the policy language PSML-P and defines the collaboration policies. Section 5 elaborates the policy enforcement process during service collaboration. Section 6 proposes the detection and resolution of conflicts in collaboration policies. Section 7 demonstrates a collaboration policy enforcement example followed by quantitative analysis of policy enforcement time. Section 8 concludes this chapter.

6.2 Pi4SOA: a Policy Enforcement for SOA

A policy infrastructure should support policy modeling, specification, enforcement, and management. Thus, a policy infrastructure should be a multi-layer architecture. In [9], Anderson proposed that a SOA policy infrastructure consisting of five layers (bottom up): a vocabulary layer, an assertion or predicate layer, a policy layer, a domain binding layer, and a service interface binding layer. The infrastructure does not consider policy enforcement.

This section uses a three-layered SOA policy infrastructure: a model layer, a policy language layer, and a policy enforcement layer.

- Model Layer: It provides the vocabulary to specify and model policies.
- Policy language layer: It defines the syntax and semantics of the policy language.
- Policy enforcement layer: It defines the process of policy enforcement. The policy enforcement process involves monitoring, policy analysis, and policy coding.

SOA applications are distributed and their policy management can follow the IETF model. However, SOA are different from traditional distributed systems because SOA allows dynamic composition and service collaboration. These features add additional dimensions to traditional distributed policy management. Two existing policy infrastructures are specifically designed for SOA: WS-Policy framework [201], and OASIS XACML-based Policy infrastructure [202].

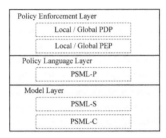

Figure 79 Three Layers of Pi4SOA Framework

Neither WS-Policy nor OASIS XACML-based policy infrastructure has a process model in their respective model layers. Thus, they cannot handle policies related to workflows yet. This section proposes a PSML-based Policy infrastructure for Service-Oriented Architecture (Pi4SOA) as shown in Figure 79. Pi4SOA is based on a process model consisting of two modeling language: the PSML-S (Process Specification and Modeling Language for Service) and its related PSML-C (Process Specification and Modeling Language for Collaboration) [184]. The policy language of Pi4SOA is PSML-P (Process Specification and Modeling Language for Policy), and it is a general policy language and supports distributed policy enforcement.

The model layer of Pi4SOA is the foundation because policies are specified in the vocabulary defined in the model layer, thus the capability of a policy infrastructure primarily depends on the model layer. Pi4SOA uses PSML-S to specify workflow and services, and uses PSML-C, extended from PSML-S, to specify service collaboration. PSML-P can be applied to both PSML-S and PSML-C as shown in Figure 80.

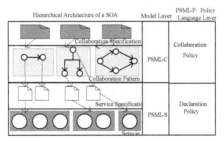

Figure 80 the Model Layer of Pi4SOA

The system structure is modeled by model elements: actors, conditions, data, actions, attributes, and events. PSML-C is used to model collaboration among services. Service collaboration processes can be categorized into reusable collaboration patterns with service stubs. Each service stub is a placeholder in the collaboration pattern. Multiple candidate services can be linked to a service stub, but only one concrete service will be selected and bound to a service stub at runtime.

After policies are specified in PSML-P, they can be enforced in the policy enforcement layer of Pi4SOA. Policy enforcement includes policy dissection, policy analysis, policy dispatching, policy checking, policy compensation, and policy profiling. Figure 81 shows the policy enforcement framework.

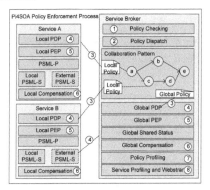

Figure 81 the Policy enforcement in Pi4SOA

To participate into the collaboration process, the services need to enforce the policies assigned to it. Local policies are enforced on each local policy decision points (PDP) and policy enforcement points (PEP), while global policies are enforcement on global PDP and PEP. If a policy fails to enforce due to system failure, then compensation actions will be taken to compensate this failure.

6.3 Collaboration Policy Specification with PSML-P

A policy language can be declarative or collaborative. A declarative policy language deals with policies related to services. PSML-P supports both declaration policies and collaboration policies.

The syntax and semantics of PSML-P are shown in the left part of Figure 82. The XML format of the syntax is shown on the right side. In the XML format, there are four first-level tags: <Actor>, <sharedStatusSet>, <DeclarationPolicySet>, and <CollaborationPolicySet>.

Figure 82 the basic syntax of PSML-P

<Actor> specifies the owner of the policy, which is also the owner of the service. <SharedStatusSet> is a set of statuses of subjects belonged to the actor. <Subject> obtains the reference to element whose status is required to be shared by other services. Policy triggering may depend on other service's condition, value of data, status of action, and value of attribute, thus <Subject> can be the reference to Condition, Data, Action, or Attribute. These statuses of the subjects are required to be shared to other services whose behaviors depend on these statuses.

DeclarationPolicySet and *CollaborationPolicySet* specify declaration and collaboration policies respectively.

Figure 83 Declaration Policy

Declaration policies are those that comply with the "Must be" and "Must not be" semantics. Declaration policies are not related to the action and the workflow. The syntax and XML format of declaration policy are shown in Figure 83, where <Subject> and <value> form a variable-value pair. The value in <Type> can be "MustBe" or "MustNotBe", which is used to assert if the <Subject> must be the <value>, or must not be the <value>. Collaboration policies are those that comply with the "Must do" and "Must not do" semantics. Collaboration policies are related to the action, and it focuses on the workflow of the process. The syntax and XML format of collaboration policy are shown in Figure 84, where <Type> can be "MustDo" or "MustNotDo", which is used to assert if the <Action> must be done or must not be done by the actor. Note that a policy cannot be declaration policy and collaboration policy at the same time.

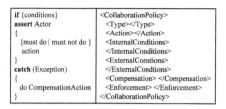

| if {conditions}
assert Actor
{
  {must do \| must not do }
  action
}
catch (Exception)
{
  do CompensationAction
} | <CollaborationPolicy>
  <Type></Type>
  <Action></Action>
  <InternalConditions>
  </InternalConditions>
  <ExternalConstions>
  </ExternalCondtions>
  <Compensation> </Compensation>
  <Enforcement> </Enforcement>
</CollaborationPolicy> |

Figure 84 Collaboration Policy

Policy should be checked and enforced under given conditions. A Condition is a subject-value pair in PSML-S. The owner of the subject and the owner of the condition is the same actor. Conditions can be further divided *into Internal Conditions* and *External Conditions*. Internal Conditions refer to those whose owner is the same as the <actor> of the policy. Thus, the actor has the full access to its own condition and can check if the subject-value pair is satisfied before the policy enforcement. External Conditions refer to those whose owner is different from the <actor> of the policy. The actor of the condition must have been specified. Thus, before the policy enforcement, the subject-value pair can be checked through the actor. Both declaration policies and collaboration policies may have <InternalConditions> and <ExternalConditions>. If a policy has external conditions, it is a global policy. Otherwise, it is a local policy.

<Compensation> is used to specify a compensation action which will be invoked once the policy is violated. The actor of the policy must have the access to the compensation action.

<Enforcement> is used to specify how the policy will be enforced. Since policy enforcement takes system execution time, different policy enforcement algorithms can lead to different system execution time. The more policies need to be enforced, the slower the system will execute. The policy engine supports three policy enforcement algorithms [186]: FYI (For Your Information) algorithm, conservative algorithm, and greedy algorithm. Depending on the safety and performance requirements, each of these three enforcement algorithms can be used to address different environment so that policies enforcement can be more flexible and efficient. The <Enforcement> can also act as an extending point of policy enforcement by containing the address of an external enforcement engine.

6.4 Collaboration Policies

Collaboration policies can be specified with PSML-P. PSML-P can specify the following collaboration policies: pre-condition policies, choreography policies, mutual exclusive policies, transaction policies, reliability policies and timing policies.

Choreography Policies: In service collaboration, execution order of involved services is a critical consideration. Services are required to follow a given execution order. Choreography policies specify such sequence relationships among services. Figure 85 illustrates this policy where one action must happen before another action.

Figure 85 Choreography Policy

Mutual Exclusive Policies: Mutual exclusive policies are used when multiple actions are exclusive to each other in a process. Figure 86 shows this policy on two actions B1 and B2. The policies specify that B1 and B2 can not happen in a same process.

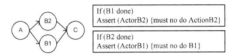

Figure 86 Mutual Exclusive Policy

Transaction Policies: Transaction policies are used to specify the relationship among actions that either all of them execute, or none of them are executed. Figure 87 shows this policy for three actions A, B and C. In this process, either action A, B and C happen all together, or none of them happen.

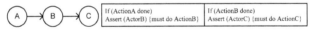

Figure 87 Transaction Policy

Reliability Policies: Reliability is a critical concern for service collaborations. When collaborating with services, the client usually requires a minimal reliability value. In order to track the reliability of services, a reliability monitor is presented in Pi4SOA. The reliability of services can be collected and analyzed by an evaluation system called Web Services Testing, Reliability Assessment, and Ranking (WebStrar).

For example, Figure 88   shows a reliability policy.   Actor A consists of an Action A. If reliability of actor A fails to meet the minimal reliability requirement, action A can not be invoked by external services.

Figure 88 Reliability Policy

Timing Policies: In some scenarios, timing is an important issue.   For example, an action must happen after certain delay. In other cases, an action must happen before a deadline.

Timing policies specify such constraints with respect to timing on collaboration participants. Figure 89 shows that action B must happen between the delay time and the deadline.

If ((action A is done) && (time<delay)) Assert (must not do Action B)	If (action A is done && time<deadline) Assert (must do Action B)

Figure 89 Timing Policy

6.5 Policies Enforcement for Service Collaboration

Collaboration policies specify the constraints on these collaboration protocols. A collaboration policy is simply a rule that will be triggered during service collaboration if the associated condition occurs. For example, a collaboration policy can check the validity of data received from the other party before accepting the data for processing. A dynamic service collaboration can be divided into four phases [184]: preparation phase, establishment phase, execution phase, and termination phase as shown in Figure 90. Policy enforcement can be carried out in all four collaboration stages.

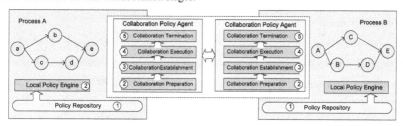

Figure 90 the Policy Enforcement for Collaboration

6.5.1 Policy Enforcement during Collaboration Preparation

In this stage, each service that wishes to participate in the collaboration process must prepare a list of collaboration protocols that the service can understand. In this phase, collaboration policy engine conducts two operations:

Policy consistency checking: Two kinds of conflicts may exist in a policy-based system: inconsistency and incompleteness. In the collaboration preparation phase, as the collaboration partners are not known yet, each service has a partial view. Thus, completeness policy checking can not conduct at this phase. Inconsistent policies are policies that conflict each other. Inconsistent policies can occur and can be identified by simply analyzing the syntax of policy specification without any knowledge of system model.

Local policy enforcement: At this phase, policy can be used to specify the local constraints that must be met before collaboration establishment. For example, in the debit card payment service of a banking system, there exists a policy specifying this constraint: the user account balance must be greater than zero before establishing the collaboration. This policy can be expressed as Figure 91.

```
if (debitcard payment request
received)
{
    assert account.balance
    {
        must not be 0
    }
    catch (exception)
    {
        do Action.RejectTransaction
    }
}
```

Figure 91 a policy example during collaboration preparation

6.5.2 Collaboration Establishment

In this stage, participating services will exchange their collaboration protocols, and agree on a common protocol agreement that all participating services share. In this phase, collaboration policy engine conducts two operations:

Global policy negotiation: Collaboration participants need to find the global policies that work for all parties through the policy negotiation process. The policy engine will generate formalized global policy scripts into the policy repository. For example, if a bank client can support three kinds of encryption protocols including: A, B and C, while a bank system can accept two kinds of encryption protocols including C and D. After the policy negotiation process, the bank client and banking system can agree on the encryption protocol C.

Policy completeness checking: In the collaboration establishment phase, the collaboration partners are known and protocol agreement can be established. Thus the service can have a complete view of the collaboration partners and the overall collaboration process. Since the service specification is now available for all collaboration partners, so policy completeness checking can be conducted. Incomplete policies refer to those constraints that are unable to enforce due to missing properties. For example, a policy on process A depends on a property of its collaboration partner process B, while the property does not exist, thus the policy becomes incomplete.

6.5.3 Collaboration Execution

In this stage, participating services will collaborate based on the common protocol agreement established earlier.

Runtime Policy enforcement: In the collaboration execution phase, the collaboration partners are known and the collaboration protocols are established. Both global and local policies can now be enforced at runtime. Policy enforcement agents will be deployed to the composite application for execution monitoring and policy enforcement. Runtime monitoring services listen to the outputs of the collaboration, retrieve the data, and report to the backend service center for policy enforcement.

The runtime enforcement can be implemented in two manners, Detection Only and Detection and Prevention.

Detection only means the policy agents can be inserted in a non-intrusive manner, which monitor and detect any violation without taking any action. In this approach, the policy agent acts like an information sink. It collects runtime data for future offline analysis.

Detection and prevention means policy agents are inserted as an intrusive manner, besides serve as the information sink, it also raises exception to interrupt the current execution and force the process to correct the erroneous conditions.

6.5.4 Collaboration Termination

In this phase, participating services terminate the collaboration. The collaboration process may be evaluated so that future collaboration can be improved. The policy agents continue executing and monitoring the collaboration participating services to ensure the services properly finished their collaboration and prepare for the next collaboration process. Policy enforcement data can be collected and analyzed by policy profiling component.

6.6 Experiment

This section presents a service-oriented air ticket ordering system and its collaboration policies, and shows the cost of policy enforcement.

6.6.1 An Air Ticket Ordering System

Figure 92 illustrates an air ticket booking system predefined in a service registry, which is composed of six service stubs: ticket ordering service stub, credit card charge service stub, Ticket printing service stub, Ticket Shipping service stub, eTicket service stub, and Email Notification service stub. Each service stub binds with one policy specification.

Figure 92 an Air Ticker Ordering Example

We implemented this example with the Windows Workflow Foundation (WWF) and the

Windows Communication Foundation (WCF) [108] as shown in Figure 93.

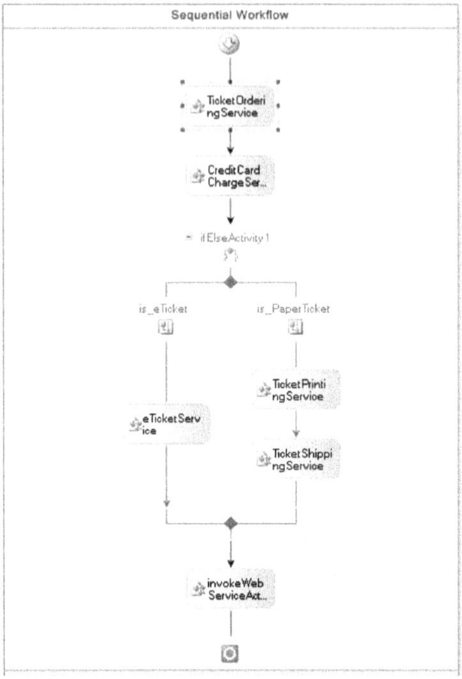

Figure 93 the Implementation of the air ticket ordering system with WWF and WCF

If (TicketPrinting not done) Assert FastShipper {must no do TicketShipping }
If (eTicket is done) Assert FastShipper {must no do TicketShipping}
If (TicketPrinting done) Assert FastShipper {must do TicketPrinting}

Figure 94 Collaboration Policies specified with the Ticket Shipping Service

Two kinds of tickets are available for customers to choose from: electronic ticket (eTicket) or a paper ticket. If a customer chooses an eTicket, no ticket will be printed or shipped to the customer. The customer can download the eTicket from the website once the ticket is purchased. If the customer chooses to order a paper ticket, the travel agency will print the ticket and then ship the ticket to the customer. After the ticket is shipped, an email will be sent to notify the customer that the transaction is completed.

If one shipping company called "FastShipper" subscribes the Ticket Shipping service stub, then FastShipper must enforce the policy specification associated with the Ticket Shipping service stub. We can identify the following policies for Ticket Shipping service stub.

1. Ticket shipping service stub and Ticket Printing service stub constitute a choreography policy.

2. Ticket shipping service stub and Ticket printing service stub constitute a transaction policy.

3. Ticket Shipping service stub and eTicket service stub constitute an XOR policy.

At run time, FastShipper must enforce the collaboration policies showed in *Figure 94*.

6.6.2 Quantitative Analysis of Collaboration Policy Enforcement

The experiment is run on a Windows box with two Pentium 3GHz CPUs underlying, and the remote services are hosted on a Windows 2003 server connected to the 100M intranet. This experiment uses three parameters: number of $\overline{X}$ services involved in the collaboration process (s), total number of policies specified with the collaboration process (p), and the running time (r).

We measure the running time when increasing p and s from 0 to 100 respectively. The experiment data is shown in Table 38. Note that every running time is not a single run of the test. Instead, the running time is a statistical result which is the average value of 20 samples. The numbers in the cells denote the running time in millisecond.

Table 38 Quantitative analysis of the running time.

	s=10	s=20	s=30	s=40	s=50	s=60	s=70	s=80	s=90	s=100
p=0	80	158	239	317	399	494	583	668	743	869
p=10	81	166	241	318	402	503	594	673	744	874
p=20	81	167	246	334	416	513	598	677	771	878
P=30	83	168	253	342	418	525	608	688	787	907
p=40	89	175	263	350	434	528	628	708	801	912
p=50	89	180	265	349	442	532	637	728	825	914
p=60	90	187	273	357	452	549	645	746	834	931
p=70	91	186	272	360	453	551	647	752	847	937
p=80	92	183	278	368	466	555	661	757	850	951
p=90	92	185	277	375	470	579	670	764	858	970
p=100	92	187	284	376	486	601	693	782	860	986

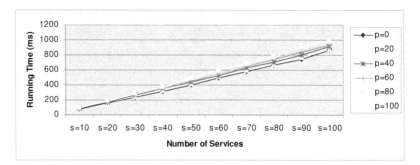

Figure 95 Running time increases when more services are involved

Figure 95 shows that the running time increases as more services are involved in the collaboration process. Since each service is a method on a remote server, more services may considerably increase execution time. From

Figure 95 we can observe that the running time is a function of s and p.

$$r=g(s)+ f(p), \qquad (1)$$

As can be observed from

Figure 95, running time linearly increases with the number of services. Thus, the relationship between running time and number of services g(s) is:

$$g(s)=K*s, \qquad (2)$$

where K is a constant. From Table 38, we can calculate the value of K from the row of p=0:

$$K=(r_{100}-r_{10})/(s_{100}-s_{10})=(869-80)/(100-10)=8.8$$

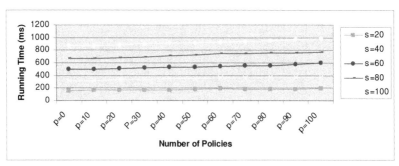

Figure 96 Running time increases slightly along with the increasing of policy amount

As can be seen from Figure 96, the running time also increases when more policies are enforced during the collaboration process. However, the number of policies does not have as much impact on the running time as the number of services does.

It is worth to notice that the mean time of policy enforcement (denoted as $\bar{t}$) increases as more services are involved in the collaboration process. For example, in the column where s=10 of Table 38,

$$\bar{t}=(92-80)/100=0.12 \text{ ms,}$$

while in the column where s=100,

$$\bar{t}=(986-869)/100=1.17 \text{ ms,}$$

Table 39 shows that $\bar{t}$ increases as s expands from 10 to 100.

Table 39 $\bar{t}$ increases as more services are involved in the collaboration process

	s=10	s=20	s=30	s=40	s=50	s=60	s=70	s=80	s=90	s=100
$\bar{t}$	0.12	0.29	0.45	0.59	0.87	1.07	1.1	1.14	1.17	1.17

The reason that $\bar{t}$ increases along with s is because the dependency among services is increasing when there are a big number of services in a collaboration process. Consequently, as a specification of these dependencies, each policy may be correlated more services and has to wait the feedback from all its correlated services before enforcement. The overhead spending on the communication and synchronization of the policy enforcement considerably increases as the number of services increase.

However, the $\bar{t}$ value does not expand infinitely when the number of services keeps increasing as shown in Figure 97. After the collaboration pattern includes a big number of services, the increasing of services will not influence the running time. Thus, the value of $\bar{t}$ becomes stabilized. This is because the number of services specified in each policy can not be too many. If a collaboration policy correlates too many services, then the collaboration policy is too complicated and decomposition of the policy is mandatory. On average, each policy is capable of specifying the dependency relationship between two (e.g, choreography policies) or three (e.g., transaction policies) services.

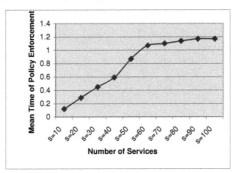

Figure 97 $\bar{t}$ increases exponentially in the beginning but then become stabilized.

From Figure 97, we can find that the relationship between $\bar{t}$ and s is approximate to

$$\bar{t} = 1.2 - 1.2^{-s/10} \qquad\qquad (3)$$

Thus,

$$f(p) = p \ast \bar{t} = p \ast (1.2 - 1.2^{-s/10}) \qquad (4)$$

With equation (1), (2) and (4), we can have the running time in the air ticket ordering system as

$$r = 8.8 \ast s + p \ast (1.2 - 1.2^{-s/10}) \qquad\qquad (5)$$

6.7 Conclusion

This chapter proposed a policy-based verification mechanism and an implementation infrastructure named Pi4SOA for verification and control of service collaboration. We used PSML-C to model the collaboration process. The process was composed of service stubs, each of which is a place holder for a genuine service. The obligations of each service stub are specified by the policy language PSML-P, and are stored in the policy specification file associated with the service stub. Genuine services can subscribe to the service stubs in the collaboration process. The corresponding policy specifications will be dispatched to appropriate policy engines. At runtime, the policies are enforced by the Pi4SOA to verify the collaboration process. The relationship between running time, number of services and number of policies are also studied and analyzed quantitatively in collaborative SOA environment. The experiment result shows that the number of services can considerably impact the running time, while the policy enforcement only increases the system execution time slightly.

CHAPTER 7

PSML-P LIFECYCLE

7.1 Introduction to PSML-P

Policies can be system constraints, commands, or regulations, and the new policy-based computing decouples the system from policy enforcement so that both can be changed independent of each other. Policy enforcement works in parallel with system execution, thus policy can be considered as a runtime verification and compensation mechanism. Figure 98 shows the model-driven approach to specify policies.

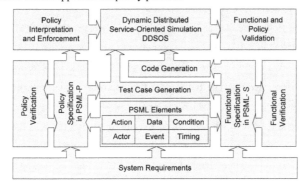

Figure 98 Model-driven Policy Specification

The lifecycle of policy includes policy specification, policy refinement, policy verification and validation, policy enforcement, and policy compensation.

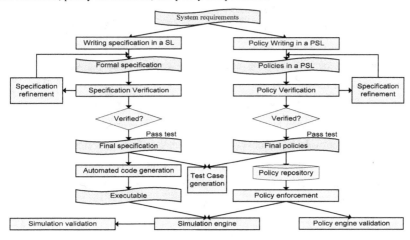

7.2 Policy Specification

Domain-Independent: a number of policy specification languages are designed to specify policies in a particular domain or application (i.e. network administration or access controls). If a policy specification language can only specify policies for a particular domain or application, this policy specification language is domain-specific. In contrast, if a policy specification language can specify generic policies for all domains or applications, this policy specification language is considered to be domain-independent.

Obligation Policy: defines an actor's responsibilities (Section 5.3.1). Normally, obligation policies are ECA (Event- Condition-Action) rules that obligate an actor to perform action A if triggering event E occurs and condition C is true.

Authorization Policy: defines an actor's rights that give the actor permissions to perform certain actions (Section 5.3.2). Authorization policies normally are specified in two different approaches. The first approach is to explicitly specify an actor's rights, allowing or denying the actor to perform actions. The problem of this approach is that policy-makers have to specify the rights for every actor, which can be a lot of workload in a system with numerous actors. The second approach is to employ access control models (such as the BLP model or RBAC model) to specify authorization policies. Properties (such roles or security levels) relevant to access controls are attached to entities (actors, data or actions) when they are defined. The policy enforcer uses these properties to decide whether actions are allowed or denied.

System Constraints: are policies that constrain system behaviors and system states (Section 5.3.3). Generally speaking, there are two types of system constraints: system constraints on actions and system constraints on data. System constraints on actions use temporal logic to constrain system behaviors (i.e. action B must occur after action A is performed). System constraints on data constrain system states (i.e. temporal must be maintained above 100 degrees).

Role Support: a role defines a management position in an organization and its associated responsibilities (represented by obligation policies) and rights (represented by authorization policies). Roles provide an intuitive way to organize policies and significantly simplify policies specification and management. By specifying policies on roles and assigning roles to actors, policies defined on a role can be reused by actors who take this role. In addition, roles are the foundation of the role-based access control.

Role Hierarchy: management positions in an organization are normally organized in a hierarchical structure. Role hierarchy provides a natural way to represent the hierarchical structure. If role A is superior to role B, it obtains all permissions given to role B.

Delegation Policy: allows an actor (or a role) to temporarily transfer its responsibilities or rights to another actor (or another role). The delegation can also be revoked at a later time.

Hierarchical Policy: allows policy-maker to specify policies at different levels. High-level policies are normally abstract and non-enforceable, and define the goals to be refined by low-level concrete enforceable policies. Low-level policies are the plans that implement high-level policies.

Meta-Policy: specify application-dependent constraints, such as separation of duties. Meta-policies are also used to resolve policy conflicts (such as precedence of modalities).

Policy Attributes: In our policy model, we are concerned with three types of policies: authorization policies, obligation policies and system policies. We don't claim these three types of policies cover all possible policies in real life, but they represent the most useful management policies in a computing system. A typical policy has the following attributes:

Keyword: defines the type of a policy. Since we have three types of polices in our policy model, there are correspondingly three types of keywords: authorization policy keywords (allow & deny), obligation policy keyword (mustdo & mustnotdo), and system policy keywords (mustbe & mustnotbe). Each type of keywords contains a positive keyword (allow, mustdo, mustbe) and a negative keyword (deny, mustnotdo, mustnotbe).

Subjects: are the entities (actors or automated agents) to whom a policy is applied. As we mentioned before, policies in our policy model is defined on roles rather than on individual entities. Consequently, subjects of a policy in the policy model are roles instead of entities. Sometimes, we may need finer granularity in policy specification. For instance, there may be a policy applying only the department manager of Department A, but not department managers of other department. In this case, a subordinate role (say the department A manager role) of the department manager role is to be defined, and this policy is defined on the subordinate role.

Triggering Events: trigger the policy enforcement of a positive obligation policy on receiving the events. A positive obligation policy is essentially an ECA (Event-Condition-Action) rule, which executes an action sequence under certain conditions when receiving the triggering event.

Actions: represent the policy goal according to the policy keyword. For instance, actions in authorization policies specify which actions are allowed or denied, and actions in obligation policies specify which actions should be obliged or forbidden. The actions in a policy could either be an abstract action in an intermediate node of the action hierarchy or a detailed action in the leaf node. In the former case, this policy needs further refinement.

Objects: are the objects onto which actions perform. The objects in the policy model are defined on domains instead of individual data. Same as subject, if we need finer granularity in policy specification, sub-domains can be defined to include more specific objects.

Condition: defines a condition under which a policy is valid. If condition is not specified, the policy is valid at all times.

Compensation: defines an event that will trigger remedial actions when a failure of policy enforcement is detected.

As we will see later, not all policies contain all of these attributes. The way attributes are organized depends on the type of a policy and its semantics.

7.3 Policy Verification and Validation

7.3.1 Policy Analysis

The conditions of collaboration policies can be represented in various standard forms including the disjunctive normal form (DNF) [47].

Table 40 Sample Policies

if (condition A and condition B)
Assert {Policy P1}
if (condition C and condition D)
Assert {Policy P2}

Policies in DNF can be represented in Karnaugh maps (K-maps) [91]. The policy in Table 40 can be represented in the following K-map, shown in Figure 99. In the K-map, cells representing "condition A and condition B" and cells representing "condition C and condition D" are represented with different strips.

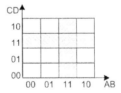

Figure 99 K-map of the policy

Observed from the above K-map, there is an overlap in the K-map: the cell "ABCD". Two policies may be inconsistent when condition overlaps exist because two actions associate with the same condition. For example, suppose policy P1 and policy P2 in Table 40 are defined as following:

- P1: Set data 1 to value 10

- P2: Set data 1 to value 0

P1 is clearly inconsistent with P2 if ABCD holds. This problem can be solved by modifying the actions associated with the overlap conditions. For example, in the above example, the policy designer will reevaluate the action associated with the overlay condition: "ABCD". Suppose one decides that P1 should be should be enforced under the condition "ABCD" instead of P2, the policy changes to Table 41.

Table 41 Updated Composite Policy

if (condition A and condition B)
    Assert {Policy P1}
if ((condition C and condition D and condition $\bar{A}$) or (condition C and condition D and condition A and condition $\bar{B}$))
    Assert {Policy P2}

Anomaly can still arise even if all policies are consistent with each other. For example, condition A, and condition can have the same actions, this is not inconsistent but odd, and thus the user should be alerted.

Besides inconsistency issues, collaboration policies may be incomplete. For example, the policies in Figure 99 are incomplete, because the actions associated with conditions "$\overline{AC} + \overline{AD} + \overline{BC} + \overline{BD}$" are not specified. Policy incompleteness can be detected and eliminated through the following six steps [175]:

1. Derive policies from the system requirements.

2. Parse each policy and extract the combinations of conditions and events.

3. Perform C&C analysis on C-E combinations. A C-E combination is the pair of conditions in a policy specification together with the trigger event.

4. Identify those covering policies to eliminate those missing C-E combinations.

5. Classify each covering policy into three categories: 1) incorporate it as a functional policy; 2) treat it as an exception with an exception handling; or 3) don't care due to physical constraints.

6. Update policy specification using the completeness analysis results.

7.3.2 Policy Coding Algorithm

The policies that passed C&C analysis can be organized into C-E (conditions-events) trees for efficient policy enforcement. A C-E tree is a data structure to compose a Policy Map [186]. A Policy Map connects a triggering data to its associated policies. As a data may trigger multiple policies, thus all the associated policies will be represented in a C-E tree with the corresponding events and conditions. For example, two policies, policy11 and policy13, may be triggered by the same data annual income, and another policy, policy12 may be triggered by another data annual expenditure. Those two data correspond to two different C-E trees. Figure 100 gives an example C-E tree, where three policies: policy1, policy2 and policy3 with their triggering data data1. These three policies have different triggering conditions but they share a triggering data. For example, policy2 has the conditions C1 and $\overline{C_2}$, while policy3 has condition $\overline{C_1}$. As a policy may have multiple triggering data, a policy may be associated with multiple C-E trees.

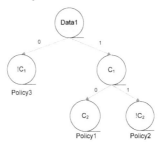

Figure 100 Example C-E Tree

Similar to the Hoffman tree [73], C-E trees use variable bit length binary words to encode policies. Policies used more frequently have length as small as possible, which speeds up the enforcement. The policy coding algorithm is shown in Table 42:

Table 42 the policy coding algorithm

Inputs: Data, corresponding policies, and policy invocation frequencies. Outputs: constructed C-E trees.
Step 1: Rank policies according to their invocation frequencies, from most frequent to least frequent ones and store the ordered policy indexes into queue: queuePolicy.

Step 2: for each data
{
   While (there are still selected policies triggered by current data in queuePolicy)
   {
     Select the next policy pCurr triggered by current data from queuePolicy.
     Put the conditions of this pCurr into the tree. If pCurr has multiple conditions, they should be put into different levels in the tree.
     If pCurr has common conditions with existing policies in the tree, they should be put under common nodes in the tree.
   }
}

Step 3: For each policy, acquire policy representing codes by concatenating the digits on the route from the root to the node representing that policy in the C-E tree.

There are no condition overlaps between different policies in the constructed C-E trees after policy analysis. The proposed algorithm guarantees that the most frequently used policies are coded with the minimum bits for speedy discovery. The following example illustrates the algorithm. Suppose the policy invocation frequencies of the three policies in Figure 100 are listed in Table 43.

Table 43 Policies and Frequencies

Policy	Frequency
Policy1	2.4%
Policy2	1.2%
Policy3	23.4%

From Table 43, one can see that Policy3 is the most frequently used policy, taking 23.4% of total policy invocation, while Policy2 is the least frequently invoked policy. The constructed C-E tree is shown in Figure 17. For example, policy3 is represented with code "0", and policy2 is represented with code "11". By organizing policies in this way, the most frequently triggered policies will be located first to speed up the enforcement.

The tree can be constructed using data collected from operation using the SOSE (Service-Oriented System Engineering) approach in [174]. The tree can be dynamically updated as new data are collected to reflect the changes in policies or system behavior.

7.4 Policy Enforcement

Policies are enforced during the simulation. In the initialization phase of simulation, the policy engine loads policies from the policy database and register them with the simulator according to their semantics. Policies are registered so that simulator knows when to trigger the policy enforcement. Simulator triggers the policy enforcement when a registered event occurs, a registered action is performed, or a registered datum is modified. Policy engine will enforce relevant policies registered to this event, action, or datum, and return the results of policy enforcement back to the simulator.

Policy enforcement can be classified into three categories: policy checking, policy execution, and policy compensation. *Policy checking* verifies if policy violations are detected when actions are performed or data are changed. *Policy execution* executes the action defined in the policy when receiving the triggering events. *Policy compensation* executes the compensation action defined in the policy when policy checking detects a policy violation. All checkable policies come with a compensation action.

Only positive obligation policies are executable policies. The rest types of policies (e.g. negative obligation policies, all authorization policies and all system constraints) are all checkable policies. *Executable policies* influence the paths of the simulation through the actions defined in them. When the triggering event occurs, executable policies registered to this event will be enforced, and the action specified in policy specification will be executed by the simulator. *Checkable policies* can also influence the paths of the simulation through compensation actions. When data are changed or actions are performed, checkable policies registered to the data or actions will be enforced. If there are policy violations detected, the compensation action specify in policy specification will be executed by the simulator.

Figure 101 illustrates the policy enforcement framework. After policies are extracted and specified in PSML-P, the policy editor parses policies for correctness and stores them into the policy database. During the initialization phase of simulation, the policy engine loads policies, interprets them, and registers them to the simulator. While the simulator executes system scenarios, it triggers the policy enforcement when the registered events occur, registered actions are performed, or registered data get changed. The policy engine checks or executes policies and returns the results back to the simulator. Based on the returned results, the simulator determines the next system scenarios.

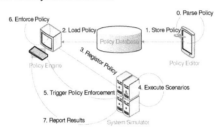

Figure 101 the Policy Enforcement Framework

Policy Enforcement should have the following Components

- *Policy Checking:* verifies whether checkable policies are violated during the system simulation / execution. Checkable define the constraints on system behaviors and system states. Negative obligation policies, authorization policies, and system constraints all belong to checkable policies in PSML-P. The policy enforcer watches over checkable policies when actions are performed or data are changed, and determines whether or not constraints defined as checkable policies are violated. For instance, if a system constraint on data specifies that the balance of a regular saving account must no less than $300, the policy enforcer will keep an eye on the balance of this account whenever it gets changed.

- *Policy Execution:* executes the action defined in an executable policy when triggering events are triggered. Executable policies (such as positive obligation policies) are essentially ECA (Event-Condition-Action) rules with the semantics that "On receiving triggering event E, action A must be performed if condition C holds". The policy enforcer is informed when a registered event is triggered, and actions defined in this executable policy will be executed by the system simulator / executor.

- *Integrated System Model:* policies are enforced on the system during the system simulation / execution. An integrated system model provides a mechanism that allows the system and policies to be modeled on a single model. However, a number of policy specification languages do not mention how the system should be modeled. They just provide a set of syntax for policy specification and assume there are a policy engine that can parse and interpret policies and domain servers that can provide information on system models. Lacking of an integrated system model for both system modeling and policy modeling makes policy enforcement and analysis difficult to achieve.

- *Failure semantics* defines how policies are violated and how system should respond to policy violations. For checkable policies, the failure semantics can be defined as the violations of constraints. After checkable policies are violated, compensation actions should be performed. For executable policies, actions defined in executable policies may not be executed due to some reasons (for example, the action is not authorized by authorization policies), which causes the failure of enforcing executable policies. As a result, the failure semantics of executable policies can be defined as the failure of executing actions.

- *Policy Parsing and Storage.* The policy editor parses policies for correctness. On successful parsing, policy editor translates policies into XML and stores them into the policy database. The policy parser is implemented by ANTLR (ANother Tool for Language Recognition). According to the policy syntax, ANTLR creates an abstract syntax tree (AST) for each policy. Policy elements (roles, actions, condition, etc) are extracted by traversing the tree, and translated to the XML representation. The XML representation of a policy is then stored into the policy database as a string.

- *Policy Registration.* Policy registration lets the simulator know when policy enforcement should be triggered. In IASM, three out of the six ACDATE elements can trigger the policy enforcement: *event, action, and data.* Events occurrences will trigger the enforcement of positive obligation policies; action performances will trigger the enforcement of negative obligation polices, authorization policies, and system constraints on actions; data changes will trigger the enforcement of system constraints on data.

- *Policy Map.* To improve performance, a policy map is created, mapping a particular event, action or datum to a list of relevant policies to which it has been registered with. All policies registered to a particular action, event or datum forms a linked list. The linked list and the ID of action, event or datum are then organized as a policy map. When policy enforcement is triggered, the policy engine locates the policy linked list of a particular action, event or datum, and enforces all policies in the list.

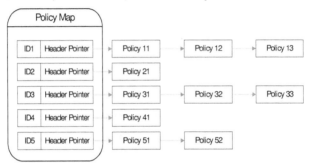

Figure 102 Policy Map

- *Policy Enforcement Triggering.* After policies have been registered, the simulator initializes the data and starts running the system scenarios. The simulator keeps an eye on the system scenarios, and triggers the policy enforcement by invoking the EnforcePolicy() method in the policy engine whenever an event is triggered, an action is performed or a datum is changed. The policy engine enforces all relevant policies, records all violations in the policy log, and returns the policy log back to the simulator. When policy enforcement is triggered, the simulator invokes the EnforcePolicy() method in the policy engine, passing the ID of the event, action or datum that triggers the policy enforcement. The policy engine looks up its policy map, maps the ID to a list of policies to which it has registered, and enforces them one by one. Authorization policies are not registered in the policy map, and they are enforced before obligation policies and system constraints are enforced. When policies are enforced, all violations are recorded into a policy log that is returned to the simulator. The EnforcePolicy() method returns a Boolean value indicating whether policy violations are detected.

- *Policy Compensation.* If a checkable policy is violated, the system simulator / executor must be capable of doing something to minimize the damages caused by the policy violation. Policy compensation mechanism is employed to achieve this goal. In the specification of a checkable policy, a compensation action is defined and this action will be performed when the policy is violated. For instance, if the balance of a regular saving account goes under $300, a compensation action could be "charge a monthly maintenance fee".

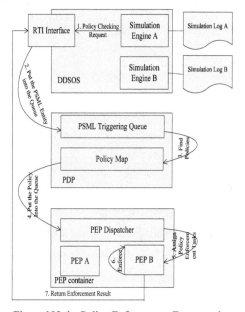

Figure 103 the Policy Enforcement Framework

Figure 103 illustrates our policy enforcement framework. After policies are extracted and specified in PSML-P, the policy editor parses policies for correctness and stores them into the policy database. During the initialization phase of simulation, the policy engine loads policies, interprets them, and registers them to the simulator. While the simulator executes system processes, it triggers the policy enforcement, when the registered events occur, registered actions are performed, or registered data are changed. The policy engine checks or executes policies and returns the results back to the simulator. Based on the returned results, the simulator determines the next system processes.

A similar policy enforcement framework, the IETF Policy Core Information Model, is reported in [115]. Different from IETF, this framework is a distributed policy enforcement framework, which consists of three main components: Dynamic Distributed Service-Oriented Simulation framework (DDSOS), Policy Decision Point (PDP), and Policy Enforcement Point (PEP) Container.

- DDSOS is a modeling and simulation framework that supports the simulation, development, and evaluation of large scale systems such as network-centric and system-of-systems applications.

- PDP is used to determine what policy should be applied under certain circumstance. PDP includes two components: PSML Triggering Queue and Policy Map.
  - PSML Triggering Queue is used to handle policy enforcement requests from multiple simulation engines.
  - Policy Map is a hash table used to maintain the relationship between policies and PSML elements.
- PEP Container includes one PEP Dispatcher and a set of PEPs.
  - PEP Dispatcher is used to schedule policy enforcement tasks
  - PEP is responsible for the enforcement of policies.

The overall process of policy enforcement is as follows:

1. The policy enforcement process is initiated by a policy checking request issued by one of simulation engines of the DDSOS. If the policy is a local policy, the local policy engine will handle the policy enforcement. If the policy is a global policy, the policy checking request is sent to the RTI (RunTime Infrastructure) of the DDSOS.

2. After receiving the global policy checking request, the RTI will put the PSML element which makes the request into the Triggering Queue.

3. Policy Map takes the first PSML element in the queue, and retrieves corresponding policies which already registered with the PSML element at policy specification time. The relationship between PSML elements and Policies is a hash table, as shown in Figure 4. PSML-Policy Map retrieves all policies related to this element from the hash table.

4. The Policy Map sends these policies to the PEP Dispatcher.

5. The PEP Dispatcher assigns policy enforcement tasks to specific PEPs. Different policy enforcement algorithms will be described in section 4.5. The following steps 6 and 7 describe one of those possible algorithms. Note that in other algorithms policy engines can also be built into PDP or DDSOS in order to save policy enforcement time.

6. The PEP will check whether the current status of the concerned PSML element violates involved policies or not.

7. The PEP returns the policy checking result to RTI for further processing.

7.4.1 Policy Parsing and Storage

The policy editor parses policies for syntax checking. On successful parsing, policy editor translates the policies into XML text and stores them into the policy databasePolicy elements (roles, actions, condition, etc) are extracted by traversing the tree, and translated it into the XML representation.

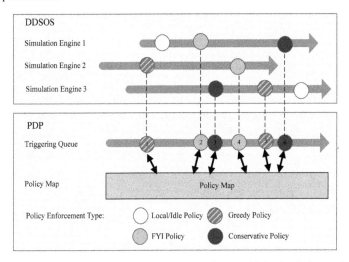

Figure 104 Receive policy enforcement requests from multiple simulation engines

7.4.2 Policy Registration & Policy Map

Policy registration lets the simulator know when policy enforcement should be triggered. In PSML-S, three out of the six model elements can trigger the policy enforcement: event, action, and data. Events occurrences can trigger the enforcement of positive obligation policies; an action execution can trigger the enforcement of negative obligation polices, authorization policies, and system constraints on actions; and data changes can trigger the enforcement of system constraints on data.

To improve performance, a policy map is created, mapping a particular event, action or data to a list of relevant policies to which it has been registered with. All policies registered to a particular action, event, or data form a linked list. The linked list and the ID of action, event or data are then organized as a policy map, as shown in Figure 4. When a policy enforcement is triggered, the policy engine locates the policy linked list of a particular action, event or data, and enforces all policies in the list.

This Policy Map is also useful to detect if there exists conflict among policies registered with the same model element. For example, assume that two policies, "policy 11" and "policy

13", are registered with the same Data "annual income". "Policy 11" claims "annual income must >= 30K", while "policy 13" specifies that "annual income must <2k". This policy conflict can be detected by the policy conflict detecting procedure in the policy parser.

In our policy enforcement framework, policies can be dynamically changed at simulation time. A locking mechanism is implemented in the policy database to resolve the potential read-write conflicts between the PDP and the Policy Editor. The locking algorithm is shown in Figure 105 and explained as follows:

- Before the policy editor begins to write/change/add a policy entry, a lock will be added to the policy entry. The lock is released as soon as the write/change/add operation is completed.

- Whenever the PDP begins to read a policy, the policy entry is locked by the locking mechanism. After the PDP finishes reading operation, the lock will be released.

By introducing the locking mechanism, the policy editor and PDP can write/read at run time without causing conflicts.

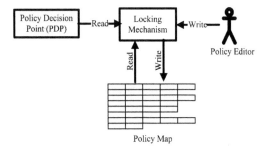

Figure 105 the Locking mechanism for the policy map

7.4.3 Policy Triggering and Enforcement Algorithms

After policies have been registered, the simulator initializes the data and starts running the system processes. The simulator keeps monitoring the system processes, and triggers the policy enforcement by invoking the EnforcePolicy() method in the policy engine whenever an event is triggered, an action is executed, or a data is modified. The policy engine enforces all relevant policies, stops simulation or records all violations in the policy log, and returns the policy log back to the simulator.

When a policy enforcement is triggered, the simulator invokes the EnforcePolicy() method in the policy engine, passing the ID of the event, action or data that triggers the policy enforcement. The policy engine looks up its policy map, maps the ID to a list of policies to which it has registered, and enforces them one by one. Authorization policies are not registered in the policy map, and they are enforced before obligation policies and system constraints are enforced. The EnforcePolicy() method returns a Boolean value indicating whether policy violations are detected.

Policy enforcement takes simulation time. Therefore, different Policy enforcement algorithms can lead to different simulation time. The more policies need to be enforced during simulation, the longer the entire simulation process will take. Our policy engine supports three policy enforcement algorithms at one simulation run, depending on the safety and performance requirements.

1. For Your Information (FYI) Algorithm

In this case the policy engine does not need to perform policy checking at run time. Instead, it can perform static policy conflict detection before simulation. At run time, the policy engine just keep the track of relevant information into a log file. This algorithm saves simulation time, but is not appropriate to safety-critical processes.

As shown in Table 44, on receiving a policy checking request, the FYI policy engine appends a new log at the end of the log history. A policy log includes the type of the policy, the time that the policy is enforced, the ID and name of the model subject that the policy is registered with, and the new value is about to assign to the model subject. FYI Policies do not have to be enforced through PDP and PEP. They can be enforced in local simulation engines to save the simulation time.

Table 44 FYI Policy Enforcement Algorithm

```
Bool onReceiveFYIPolicy (Policy policy, Value value)
{
    policy.appendLog (policy.Type, currentTime, policy.Subject.ID,
    policy.Subject.Name,value);
    Return true;
}
```

2. Conservative Algorithm

The simulation engine stops whenever it needs to invoke the PEP to check if the next simulation step is valid. The simulation process hold at each step until the PEP performs policy checking and confirms that this simulation step is safe. Conservative algorithm can guarantee that every simulation step complies with the policy if the policy has been specified in the policy map. However, if the PEP needs to check a large number of policies during the simulation, the conservative algorithm will consume a large amount of simulation time.

A policy is triggered just before the "write" operation of a model element. While the PEP dispatcher receives a conservative policy checking request, it will forward both the policy and the value that subject want to take to the conservative PEP. The conservative PEP will browse through the policy map, and query if the current simulation results satisfy the predictive (condition) that the policy can take effect. For example, if there is a "must be" policy in simulation engine A specified as:

If (rank=Department Manager) {Monthly Salary must be >=3k}

This policy has only one predictive: rank= Department Manager. The conservative PEP sends an inquiry about the current status of the rank to the RTI of the DDSOS. The RTI may find the rank variable is in another simulation engine B, and then it will search the simulation log to determine if the current value of rank is "Department Manager". If the rank is not "Department Manager", the conservative PEP will return true. Otherwise, the conservative PEP will continue to check if the value that will be assigned to the subject "Monthly Salary" satisfy the predictive "Monthly Salary must be >=3k". If the value will be assigned to monthly salary is greater than 3k, then the conservative will return true to the simulation engine A. After the simulation engine A receives the acknowledgement that conservative PEP has validated the "write" operation, the simulation process can proceed. The overall process is shown in Figure 106.

```
Bool onReceiveConservativePolicy (Policy policy, Value value)
{
  foreach (predictive of policy)
  {
    predictive.Element.CurrentStatus=theRTI.getElementLog(predictive. Element);
    If (predictive. Element.CurrentStatus does not satisfy predictive. Element.Condition)
    {
      policy.appendLog(policy.Type, currentTime, policy.Subject.ID,
      policy.Subject.Name,value);
      return true;
    }
  }
  If (value does not satisify policy.Subject.status)
  {
    policy.appendLog(policy.Type, currentTime, policy.Subject.ID,
    policy.Subject.Name,value);
    return false;
  }
  policy.appendLog(policy.Type, currentTime, policy.Subject.ID, policy.Subject.Name,value);
  Return true;
}
```

Figure 106 the Conservative Policy Enforcement Algorithm

3. Greedy Algorithm.

The greedy policy enforcement algorithm is similar to the conservative policy enforcement algorithm except that the simulation engine does not stop while waiting for the acknowledgement from the PEP. The simulation engine and the PEP are two parallel threads. The simulation engine can save a rollback point of the system as it proceeds assuming no policy violation will occur. Notice that, everything is reversible in simulation. In a real system, some processes easy to reverse or to compensate (e.g., under pay an employee), some are more difficult (e.g., overpay a contractor), and some are impossible to reverse.

Although this algorithm usually takes memory and time to save the rollback points and to reverse to a rollback point, it may still be more efficient if the frequency of policy violations is not high. In addition, incremental backup algorithm can be applied to the simulation engine to save backup memory and rollback time. Another feature of this algorithm is that the PEP can be set to tolerate minor policy violations. In this case, the simulation engine can choose to roll back to previous rollback point, or to ignore the policy violation based on the evaluation of to what extent the system has been compromised due to the policy violation. Greedy algorithm improves the efficiency by performing simulation and policy enforcement simultaneous. Figure 107 shows the greedy algorithm.

```
Bool onReceiveGreedyPolicy (Policy policy, Value value, CheckPoint checkPoint)
{
    Foreach (predictive of policy)
    {
        predictive.Element.CurrentStatus=theRTI.getElementLog(predictive.Element);
        If (predictive.Element.CurrentStatus does not satisfy
        predictive.Element.Condition)
        {
            policy.appendLog(policy.Type, currentTime, policy.Subject.ID,
            policy.Subject.Name,value);
            return true;
        }
    }
    If (value does not satisify policy.Subject.status)
    {
        policy.appendLog(policy.Type, currentTime, policy.Subject.ID,
        policy.Subject.Name,value);
        theRTI.rollback(checkPoint);
        return false;
    }
    else
    {
        policy.appendLog(policy.Type, currentTime, policy.Subject.ID,
        policy.Subject.Name,value);
        Return true;
    }
}
```

Figure 107 the Greedy policy enforcement algorithm

The three policy enforcement algorithms can be applied separately or mixed, and the configuration can be done at runtime. Before or during simulation, one policy can be specified as one of these three enforcement algorithms. Table 6 shows detailed criteria of specifying policy enforcement types.

7.5 Comparative study between the three policy enforcement algorithms

In this section we will design and implement a payroll example, and then compare the memory cost and time cost among different policy enforcement algorithms.

7.5.1 Design of the payroll System

To compare the three different policy enforcement algorithms, we present a sample system (Payroll System) in this section. The system descriptions below serve as the system requirements that are the inputs to the modeling process.

The Employee (an actor) can file a DDA (Direct Deposit Application) to the AAS (Accounting Assistant Senior). The DDA must include the employee's name, SSN (Social Security Number), Bank Routing Number, and Account Number. On receiving the DDA, the AAS must confirm receiving the file. Confirmation process can be broken down into a sequence of sub-actions: check if the SSN is correct, contact the bank to see if the routing number is correct, and contact the bank to check if the account is correct. After a direct deposit application is confirmed, the AAS must send an IDDA (Input Direct Deposit Application) order to the Payroll Accountant. On receiving the IDDA, the Payroll Accountant will input the direct deposit application information into the payroll. Then, the Payroll Accountant will acknowledge the AAS by sending a CDDA (Confirmation of Direct Deposit Application). On receiving the CDDA, the AAS will register the employee's name into the DDP (Direct Deposit Payroll).

On the PPED (Pay Period End Date), the AAS calculates the employee's payment. Then, the AAS will search the employee's name in the DDP. If the employee is in the DDP, then a DDR (Direct Deposit Request) is sent to the Payroll Accountant. Otherwise, a payment check will be sent to the employee by mail. On receiving the DDR, the Payroll Accountant will add the Company Account information into the DDR, forward the DDR to the bank, and then send a CDDR (Confirmation of Direct Deposit Request) to the AAS. On receiving the CDDR, the AAS will send a receipt to the employee by mail.

Here are the acronyms used in this example:

AAS: Accounting Assistant Senior

CDDA: Confirmation of Direct Deposit Application

CDDR: Confirmation of Direct Deposit Request

DDA: Direct Deposit Application

DDP: Direct Deposit Payroll

DDR: Direct Deposit Request

IDDA: Input Direct Deposit Application

SSN: Social Security Number

The modeling process consists of the following steps. In Step 1, system requirements are carefully analyzed and decomposed into the model elements. In Step 2, both system process (functional specification) and policies are extracted from system requirements. In Step 3, system processes and policies are formally reconstructed by the model elements.

Step 1: Decompose System Requirements into Model Elements

After analyzing the system requirements, the model elements can be identified. Table 1 lists several model elements extracted from the system requirements of the payroll system. To simplify the system model, attribute is not defined for this system.

Step 2: Extract Processes & Policies

From the user's point of view, a system process consists of a sequence of atomic processes. In each atomic process, actions are performed, conditions are evaluated, data are accessed, and events are emitted to trigger other atomic processes. Through event triggering, atomic processes are brought together to represent a complete system process. Table 46 and Table 47 list several processes and policies.

Table 45 the Model Elements

Actors	Bank, Company, Employee, EmployeeAccount, CompanyAccount, …
Conditions	TodayIsPayDay, AccountNumberIsValid, RoutingNumberIsValid, …
Data	SSN, RoutingNumber, AccountNumber, Payment …
Actions	CheckRoutingNumber, CheckAccountNumber, DirectDeposit, …
Attribute	Not defined in this example.
Events	ConfirmBankroutingNumber, ReceiveDirectDeposit, , …

Table 46 Atomic Processes

Process01	On receiving a DDA from the employee, the AAS checks if the SSN, bank routing number and account number is valid
Process02	After the direct deposit request is confirmed, the AAS must send the IDDA order to the Payroll Accountant.
Process03	On receiving the IDDA, the Payroll Accountant will input the direct deposit request information into the payroll.
Process04	On receiving the CDDA, the AAS will register the employee's name into the DDP.

Table 47 Policies

Policy01	On receiving a new direct deposit application, the AAS must check if RoutingNumber is valid.
Policy02	If the AAS receives a valid DDR, s/he may not reject the request
Policy03	The payment must always be <=10k
Policy04	Action CheckRoutingNumber must occur before action DirectDeposit
Policy05	A DDR can be issued only once during one payment process
Policy06	On receiving the DDR, the Bank must deposit the payment to the

account if the deposit >= 0.

Step 3: Reconstruct Processes & Policies

System processes and policies are usually informally stated in the system requirements as we have seen in Step 2. The purpose of system modeling is to create a formal model to represent the system structure (model elements), behaviors (system processes), and various constraints (policies). After the model elements are identified and system processes and policies are extracted, system processes and policies are formally reconstructed based on the model elements as well as constructs that control the flow of process execution.

7.5.2 Policy Enforcement Analyses

If the system does not behave as the policies state, the manifestation can be caused by the system model, the simulation program, the simulation engine, or the interactions among them. For example, Policy06 states that "On receiving the DDR, the Bank must deposit the payment to the account if the deposit >=0". In the system model, this process is incorrectly implemented as:

$$\text{if (DATA:Deposit > 0) \{do ACTION:DirectDeposit \}}$$

Policy enforcement will detect the violation given the deposit equals to 0, which indicates a fault in the system model. However, policy enforcement is based on the simulation and simulation may not execute a particular system path. A fault in the system model may not manifest as an error during a particular simulation. For example, the problem of system modeling can not be detected if the deposit equals 1 or more. In other words, performing simulation V&V using dynamic policy enforcement can not guarantee all faults to be detected or to be detected immediately. We deliberately injected the fault mentioned above into the system model that could violate Policy06, and run the simulation 20 times with policy enforcement to test if or how many times the fault is detected. In the 20 tests, only one violation occurred and detected by Policy06.

Table 48 Contrast among policy enforcement algorithms

		Policy Enforcement Type		
		FYI	Greedy	Conservative
Probability of Failure	High	X		
	Medium	X	X	
	Low	X	X	X
Frequency Of Checking	High	X		
	Medium	X	X	
	Low	X	X	X

Safety Critical / Mission Critical	High			X
	Medium			X
	Low	X	X	X
Requirement of Efficiency	High	X		
	Medium	X	X	
	Low	X	X	X

7.5.3 Overhead Analyses

Police-based computing enables dynamic V&V and brings flexibility in governing constraints on system status and system behaviors. By specifying and enforcing policies on the fly rather than hard-coding policies into the system implementation, policy changes can take effect immediately. However, flexibility comes with a cost. Dynamic policy specification and enforcement inevitably increase the system overhead in terms of space complexity and time complexity. We conducted a series of experiments on the Payroll System, where 25 policies are extracted from the system requirements and enforced in the experiments, to explore the cost of dynamic policy specification and enforcement. The experiments are conducted in four policy enforcement algorithms:

- For Your Information (FYI) policy enforcement.
- Conservative policy enforcement.
- Greedy policy enforcement
- Policies are hard-coded into system processes.

Memory Cost Analysis: During the simulation, the simulator and system processes are loaded into the memory. When the policy enforcement is disabled, the memory size (5376k) is the combined size of the simulator and system processes. When policy enforcement is enabled, the policy engine is also loaded to the memory. The difference between the memory sizes (575k = 5951k – 5376k) is the size for the policy engine. The greedy algorithm consumes more memory than FYI because the simulation engine needs to backup all data at each policy enforcement point. Every data entry is a pair of data ID and data value which is 8 Bytes each, and we have 15 data in the Payroll System experiment. Thus, every rollback point needs 8*2*15=240 Bytes, and total memory for 10 rollback points is nearly 2400 KB. Thus, the total memory size for greedy algorithm is 5953KB (5951k+2k). When policies are hard-coded into system processes, the increase of memory size (226k = 5602k – 5376k) is brought by the increase of code of policies that is hard-coded into system processes. From the collected data, we can see the space complexity increases by 11% (575k / 5376k) when dynamic policy enforcement is employed. In contrast, the hard-coded policy enforcement only increases the space complexity by 4.2% (226k / 5376k).

Time Cost Analysis: In our experiments, the system processes are translated into LUA code [105] when the simulation is being initialized. The simulator then interprets LUA code and feed it to the LUA Virtual Machine for execution. When policy enforcement is disabled, the simulation time (2880ms) is totally dedicated to LUA code execution. When policy enforcement is enabled, the simulator triggers the policy engine to enforce policies. Since policy engine is written in C++, which is about 20 times faster than LUA code, we converted the time spent on policy enforcement (C++ time) to LUA time, in order to make a fair comparison. After converted, the difference between simulation time (13363ms = 16243ms − 2880ms) is the time spent on policy enforcement and network communication. The time complexity of greedy algorithms depends on how many rollbacks occur during the simulation. In this experiment, three policies are violated during the simulation, and the overall time is 3150ms, which means each rollback will consume about 100ms. When policies are hard-coded into system processes, more LUA code is executed and the increase of simulation time (346ms = 3226ms − 2880ms) is brought by the LUA code of hard-coded policies. From the collected data, we can see the time complexity is increased by 464% (13363ms / 2880ms) when conservative policy enforcement is employed. In contrast, the greedy policy enforcement only increases the time complexity by 9.4% (270ms/2880ms) ,and the hard-coded policy enforcement increases the time complexity by 12% (346ms / 2880ms). Greedy algorithm may consume less time than hard-coded policy enforcement if the system has a low frequency of policy violation.

Table 49 Summary of the experiment result

Direct Deposit	Policy Enforcement Algorithms	FYI	Conservative	Greedy	Hard-coded Policies
Space Complexity	Memory Size (KB)	5376	5951	5953	5602
	Compared to No Policies	100%	110.7%	110.7%	104.2%
	Memory Composition	SIM + SP	SIM + SP + PE	SIM + SP + PE + RB	SIM + SP + HCP
Time Complexity	Simulation Time (ms)	2880	16243	3150	3226
	Compared to No Policies	100%	564%	109.4%	112%
	Time Composition	SP	SP + PE + NC	SP + RB	SP + HCP
Comments	SIM = Simulator, SP = System Processes, PE = Policy Engine, HCP = Hard-Coded Policies, RB=Roll Back, NC=Network Communication				

This experiment result is compliant to our analysis of different policy triggering and enforcement algorithms. The policy enforcement can be disabled once the system is proven to be correct.

CHAPTER 8

EDPE: EVENT-DRIVEN POLICY ENFORCEMENT FOR PI4SOA

In the service oriented development paradigm, a number of candidate services are composed rapidly to form a Service-Oriented Architecture (SOA). The verification of SOA applications is important. Among various verification mechanisms, simulation is a promising method because it provides runtime behavior and performance analysis. This section uses a BPEL engine as a simulation engine to simulate the execution of SOA, and proposes an event-driven policy enforcement framework to verify the SOA applications by simulation.

8.1 Introduction

Service-Oriented Architecture (SOA) and Web Services (WS) received significant attention recently as they have been adopted by major computer and software companies. The verification and validation (V&V) of SOA application is important to ensure successful applications. Among various verification mechanisms such as model checking [77][117]and testing[117], simulation plays an important role because it can provide runtime behavior and performance analysis.

Service-oriented simulation is supported by a number frameworks, including SIMPROCESS [155], ISTF [83], XMSF (Extensible Modeling and Simulation Framework) [28][209]and the simulation grid system Cosim-Grid [97]. SIMPROCESS is a simulation tool that can simulate and monitor SOA applications on-demand. It uses a simulation language called SIMSCRIPT to build discrete event and/or continuous simulation models. ISTF (IONA Interface Simulation and Testing Framework) provides a simulation and testing platform for SOA applications. ISTF can simulate the behavior of both service consumers and service providers. XMSF creates a modeling and simulation framework that utilizes a set of web-enabled technologies to facilitate modeling and simulation applications. A significant contribution by XMSF is its web-based RTI (Runtime Infrastructure). Cosim-Grid is a service-oriented simulation grid based on HLA, PLM (Product Lifecycle Management) [81], and grid/Web services. It applies OGSA (Open Grid Services Architecture) [166] to modeling and simulation to improve HLA in terms of dynamic sharing, autonomy, fault tolerance, collaboration, and security mechanisms.

In our previous works, we proposed a Dynamic Distributed Service-Oriented Simulation Framework (DDSOS) [186] to simulate SOA applications. DDSOS can generate code from the service specification and then execute the code. In addition, we also proposed a dynamic policy infrastructure Pi4SOA (Policy infrastructure for SOA) [216] to verify SOA during simulation. Pi4SOA is 3-layer infrastructure, including a service modeling language PSML-C at the bottom layer, a policy specification language PSML-P in the middle layer, and a policy enforcement layer at the top layer.

This chapter introduces an SOA simulation technique that use the BPEL (Business Process Execution Language) [25] engine as a simulator to simulate the SOA application. In addition, this chapter proposes an Event-Driven Policy Enforcement (EDPE) framework. The EDPE framework can enforce various SOA policies including negotiation policies, authorization policies, and temporal policies. During simulation, events are sent to the policy-enforcement agent to enforce these policies.

This chapter is organized as follows: section 2 introduces SOA simulation using the BPEL engine and various SOA policies and their enforcement. Section 3 presents the EDPE where triggering events are sent to policy-enforcement agents for execution. Section 4 describes the temporal dependency among events including both continuous time and discrete time models. Section 5 uses PSML-P to specify negotiation policies, authorization policies and temporal policies. Section 6 uses an example to show the SOA simulation process and policy enforcement and optimization by EDPE. Section 7 concludes this chapter.

8.2 SOA Simulation and Verification

This section introduces the BPEL engine as a SOA simulation platform, and then describes the policy enforcement Pi4SOA during SOA simulation.

8.2.1 SOA Simulation with BPEL

BPEL is a modeling language to specify the workflow and data of a composite service, and it is in the XML format. In a BPEL specification, the *<portType>* defines the input and output interfaces, the *<partnerLink>* defines the external WS it invokes, the *<variables>* defines the data it uses, and the *<process>* defines the workflow it executes. BPEL is a suitable description language to compose a SOA from   candidate services.

BPEL is executable. After the SOA is specified with BPEL, BPEL engines can execute the BPEL workflow. Many BPEL engines are available, such as ActiveBPEL Engine [1], IBM BPEL4J [78], and Oracle BPEL Process Manager [125]. Because BPEL engines can execute the specification, it can be used as a simulator to preview the behavior before the application is deployed.

8.2.2 Pi4SOA with Simulation

The essential information about an atomic service, such as the input/output and the workflow, can be specified by a service specification language such as Web Services Description Language (WSDL) [195] or OWL-S [130]. Additional information about the service, such as the constraints of the service, can be specified into other forms along with the service specification file. Policies are used to specify the constraints of its subject in a SOA. The subject can be services, data, and workflow as shown in Figure 108. Both service providers and service consumers can have policies. Service providers declare the constraints of invoking the service into its policy specification, and service consumers declare the requirements of services into its policy specification.

Pi4SOA is a framework to specify and enforce SOA policies, as shown in Figure 108. It is comprised of three layers: the service model layer, the policy language layer, and the policy enforcement layer. The service model layer is the foundation because policies are specified by the vocabulary defined in the model layer. The service model layer consists of the building elements of a SOA: data, workflow and service properties. On the policy specification layer, PSML-P is used to specify the constraints on data, workflow and service properties. After policies are specified in PSML-P, they can be enforced on the policy enforcement layer by the Event-Driven Policy Enforcement (EDPE). The service model layer can use BPEL or PSML-C as the modeling language. If the SOA is specified by BPEL, a BPEL engine can simulate the SOA by executing the BPEL. During simulation, the EDPE collects the runtime events and verify the SOA against the policies specified in PSML-P.

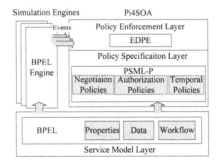

Figure 108 an SOA Policy Enforcement and Simulation Framework

8.3 EDPE Framework

Event-Driven Policy Enforcement (EDPE) is the third layer of Pi4SOA. This section shows the EDPE framework.

8.3.1 EDPE Architecture

The main feature of EDPE is an event broker. It offers collaboration between service providers and consumers with an event mechanism. EDPE consists of the following components as shown in Figure 109:

- A policies repository: This stores the negotiation policies from service providers and consumers. Service providers and consumers can publish negation policies on the policy repository.

- An event registry: This stores the event information, and supports events publishing and subscribing. Service providers can register their runtime events into the event registry. Service consumers can subscribe their interested events from the event registry.

- Event listeners: Each listener allows EDPE to receive events sent from services.

- Negotiation policy engine: EDPE can find appropriate services for clients according to the criteria specified in the negotiation policies.

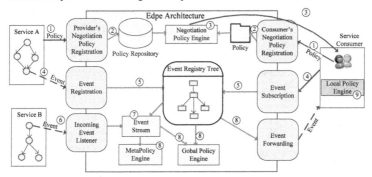

Figure 109. EDPE Architecture

- A meta-policy engine: This enforces meta-policies. A meta-policy enforced at the global policy engine on the event broker for two purposes: first meta-policies verify domain-independent policies, and detect only major faults. These policies are enforced for all clients and services. Second, the event broker has the complete event stream, the clients subscribe their interested events only.

- Global policy engines: Each global policy engine enforces those global policies.

- Event-forwarding agents: After receiving runtime events form services, an event-forwarding agent is responsible for forwarding the events to a specific local policy engine hosted by individual service consumers.

- Event-management interface: the owner of the event broker can manage the event broker through this interface. The supported management includes: delete an event, insert an event, etc.

8.3.2 Policy Enforcement

The collaboration process can be dived into four phases: preparation, establishment, execution and termination.

- Preparation phase: negotiation policy matching

The process is as follows:

1. A service provider publishes the negotiation policy into the policy repository. The provider's negotiation policy includes two aspects: the constraints of invoking this service, and the responsibilities the service including those events the service will generate. .

2. A service consumer publishes its negotiation policy into the EDPE. The consumer's negotiation policy specifies the requirements for services.

3. Negotiation policy matching: according to the consumer's negotiation policy, the negotiation policy engine finds if any services meet the requirement. For example, if a consumer specifies that only REST protocol can be used, and if a provider specifies that he can support both REST and SOAP, then a match is achieved.

4. The negation policy engine returns candidate service sets to the service consumer. The consumer binds the best service with his application.

- Establishment phase: event registration

5. Service providers register their events into the event registry. If an event is registered into the registry, the corresponding service provider promises that it will deliver the events to the EDPE during runtime.

6. A service consumers check if the required events are registered on the event registry. If all interested events are registered, the consumer will subscribe to these.

Note that the events can be automatically registered and subscribed if sufficient information is provided in the provider's and consumer's negotiation policies.

- Execution phase: policy enforcement

7. During service runtime, a service provider sends events to an event listener on the EDPE.

8. The event listener puts all incoming events into the event stream. The event stream filters out uninterested events and keeps subscribed events only.

9. The meta-policy engine checks if the meta-policies are satisfied.

10. According to the preference specified by the service consumer, the event registry will forward the event to the local policy engine.

11. The local policy engine will enforce the policy.

- Termination phase: compensation

12. When the collaboration terminates, the policy engine determines if any policy failed. For failed policies the corresponding compensation action will be executed.

13. Used events in the event stream are cleaned up.

8.3.3 Event Registry and Event Tree

The event registry stores all the events interested by various policy engines. The event registry has two responsibilities:

- Organize event registration, subscription and un-subscription.
- Trigger policies.

The major component in the event registry is an event tree. The events are organized hierarchically by their category relationship in the tree as shown in Figure 110.

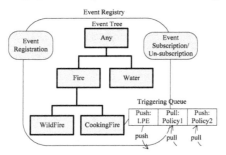

Figure 110. Event Registry

The root event in the event tree is the *any* event. If a policy does not specify any the triggering event explicitly or implicitly, its triggering event is set to *"any"* by default, as a policy may be triggered during execution.

Whenever an event is triggered, its parent events should be triggered as well because the parent event is a more general event. For example, the event *"Wildfire"* is a child of event *"Fire"*, all clients subscribed with the *Fire* should also be notified. However, this kind of cascading triggering mechanism can consume considerable resources. Cascading triggering can be prohibited globally or at some given nodes to save cost. For example, if the event *WildFire* is set as non-cascading, the event *Fire* would not be triggered when a *Wildfire* occurs.

In the event tree, each event is associated with a triggering queue. Whenever the event occurs, the items in its triggering queue will be triggered. According to the consumer's preference, the items in the triggering queue either can be global or local policies enforced by global or local agents. In the later case, EDPE does not have the local policy so it will forward these event to the relevant local policy engines. Two forwarding mechanisms are supported by EDPE: pull and push. In the pull mechanism, the EDPE will deliver the events to the destination actively; in the push mechanism, the EDPE will wait the local policy engines to retrieve the events.

8.4 Service Temporal Dependency Model

One critical requirement of SOA verification is to verify the temporal dependency in SOA. EDPE provides such a function by introducing the temporal policies. Temporal policies are based on a formalism called Temporal Dependency with Delay (TDD). This section presents some common temporal dependencies in SOA, and then introduces the TDD model.

8.4.1 Temporal Dependency in SOA

In SOA, each service is an execution interval of code. Service consumers are responsible to ensure the correctness of the temporal relationship in a SOA. One major motivation of SOA policies is to specify and verify such temporal constraints.

Let a capital letter such as A denote a service. The temporal dependencies between two services are identified in Figure 111:

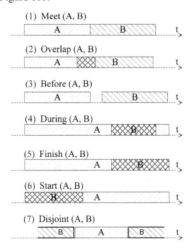

Figure 111. Pi4SOA and simulation engine

Seven predicates can be identified and these are similar to those in [4], but they are modified for SOA applications.

- Meet (A, B): This denotes that service B starts immediately after service A terminates.
- Overlap (A, B): This denotes that service A starts before service B starts, terminates when B is still executing.
- Before (A, B): This denotes that service A terminates before service B starts.
- During (A, B): This denotes that service B executes during the interval that A executes.
- Finish (A, B): This denotes that service A and service B terminate at the same time. Finish (A, B) and Finish (B, A) have the same meaning, i.e., Finish (A, B) $\equiv$ Finish (B, A)
- Start (A, B): This denotes that service A and B start at the same time. Start (A, B) and Start (B, A) are equivalent, i.e., Start (A, B) $\equiv$ Start (B, A).
- Disjoint (A, B): This denotes that service A and B cannot execute simultaneously. Disjoint (A, B) and Disjoint (B, A) are equivalent, i.e., Disjoint (A, B) $\equiv$ Disjoint (B, A).

Note that in some SOA operations, one may assume they are instantaneous, e.g., read/write individual items, and this is consistent with traditional databases. For one instantaneous operation and one interval, only *before*, *during*, and *disjoint* apply. For two instantaneous operations, only the predicate *before* and its derivative *after* apply.

8.4.2 Events in SOA

The predicates are based on a continuous time model. In EDPE, policy enforcement is triggered by events. Therefore, it is necessary to introduce events into this model. Three types of events can be identified in a SOA: *service* events, *data* events, and *arbitrary* events.

- Service Events

The service execution interval can be identified by its start event and its termination event. For example, when service A starts, it will trigger a start event, denoted as A^+. Similarly, A^- is used to denote the event that occurs when A terminates. Capital letters with +/- are used to specify service events, such as A^+, B^-.

- Data Events

Two types of events can be triggered by data access: the read data event, denoted as d^-, occurs when a read request happens on data d; write data event, denoted as d^+, happens when a write request happens on data d. Lower case letters with +/- are used to denote data events, such as d^+, a^-;

- Arbitrary Events

In addition to service events and data events, any point in the workflow of the SOA can be associated with an event. During the execution of the service, these arbitrary events will be triggered. For example, the following events can occur during the execution of an SOA application:

- OnEnteringMethod: This occurs when the SOA enters an internal method.
- OnExistMethod: This occurs when the SOA exists an internal method.
- OnDecision: This occurs when the service is going to branch.

Lower case letters are used to denote arbitrary events.

8.5 Continuous Time to Discrete Time

Events can form an event stream according to their occurrence sequence. In this way, the SOA execution can be converted form a continuous time model to a discrete time model. For example, a possible execution sequence can be $A^+d^-B^+C^+B^-C^-d^+A^-$. This stream shows the following temporal sequence: service A starts, then a read request on data d,   then service B starts, then service C starts, then service B terminates, then service C terminates, then a write request on data d, then service A terminates. One client might be only interested in the occurrence sequence of service C and data d, thus the sub-stream "$d^-C^+C^-d^+$ is sent to the client. This sub-stream shows that service C does not read or write data d.

8.5.1 Policy Refinement from HLP to LLP

Policies can be specified on the continuous time model or the discrete time model. A policy is called a High Level Policy (HLP) if it is based on the continuous time model, because in the continuous time model the execution is represented by high level intervals.   A policy is called a Low Level Policy (LLP) if it is based on the discrete time model, because in a discrete time model an interval breaks into low level events. Both HLP and LLP have pros and cons, listed as follows:

- HLP
  - Pros: straightforward to specify the temporal dependency
  - Cons: Cannot be used by policy engine directly, because policies are event triggered.
- LLP
  - Cons: cumbersome to specify
  - Pros: Can be used by policy engine directly.

Because HLP cannot be enforced by policy engine, it is necessary to refine the HLP to LLP. Let Te denote the timestamp that event e occurs, let $T+t$ denote the timestamp that t time after T, and let T-t denote the time stamp that t time before T. For any two events e_1, e_2, the following definitions are introduced:

- $Te_1 < Te_2$ *iff* e_1 occurs before e_2, and denoted as $e_1 \prec e_2$
- $Te_1 > Te_2$ *iff* e_1 occurs after e_2, and denoted as $e_1 \succ e_2$
- $Te_1 = Te_2$ *iff* e_1 and e_2 happen simultaneously, and denoted as $e_1 = e_2$.

A HLP can be refined to a LLP automatically by following Table 50.

Table 50 From HLP to LLP

Continuous time	Discrete time with events
Before(A, B)	$A^- \prec B^+$
Meet(A, B)	$A^- = B^+$
Overlap(A, B)	$(A^+ \prec B^+) \wedge (A^- \prec B^-) \wedge (A^- \succ B^+)$
During(A, B)	$(A^+ \prec B^+) \wedge (A^- \succ B^-)$
Finish(A, B)	$A^- = B^-$
Start(A, B)	$A^+ = B^+$
Disjoint(A, B)	$(A^- \prec B^+) \vee (B^- \prec A^+)$

8.5.2 Tolerating Delays

However, such a strict dependency model is not practical in SOA because it does not consider the possible message delay in a distributed environment. The dependency can be relaxed by introducing the tolerance on delay. For example, a requirement might be: if e_1 happens within delay t, $e_1 = e_2$ is still considered as satisfied. To address this need, the predicates are extended by adding an additional parameter called "tolerance on delay", denoted as t. Therefore, in the continuous time model, the predicate *Before* (A, B) becomes *Before* (A, B, t). This model assumes that for any service A, A^+ and A^- have the same delay t_A. The delay t can happens to both services A and B, thus it is a signed delta between A and B, i.e., $t = \Delta(t_A, t_B) = t_B - t_A$.

Accordingly, in the discrete time model, a subscript t is used to denote the delay.

- $e_1 \prec_t e_2$ *iff* $Te_1 < Te_2 + t$
- $e_1 \succ_t e_2$ *iff* $Te_1 > Te_2 - t$
- $e_1 =_t e_2$ *iff* $Te_2 - t < Te_1 < Te_2 + t$

For example, if e_1 occurs at timestamp 10 and e_2 occurs at timestamp 8, the proposition $e_1 \prec_3 e_2$ still holds. The tolerance on delay model can be applied to both continuous time and discrete time, as shown in Table 51.

Table 51 Discrete time with tolerance on delay

HLP with delay	LLP with delay
Before (A, B, t)	$A^- \prec B^+ + t$
Meet(A, B, t)	$B^+ - t \prec A^- \prec B^+ + t$
Overlap(A, B, t)	$(A^+ \prec B^+ + t) \wedge (A^- \prec B^- + t) \wedge (A^- \succ B^+ - t)$

During (A, B, t)	$(A^+ \prec B^+ +t) \wedge (A^- \succ B^- -t)$
Finish (A, B, t)	$B^- -t \prec A^- \prec B^- +t$
Start (A, B, t)	$B^+ -t \prec A^+ \prec B^+ +t$
Disjoint (A, B, t)	$(A^- \prec B^+ +t) \vee (B^- \prec A^+ +t)$

8.6 SOA Policy Specification

Constraints in SOA can be categorized into three classes: negation policies, authorization policies and temporal policies. After the temporal dependencies are identified, they can be specified into temporal policies. In Pi4SOA, temporal policies can be specified with the policy specification language PSML-P. In addition, PSML-P is also capable of specifying negotiation policies and authorization policies.

8.6.1 PSML-P

In PSML-P, policies are specified in the form of the tuple <Event, Condition, Proposition, Action>. The syntax of PSML-P is

$$\text{on } (E) \text{ if } (C) \text{ then } P \text{ do } A.$$

- E: denotes an event. In PSML-P, policies enforcement is triggered by events;
- C: denotes conditions. In PSML-P, conditions are the prerequisites to enforce policies;
- P: denotes a proposition that the system must hold. If the proposition holds, then the policy is valid;
- A: denotes a compensation action. If the proposition does not hold, then EDPE will take over the system and execute the compensation action. The compensation action compensates for the loss caused by the system failure. Compensation actions can be as simple as a logging function, or can be very complicated such as a failure-proof mechanism.

8.6.2 Negotiation Policy Specification

Negotiation Policies refer to the constraints defined at the service level, i.e., the static properties of the service. Since the properties of the service do not change, negotiation policies can be enforced without the knowledge of any runtime information. Negotiation policies function as a gatekeeper procedure to ensure the compatibility of SOA and to achieve Service-Level Agreement (SLA). Every party in SOA can have negotiation policies. Negation policies specify the service level agreement that all collaboration parties must comply before service invocation. For example, there are two types of protocols in the web service technology stack: SOAP and REST. These two protocols are not compatible. A service consumer can have such a negotiation policy: the service consumer supports SOAP only. The negotiation policy a service provider can have is: the provider supports both SOAP and REST.

In this example, the agreement between the consumer and the provider can be achieved: the consumer and the provider collaborate with SOAP protocol. Since the negotiation policy must hold although the collaboration process, the condition should be "true". The service provider's policy is:

if (true) **then** (consumer.protocol=SOAP ∨ REST)

In this policy, the subject is the property "protocol" of the consumer, the proposition is (consumer.protocol=SOAP ∨ REST), and the triggering event can be anytime before the runtime.

Similarly, the negotiation policy on the client can be specified as:

if (true) **then** (provider.protocol=SOAP)

8.6.3 Authorization Policy Specification

Authorization Policies are those constraints that control the access to the resources in a SOA. The resources can be data, method, and service. Authorization policies are enforced at runtime.

Data Authorization Policy specifies the access control on any protected data d. The subject of the policy is data d, the triggering event is the access request on d, i.e., $d^{+/-}$. The policy can be specified as:

on $(d^{+/-})$ **if** (C) **then** (¬(d.get()/set()))

For example, in a banking system, the constraint that "only clerk role can read customers' deposit" can be specified in the following policy:

on (customer.deposit$^{+/-}$) **if** (requestor.role!=clerk) **then** (¬(customer.deposit.get()))

Service Authorization Policy specifies the access control on any services. The subject of the policy is any protected service S, the triggering event is the access request on d, i.e., S^+. The policy can be specified as:

on (S^+) **if** (C) **then** (¬S.invoke())

In the same banking example, the constraint that "only clerk role can call the denyCheck service" can be specified as the following policy.

on (denyCheck()$^+$) **if** (requestor.role!=clerk) **then** (¬(denyCheck()))

8.6.4 Temporal Policy Specification

Temporal Policies define the temporal dependencies in a SOA. Temporal policies specify the temporal dependency in SOA. The subject of the temporal policy can be data or services. Temporal policies are enforced at runtime.

Data Temporal Policy: Data access may have temporal dependency with services or other data. For example, data d can be accessed only until/during/before/after some services or until/before/after another data is accessed. The subject of this policy is data d, and the triggering event is $d^{+/-}$. The policy can be specified as follows:

- If d depends on the a service S,

$$\text{on } (d^{+/-}) \text{ if } (C) \text{ then } (P(d^{+/-}, S))),$$

where P is the predicate.

Where P can be the predicate of *before, after, during, start, finish,* or *disjoint.* Since data is instantaneous, P can not be *Overlap.*

- If d depends on the occurrence of another data b,

$$\text{on } (d^{+/-}) \text{ if } (C) \text{ then } (P(d^{+/-}, b^{+/-}))),$$

where P is the predicate, can be *before* or *after.* The predicate for two data can not be *meet, overlap, during, finish,* or *start.*

Service Temporal Policy: Services themselves may have temporal dependency. For the temporal policy between any two services, S_1 and S_2, the subject of this policy can be either S_1 or S_2, and the triggering event can be $S_1^{+/-}$ or $S_2^{+/-}$. The temporal dependency can be specified in the following policy:

$$\text{on } (S_{1/2}^{+/-}) \text{ if } (C) \text{ then } (P(S_1, S_2))),$$

Where P can be the predicate of before, *after, during, start, finish, disjoint,* or *overlap.*

The above policies are given in the form of HLP. Policies can be specified in either HLP or LLP. If the temporal policy is in the HLP form, EDPE can automatically refines them into LLP.

8.6.5 Meta Policies

A meta-policy is a domain-independent policy that holds at all time for all applications. If any policy or any application violates the meta-policy, the policy or application becomes invalid. Given any services S and any data d, three meta-policies are included in Pi4SOA:

- S^+ and S^- must interleave. For example, the $S^-S^+S^-$ is invalid because S cannot start again before it terminates.
- $S^+ \prec S^-$. This meta-policy specifies that all services should start first then terminate.
- $d^{+/-}$ must be enclosed in a pair S^+, S^-. This is because the access of data must occur within the execution of some service. For example, the stream $d^+S^+S^-$ is invalid.

8.7 Case Study

This section presents an SOA application which implements the online book shopping process. The workflow of this SOA application is specified by BPEL, and the constraints are specified in policies. The application is simulated by a BPEL engine. During simulation, the policies are enforced by Pi4SOA.

8.7.1 SOA Application and Policy Specification

Figure 112 shows the book-shopping application developed by Oracle JDeveloper [126]. In this example, the BPEL uses two external web services:

- *AmazonWS* retrieves book information by ISBN on Amazon's website, and
- *BNWS* retrieves book information by ISBN on Barnes&Noble's website.

In addition, the BPEL consists of five methods:

- *AssignISBN*: assign the input to the local data called *ISBN*;
- *InvokeAmazonWS*: invoke the *AmazonWS*;
- *InvokeBNWS*: invoke the *BNWS*;
- *AssignAmazonPrice*: assign the output of *AmazonWS* to the local data *BestPrice*;
- *AssignBNPrice*: assign the output of BNWS to the local data BestPrice;

Clearly, two local data: *ISBN* and *BestPrice* are used in this BPEL as well.

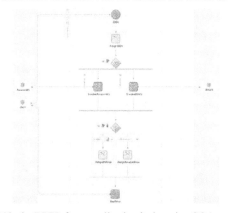

Figure 112. the BPEL for an online book shopping SOA application

The BPEL describes the following business logic: the user inputs the ISBN of a book, and then finds the prices of a book by invoking both Amazon's web service and Barnes&Noble's web service in parallel. After receiving the two prices, the user compares the two prices and chooses the lowest price only. The following policies can be identified:

- Before(*AssignISBN*, *InvokeAmazonWS*, t)
- Before(*AssignISBN*, *InvokeBNWS*, t)
- Before(*InvokeAmazonWS*, *AssignAmazonPrice*, t)
- Before(*InvokeBNWS*, *AssignBNPrice*, t)

These four policies specify the sequence relationship between two actions.

- Start(*AmazonWS*, *BNWS*, t)

This policy specifies that the two external web services should be invoked in parallel.

- Disjoint(*AssignAmazonPrice*, *AssignBNPrice*, t)

This policy specifies that the BestPrice can not be assigned to two values.

- During(*ISBN*$^+$, *AssignISBN*, t)

- During(*BestPrice*$^+$, *AssignAmazonPrice*, t)

- During(*BestPrice*$^+$, *AssignBNPrice*, t)

These three policies specify that one operation should happen within another operation.

8.7.2 SOA Simulation and Policy Enforcement

This book-shopping SOA application is simulated by three Oracle's BPEL engines [125]: one simulates the BPEL, one simulates the *AmazonWS*, and the other simulates the *BNWS*. The event listener on the EDPE puts all incoming events along with the corresponding timestamps into the event stream.

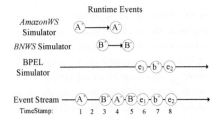

Figure 113. Simulating the SOA application by three simulation engines

In the above policies, users can customize the tolerance on delay *t*. Since policy enforcement consumes computation resources, users may choose only critical policies to enforce. For example, one user believes the following policies are critical to his application and enforce these policies only:

P1: Start(*AmazonWS*, *BNWS*, 1)

P2: Before(*InvokeAmazonWS*, *AssignAmazonPrice*, 0)

P3: During(*BestPrice*$^+$, *AssignAmazonPrice*, 0)

The simulation processes and events are shown in Figure 113, where A$^+$ and A$^-$ denote the start and termination events in *AmazonWS*, B$^+$ and B$^-$ denote the start and termination events in *BNWS*, arbitrary events e1 and e2 denote the start and termination events of *AssignAmazonPrice*, and b+ denote the write event on data *BestPrice*. When enforcing the three policies, the EDPE verifies that P2 and P3 are satisfied. However, P1 is not satisfied because BNWS starts 2 seconds after Amazon WS starts. This is probably caused by the delay on the internet. One way of relaxing the policy is to let t=3, or replace this policy with an weak one: Start(*InvokeAmazonWS, InvokeBNWS*, 1). This policy is less strict because it specifies the constraints on the local action instead of on the external web services.

8.7.3 Policy Optimization by Simulation Results

Polices optimization is an important step before policies can be used to verify the application. If the policy is inaccurate, it may cause disorders during system execution because it invokes the compensation action improperly.

Policies can be optimized by the simulation results. For example, the tolerance on delay parameter *t* can be tuned during the simulation process. *t* value is a critical parameter in SOA policies. If it is too small, the policy takes over the execution of the system when the service delays, and invokes unnecessary compensation action. If it is too large, it becomes ineffective.

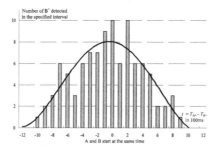

Figure 114. Optimize t value by simulation results

Figure 114 shows the optimization process for the *t* of the policy Start(*AmazonWS, BNWS,* t). In this experiment, two services *AmazonWS* (A) and *BNWS*(B) start at the same time. Calculate *t* value by using

$$t = T_A{}^+ - T_B{}^+,$$

where $T_A{}^+$ and $T_B{}^+$ are the timestamps that the EDPE receive the events A^+ and B^+ respectively. Repeat the simulation 100 times, it can be observed from the simulation results that *t* approximately follows the normal distribution of $N(0, 5^2)$. To achieve 95% tolerance, t can be set as:

$$t = 1.96*\sigma = 1.96*5 = 9.8 \ (100ms) = 0.98 second,$$

To achieve 99% tolerance, t can be set as

$$t = 2.58*5 \ (100ms) = 1.29 \ second.$$

Figure 115 shows difference of the distribution of *t* in the following two cases:

- Case 1: *AmazonWS* and *BNWS* start at the same time.

- Case 2: *BNWS* starts 1.5 second after *AmazonWS* starts.

In the first case, t still follows $N(0, 5^2)$; in the second case, t follows $N(15, 5^2)$. It can be bereaved that if t is set as 0.98 second to achieve 95% tolerance, this policy Start(*AmazonWS*, *BNWS*, 0.98) can rule out almost all incorrect instances in case 2.

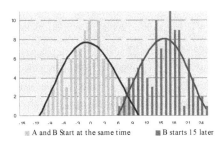

Figure 115. Optimize t value by simulation results

8.8 Conclusion

This chapter proposed an event-driven policy enforcement framework for verification of SOA applications during simulation. EDPE can enforce negotiation policies, authorization policies and temporal policies. Policies in EDPE can be specified into two levels: the high-level policies are based on a continuous time model, and the low-level policies are based on the discrete time model. EDPE can refine high-level policies to low-level policies automatically. In addition, EDPE extends the temporal predicates by introducing an additional parameter: the tolerance on delay. With those extended temporal predicates, EDPE can specify and enforce more sophisticated constraints for SOA applications.

REFERENCES

[1] ActiveBPEL, http://www.active-endpoints.com/active-bpel-engine-overview.htm

[2] D. Agrawal, J. Giles, K. W. Lee, K. Voruganti, K. Filali-Adib, "Policy-Based Validation of SAN Configuration", in Proceedings of 5th IEEE International Workshop on Policies for Distributed Systems and Networks (POLICY'04), 2004, pp. 77-86.

[3] D. Agrawal, J. Giles, K. W. Lee, K. Voruganti, K. Filali-Adib, "Policy-Based Validation of SAN Configuration", in Proceedings of 5th IEEE International Workshop on Policies for Distributed Systems and Networks (POLICY'04), 2004, pp. 77-86.

[4] J.F., Ferguson, G.: Actions and Events in Interval Temporal Logic. Journal of Logic and Computation, Special Issue on Action and Processes, 1994.

[5] A. H. Andersen, "An introduction to the Web services policy language (WSPL)," in *Proceedings of Fifth IEEE International Workshop on Policies for Distributed Systems and Networks, POLICY 2004*, Yorktown Heights, NY, United States, 2004, pp. 189-192.

[6] A. H. Andersen, "Domain-Independent, Composable Web Services Policy Assertions," in *Proceedings of the 7th IEEE International Workshop on Policies for Distributed Systems and Networks*, 2006.

[7] A. Anderson and B. Devaraj, "XACML-Based Web Services Policy Constraint Language (WS-PolicyConstraints)" Working Draft 06, 2005.

[8] A. Anderson, "Web Services Policies", IEEE Security and Privacy Magazine, Volume 4, Issue 3, pp. 84-87, 2006.

[9] A. Anderson, "Web Services Policies", IEEE Security and Privacy Magazine, Volume 4, Issue 3, pp. 84-87, 2006.

[10] J. Arias-Fisteus, L. S. Fern´andez, and C. D. Kloos. Formal Verification of BPEL4WS Business Collaborations. In Ecommerce and Web Technologies, 5th International Conference, EC-Web 2004, Proceedings, volume 3182 of Lecture Notes in Computer Science, pages 76–85. Springer, 2004.

[11] Arsanjani A, Service-oriented modeling and architecture. IBM White Paper, 2004.

[12] AUDDI: http://www.acumentechnologies.com/

[13] X. Bai, Z. Cao, Y. Chen, "Design of a Trustworthy Service Broker and Dependence-Based Progressive Group Testing", International Journal of Simulation and Process Modelling (IJSPM), Vol.3, No.1-2, 2007, pp.80-87.

[14] Luciano Baresi, Carlo Ghezzi, Sam Guinea, Smart Monitors for Composed Services, Proceedings of the 2nd international conference on Service oriented computing, pp: 193 - 202, 2004.

[15] Luciano Baresi, Sam Guinea and Pierluigi Plebani, WS-Policy for Service Monitoring, Lecture Notes in Computer Science, Springer Berlin / Heidelberg, Volume 3811, pp. 72-83, 2006.

[16] A. Bar-Noy, F. Hwang, H. Kessler, and S. Kutten. A new competitive algorithm for group testing. Discrete Applied Mathematics, 52:29--38, July 1994.

[17] BEA WebLogic Server UDDI Registry, http://www.bea.com/framework.jsp?CNT=index.htm&FP=/content/products/weblogic/server/

[18] D. Bell and L LaPadula, Secure Computer System: Unified Exposition and Multics Interpretation, Technical Report, MITRE Corporation, March 1976

[19] E. Bertino, RBAC Models – Concepts and Trends, Computers & Security, Volume 22, Issue 6, August 2003

[20] Bertolino, A. and Polini, A. The audition framework for testing Web services interoperability. In Proceedings of EUROMICRO-SEAA, pages 134-142. IEEE Computer Society, 2005.

[21] A. Bertolino, L. Frantzen, A. Polini, and J. Tretmans. Audition of web services for testing conformance to open specified protocols. In Architecting Systems with Trustworthy Components, No. 3938 in LNCS. Springer-Verlag, 2006.

[22] Domenico Bianculli, Carlo Ghezzi, Paola Spoletini. "A model checking approach to verify BPEL4WS workflows". Proceedings of IEEE International Conference on Service-Oriented Computing and Applications (SOCA'2007), Newport Beach, US, June 2007, IEEE Computer Society Press, pp. 13-20. End.

[23] Bieberstein N, Bose S, FiammanteM, Jones K, Shah R, Service-oriented architecture compass: business value, planning, and enterprise roadmap. IBM Press, Lebanour, 2005.

[24] P.A. Bonatti, P. Festa, "On Optimal Service Selection", Proc.of the International World Wide Web Conference (WWW), 2005, pp.530-538.

[25] BPEL4WS 1.1, usiness Process Execution Language for Web Services version 1.1, http://www.ibm.com/developerworks/library/specification/ws-bpel/

[26] D. Brewer and M. Nash, the Chinese Wall Security Policy, Proceedings of IEEE Symposium on Security and Privacy, May 1989

[27] Marcello Bruno, Gerardo Canfora, Massimiliano Di Penta, Gianpiero Esposito, Valentina Mazza: Using Test Cases as Contract to Ensure Service Compliance Across Releases, In the 3rd International Conference In Service-Oriented Computing (ICSOC'05), pp. 87-100, Amsterdam, 2005.

[28] Brutzman, D., M. Zyda, M. Pullen, and K. L. Morse. 2002. Extensible modeling and simulation framework (XMSF): Challenges forWeb-based modeling and simulation. In Findings and Recommendations Report of the XMSF Technical Challenges Workshop and Strategic Opportunities Symposium, 2002.

[29] R.C. Bryce and C.J. Colbourn, One-test-at-a-time heuristic search for interaction test suites, Proc. Genetic and Evolutionary Computation Conference (GECCO-2007), London, England, July 2007, pp. 1082-1089.

[30] J. Burns and D.M. Martin, "Automatic Management of Network Security Policy", Proceedings of DARPA Information Survivability Conference and Exposition, June 2001

[31] Kai-Yuan Cai: Optimal software testing and adaptive software testing in the context of software cybernetics. 841-855, Information & Software Technology, Volume 44, Number 14, 1 November 2002.

[32] Kai-Yuan Cai, Yong-Chao Li, Ke Liu, "Optimal and adaptive testing for software reliability assessment," Information & Software Technologie, volume 46, December 2004, pp. 989-1000.

[33] G. Canfora and M. Di Penta, SOA: Testing and Self-checking, International Workshop on Web Services - Modeling and Testing (WS-MaTE'06), Palermo, Italy, pp. 3-12, 2006.

[34] G. Canfora and M. Di Penta. Testing services and service-centric systems, Challenges and opportunities. IT Professional, vol. 8, no. 2, 2006, pp. 10-17

[35] Mark Chang, Jackson He, W.T. Tsai, Bingnan Xiao, Yinong Chen, UCSOA: User-centric service-oriented architecture. In proceedings of IEEE International Conference on e-Business Engineering (ICEBE'06), Shanghai, October, pp. 248-255.

[36] J. J. Chelenski and S.P. Miller, "Applicability of modified condition/decision coverage to software testing", Software Engineering Journal, Sept. 1994, Vol. 9, No. 5, pp. 193-200.

[37] Liming Chen; A. Avizienis, N-Version Programming: a Fault-Tolerance Approach to Reliability of Software Operation, Twenty-Fifth International Symposium on Fault-Tolerant Computing, 1995, pp. 113-119.

[38] Yu-Liang Chi, Ming-Hung Tsai, Chih-Wei Lee, A Petri-Net based Validator in Reliability of a Composite Service, Proceedings of the 2005 IEEE International Conference on e-Technology, e-Commerce and e-Service (EEE'05), pp. 450 – 453, 2005.

[39] J. J. Chilenski, "An investigation of three forms of the modified condition decision coverage criterion", Report DOT/FAA/AR-01/18, Federal Aviation Administration, USA, April 2001.

[40] Fernando Cuervo, Michel Sim, "Policy Control Model: A Key Factor for the Success of Policy in Telecom Applications", in Proceedings Fifth IEEE International Workshop on Policies for Distributed Systems and Networks, 2004, pp. 223-228.

[41] Guilan Dai, Xiaoying Bai, Chongchong Zhao, A Framework for Model Checking Web Service Compositions Based on BPEL4WS, IEEE International Conference on e-Business Engineering (ICEBE'07)   pp. 165-172, 2007.

[42] N. Damianou, N. Dulay, E. Lupu, M. Sloman, *the Ponder Policy Specification Language*, Proceedings of Workshop on Policies for Distributed Systems and Networks, 2001

[43] N. Davidson, "Testing Web Services" at http://www.webservices.org/, in October 2002.

[44] Wim De Pauw, et al., "Websight Visualizing the Execution of Web Services", Workshop on Testing, Analysis and Verification of Web Services, Boston, MA, July 2004.

[45] B. De, "Web Services - Challenges and Solutions", WIPRO white paper, 2003, http://www.wipro.com.

[46] Murthy V. Devarakonda, Vijay K. Naik, Nithya Rajamani, "Policy-Based Multi-Datacenter Resource Management", in Proceedings 6th IEEE International Workshop on Policies for Distributed Systems and Networks (POLICY'05), 6-8 June 2005, Stockholm, Sweden, pp. 247-250.

[47] DNF, "Definition of Disjunctive Normal Form", available at http://mathworld.wolfram.com/DisjunctiveNormal Form.html.

[48] W. Dong, H. Yu, Y. Zhang. Testing BPEL-based Web Service Composition Using High-level Petri Nets. Enterprise Distributed Object computing Conference, EDOC 2006, pp.441- 444.

[49] D. Z. Du and F. Hwang, Combinatorial Group Testing And Its Applications, World Scientific, 2nd edition, 2000.

[50] S. Dustdar, S. Haslinger, Testing of service-oriented architectures - a practical approach, 5th Annual International Conference on Object-Oriented and Internet-Based Technologies, Concepts, and Applications for a Networked World, 2004, pp 97-109

[51] EBSOA, Electronic Business Service Oriented Architecture, available at www.oasis-open.org/committees/ download.php/9325/wd-ebsoa-047.pdf

[52] Ibrahim K. El-Far and James A. Whittaker, "Model-based Software Testing", Encyclopedia on Software Engineering (edited by J.J.Marciniak), Wiley, 2001.

[53] Empirix e-test http://www.empirix.com/

[54] Endrei M, Ang J, Arsanjani A, Chua S, Comte P, Krogdahl P, LuoM, Newling T Patterns: service-oriented architecture and web services. IBM Red Books, 2004.

[55] eValid, www.soft.com

[56] H. Foster, S. Uchitel, J. Magee, J. Kramer, Model-based verification of Web service compositions, Proceedings 18th IEEE International Conference on Automated Software Engineering, 2003, pp 152-61.

[57] H. Foster, S.Uchitel, J.Magee, J.Kramer,Compatibility Verification for Web Service Choreography, IEEE International Conference on Web Services (ICWS) 2004, San Diego, CA, July 2004.

[58] H. Foster, W. Emmerich, J.Kramer, J.Magee, D.Rosenblum and S.Uchitel, Model Checking Service Compositions under Resource Constraints, in Proceedings of ESEC/FSE 2007, Dubrovnik, Croatia. Sept 2007.

[59] L. Frantzen, J. Tretmans, and R. d. Vries. Towards model-based testing of web services, International Workshop on Web Services - Modeling and Testing (WS-MaTe2006), pp. 67-82, Palermo, Italy, June, 2006.

[60] freebXML, http://ebxmlrr.sourceforge.net/2.1/ebxmlrr-client.html

[61] Fu, C., Ryder,B.G., Milanova, A. and Wonnacott,D. Testing of Java web services for robustness. In International Symposium on Software Testing and Analysis, ISSTA, 2004:23-24.

[62] X. Fu, T. Bultan, and J. Su. Analysis of interacting BPEL web services. In WWW 04: Proceedings of the 13th international conference on World Wide Web, pages 621~630, New York, NY, USA, 2004. ACM Press.

[63] X. Fu, T. Bultan, and J. Su. WSAT: A Tool for Formal Analysis of Web Services. In Computer Aided Verification, 16th International Conference, CAV 2004, Proceedings, volume 3114 of Lecture Notes in Computer Science, pages 510~C514, Springer, 2004.

[64] X. Fu, T. Bultan, and J. Su. Model checking interactions of composite web services. UCSB Computer Science Department Technical Report (2004-05). (Available at http://www.cs.ucsb.edu/~su/tmp/Map2SPIN.pdf).

[65] Chunming Gao, Rongsheng Liu, Yan Song, Huowang Chen, A Model Checking Tool Embedded into Services Composition Environment, Fifth International Conference on Grid and Cooperative Computing (GCC'06.), pp. 355-362, 2006.

[66] J. Garcia-Fanjul, C. de la Riva,; J. Tuya, Generation of conformance test suites for compositions of Web services using model checking, Proceedings of the Testing: Academic & Industrial Conference on Practice And Research Techniques, 2006.

[67] J. Garcia-Fanjul, J. Tuya, C. de la Riva. Generating test cases specifications for bpel compositions of web services using spin, International Workshop on Web Services Modeling and Testing (WSMaTe), 2006.

[68] P. Groth, M. Luck and L. Moreau, "A Protocol for Recording Provenance in Service-Oriented Grids", Proc. of 8th International Conference on Principles of Distributed Systems (OPODOS'04), 2004.

[69] Heckel, R. and Mariani, L., Automatic conformance testing of Web Services, Proceedings of FASE 05: 34-48.

[70] R. Heckel and M. Lohmann. Towards contract-based testing of web services. Electr. Notes Theor. Comput. Sci., 116:145–156, 2005.

[71] High R Jr, Kinder S, Graham S, IBM SOA foundation: an architectural introduction and overview, Version 1.0, 2005.

[72] D. Hirtle, H. Boley, B. Grosof, M. Kifer, M. Sintek, S. Tabet, and G. Wagner, "Schema Specification of RuleML 0.91," http://www.ruleml.org/0.91/, 2006.

[73] Hoffman Coding Algorithm, available at http://www.csl.mtu.edu/cs2321/www/newLectures/Hoffman_Coding.html.

[74] HP Service Test, https://h10078.www1.hp.com/cda/hpms/display/main/

[75] H. Huang, W. T. Tsai and R. Paul, "Proof Slicing with Application to Model Checking Web Services", 8th IEEE International Symposium on Object-oriented Real-time distributed Computing (ISORC), Seattle, May 2005, pp. 292-299.

[76] H. Huang, W. T. Tsai, R. Paul and Y. Chen, "Automated Model Checking and Testing for Composite Web Services", 8th IEEE International Symposium on Object-oriented Real-time distributed Computing (ISORC), Seattle, May 2005, 300-307.

[77] H. Huang, R.A. Mason, Model checking technologies for Web services, Proceedings of Second International Workshop on Collaborative Computing, Integration, and Assurance (WCCIA'06), April 2006.

[78] IBM BPEL4J, http://www.alphaworks.ibm.com/tech/bpws4j

[79] IBM WebSphere UDDI Registry, http://www-128.ibm.com/developerworks/websphere/downloads/UDDIregistry.html

[80] IBM, Unit Test UDDI Registry, http://www.ibm.com/developerworks/websphere/library/techarticles/0305_liu/liu3.html

[81] IBM. "PLM: Product Lifecycle Management." http://www-03.ibm.com/solutions/plm/index.jsp

[82] IBM, IBM SOA foundation: providing what you need to get started with SOA. White paper, September 2005.

[83] IONA Interface Simulation and Testing Framework, www.iona.com/solutions/istf.htm

[84] jUDDI: http://ws.apache.org/juddi/

[85] L. Kagal, Rei: A Policy Language for the Me-Centric Project, Technical Report, HP Laboratories.

[86] L. Kagal, T. Berners-Lee, D. Connolly, and D. Weitzner, "Self-describing delegation networks for the Web," in Proceedings of Seventh IEEE International Workshop on Policies for Distributed Systems and Networks, London, Ont., Canada, 2006, pp. 205-214.

[87] L. Kagal, T. Berners-Lee, D. Connolly, and D. Weitzner, "Using Semantic Web Technologies for Policy Management on the Web," in Proceedings of 21st National Conference on Artificial Intelligence (AAAI), 2006.

[88] Andrew B. Kahng, Sherief Reda, Combinatorial group testing methods for the BIST diagnosis problem, Proceedings of the 2004 conference on Asia South Pacific design automation: electronic design and solution fair, pp. 113 – 116, Yokohama, Japan, 2004

[89] Kaplan, J. 2006. "Software-as-a-Service Myths." < http://www.businessweek.com/print/ technology/content/apr2006/tc20060417_996365.htm > (27 February 2007).

[90] Marcel Karam, Haidar Safa, Hassan Artail, An Abstract Workflow-Based Framework for Testing Composed Web Services, International Conference on Computer Systems and Applications, 2007.

[91] Karnaugh Map, "Definition of Karnaugh Map", available at http://en.wikipedia.org/wiki/Karnaugh_map.

[92] J. Koehler and B. Srivastava, "Web Service Composition: Current Solutions and Open Problems", ICAPS 2003 Workshop on Planning for Web Services, pp. 28-35.

[93] V. Kolovski, B. Parsia, Y. Katz, and J. Hendler, "Representing Web service policies in OWL-DL," in Proceedings of the 4th International Semantic Web Conference, ISWC 2005, Galway, Ireland, 2005, pp. 461-75.

[94] M. Koshkina and F. van Breugel. Verification of Business Processes for Web Services. Technical Report CS-2003-11, York University - Department of Computer Science, 4700 Keele Street, Toronto, M3J 1P3, Canada, October 2003.

[95] M. Koshkina, and F. van Breugel, "Modeling and Verifying Web Service Orchestration by means of the Concurrency Workbench", In Proceeding of 1st Workshop on Testing, Analysis and Verification of Web Services, 2004.

[96] Alexander Lazovik, Marco Aiello, Mike Papazoglou, Associating assertions with business processes and monitoring their execution, Proceedings of the 2nd international conference on Service oriented computing, New York, 2004, pp. 94 – 104.

[97] Li, B. H., X. Chai, et al. 2005. Research on service oriented simulation grid. In Proceedings of the 8th International Symposium on Autonomous Decentralized Systems (ISADS 2005), 2005, pp. 7–14.

[98] Z. Li, W. Sun, Z. Jiang, and X. Zhang. Bpel4ws unit testing: Framework and implementation. In 2005 IEEE International Conference onWeb Services (ICWS 2005), pages 103–110, 2005.

[99] A. Lomuscio, H. Qu, M. Sergot, M. Solanki. Verifying Temporal Epistemic properties of Web service compositions. Proceedings of the 5th International Conference on Service Oriented Computing (ICSOC07). Vienna, Austria. Springer LNCS Vol 4749, pp 456-461.

[100] N. Looker and J. Xu, "Assessing the Dependability of SOAP RPC-Based Web Services by Fault Injection", In Proc. of the 9th IEEE International Workshop on Object-Oriented Real-Time Dependable Systems (WORDS'03), 2003.

[101] N. Looker, M. Munro and J. Xu, "Testing Web Services", the 16th IFIP International Conference on Testing of Communicating Systems, Oxford, 2004.

[102] N. Looker, M. Munro, J. Xu, Simulating Errors in Web Services, International Journal of Simulation: Systems, Science & Technology, vol. 5, 2004

[103] Nik Looker, Malcolm Munro, Jie Xu, WS-FIT: A tool for dependability analysis of web services, Proceedings of the 28th Annual International Computer Software and Applications Conference, COMPSAC 2004, pp. 120-123.

[104] N. Looker, L. Burd, S. Drummond, M. Munro "Pedagogic Data as a Basis for Web Service Fault Models," In Proceedings of International Workshop on Service-Oriented System Engineering (SOSE'05), Beijing, China, 2005.

[105] LUA Programming Language, www.lua.org/

[106] Khaled Mahbub, George Spanoudakis, A framework for requirements monitoring of service based systems, ICSOC '04: Proceedings of the Second International Conference on Service Oriented Computing, 2004, pp. 84-93.

[107] Philip Mayer, Daniel Lübke, Towards a BPEL unit testing framework, Proceedings of the 2006 workshop on Testing, analysis, and verification of web services and applications, 2006

[108] Microsoft .Net Framework 3.0, http://www.netfx3.com/

[109] Microsoft Enterprise UDDI Services, http://www.microsoft.com/windowsserver2003/technologies/idm/uddi/

[110] Microsoft. 2006. "Microsoft Robotics Studio." http://msdn.microsoft.com/robotics/.

[111] N. Milanovic and M. Malek, "Verifying Correctness of Web Services Composition", Proc. of the 11th Infofest, Budva, Montenegro 2004.

[112] N. Milanovic, M. Malek, "Current Solutions for Web Service Composition", IEEE Internet Computing, Nov/Dec 2004, Volume: 8, Issue: 6. pp. 51- 59.

[113] P. B. Monday, Web Services Patterns: Java Edition, Apress, April, 2003.

[114] O. Mondragon, A. Q. Gates, and S. Roach, "Prospec: Support for Elicitation and Formal Specification of Software Properties", Electronic Notes in Theoretical Computer Science, O. Sokolsky and M. Viswanathan (eds.), 2004.

[115] B. Moore, E. Ellesson, J. Strassner and A. Westerinen, "Policy Core Information Model -- Version 1 Specification", IETF, RFC 3060, February 2001.

[116] J. Myerson, "Testing for SOAP Interoperability" at http://www.webservicesarchitect.com/, Feb 2002

[117] Shin Nakajima, Model-Checking Verification for Reliable Web Service, OOPSLA 2002 Workshop on Object-Oriented Web Services (OOWS'02), November 2002.

[118] S. Nakajima. Model-Checking Behavioral Specification of BPEL Applications. In Proceedings of the International Workshop on Web Languages and Formal Methods, WLFM 2005, 2005.

[119] S. Narayanan and S. Mcllraith, "Simulation, verification and automated composition of web services", In Proc. WWW, 2002.

[120] Dmitri Nevedrov, Using JMeter to Performance Test Web Services, http://dev2dev.bea.com/pub/a/2006/08/jmeter-performance-testing.html

[121] J.R. Norris. Markov Chains. Cambridge Series in Statistical and Probabilistic Mathematics. Cambridge University Press, 237 pp, 1998

[122] Novell Nsure UDDI Server, http://developer.novell.com/uddi/

[123] OASIS, "XACML 2.0 Specification," http://www.oasis-open.org/specs/, 2005.

[124] J. Offlutt, W. Xu, "Generating Test Cases for Web Services using Data Perturbation", ACM Sigsoft Software Engineering Notes, Vol 29, Issue 5, Sept 2004.

[125] Oracle   BPEL   Process   Manager, http://www.oracle.com/technology/products/ias/bpel/index.html

[126] Oracle JDeveloper, http://www.oracle.com/ technology/products/jdev/index.html

[127] OracleAS   UDDI   Registry, http://www.oracle.com/technology/tech/webservices/htdocs/uddi/ index.html

[128] S. Osborn, R. Sandhu and Q. Nunawer, Configuring Role-Based Access Control to Enforce Mandatory and Discretionary Access Control Policies, ACM Transactions on Information and System Security, Volume 3, Issue 2, May 2000

[129] Nardine Osman, David Robertson, Christopher Walton, Run-time model checking of interaction and deontic models for multi-agent systems, Proceedings of the fifth international joint conference on Autonomous agents and multiagent systems (AAMAS'06), pp. 238-240, 2006.

[130] OWL-S: Semantic Markup for Web Services, http://www.w3.org/Submission/OWL-S/

[131] Parasoft SOAPtest, http://www.parasoft.com/j

[132] B. Parsia, V. Kolovski, and J. Hendler, "Expressing WS Policies Using OWL," in Proceedings of Policy Management for the Web Workshop, Chiba, Japan, 2005, pp. 29-36.

[133] Chris Peltz, web ser vices orchestration: a review of emerging technologies, tools, and standards, 2003, http://xml.coverpages.org/HP-WSOrchestration.pdf

[134] Marco Pistore, Paolo Traverso: Assumption-Based Composition and Monitoring of Web Services. Test and Analysis of Web Services 2007: 307-335

[135] C. Pleeger, *Security in Computing*, 3rd Edition, Prentice Hall PTR, 2003

[136] Geguang Pu, Xiangpeng Zhao, Shuling Wang, and Zongyan Qiu, Towards the Semantics and Verification of BPEL4WS. In Proceedings of the International Workshop on Web Languages and Formal Methods, WLFM 2005, 2005.

[137] Pudhota, L.; Tierney, A.; Chang, E.; Services integration monitor for collaborative workflow management, Proceedings. Fourteenth IEEE International Workshops on Enabling Technologies Infrastructure for Collaborative Enterprises, 2005, pp. 201-206

[138] S. Rajbhandari and D. W. Walker, "Support for Provenance in a Service-based

Computing Grid", UK e-Science All Hands Meeting, 2004.

[139] REST, http://www.oreillynet.com/pub/wlg/3005

[140] REWERSE Policies and Rules, http://rewerse.net/I2/

[141] W.N. Robinson, "Monitoring Web Service Requirements," presented at 11 IEEE International Conference on Requirements Engineering, Monterey Bay, CA, pp. 65-74, 2003.

[142] William N. Robinson, "A requirements monitoring framework for enterprise systems," Requirements Engineering Journal, 11 (2006): 17-41.

[143] RuleML-powered Policy specification and interchange, http://policy.ruleml.org/, 2004.

[144] R. Sandhu, E. Coyne, H. Feinstein and C. Youman, Role-Based Access Control Models, IEEE Computer, Volume 29, Issue 2, February 1996

[145] SAP, "Life-Cycle Process Support with mySAP Product Lifecycle Management", available at http://www.sap.com/solutions/business-suite/plm/brochures/index.epx.

[146] SAP, "Enterprise SOA Governance, Security, and Life-Cycle Management", available at http://www.sap.com/community/pub/showdetail.epx?itemID=8978.

[147] SAP, "Enterprise SOA: Business Process Management and Process Modeling", available at http://www.sap.com/community/pub/showdetail.epx?itemID=10586.

[148] SAP, "Implementation Concepts: Enterprise SOA Design and Governance", http://www.sap.com/community/pub/showdetail.epx?itemID=11102.

[149] SAP's UDDI Business Registry Node: uddi.sap.com

[150] SCA, Service Component Architecture SCA Policy Framework, available at http://osoa.org/display/ Main/Service+Component+Architecture+Specifications.

[151] Ina Schieferdecker, Bernard Stepien, "Automated Testing of XML/SOAP based Web Services", In Proceedings of the 13th. Fachkonferenz der Gesellschaft fur Informatik (GI) Fachgruppe Kommunikation in verteilten Systemen (KiVS), Leipzig, Germany, Feb, 2003.

[152] B.-H. Schlingloff, A. Martens, and K. Schmidt. Modeling and Model Checking Web Services. Electronic Notes in Theoretical Computer Science: Issue on Logic and Communication in Multi-Agent Systems, 126:3–26, March 2005.

[153] B. Shafiq, A. Masood, and A. Ghafoor, "Policy-Based Verification of Distributed Workflows in a Multi-Domain Environment", technical report, https://www.cerias.purdue.edu/tools_and_resources/bibtex_archive/view_entry.php?bibtex_id=2969.

[154] Reda Siblini, Nashat Mansour, "Testing Web Services", Proceedings of the ACS/IEEE 2005 International Conference on Computer Systems and Applications, 2005.

[155] SIMPROCESS, http://www.simscript.com/products/simprocessKFTP.cfm

[156] M. P. Singh, M. N. Huhns, Service-Oriented Computing, John Wiley & Sons, 2005.

[157] A. Sinha and A. Paradkar, "Model based functional conformance testing of web services operating on persistent data," In Proceedings of workshop on Testing, Analysis, and Verification of Web Services and Application (TAV-WEB'06), pp. 17–22, 2006.

[158] Colin Smythe, "Initial Investigations into Interoperability Testing of Web Services from their Specification using the Unified Modeling Language," in Proceedings of International Workshop on Web Services Modeling and Testing (WS-MaTe2006), pp. 95-119, ITALY, 2006

[159] Saas, "Software as a service. " http://en.wikipedia.org/wiki/Software_as_a_Service.

[160] Software Acquisition Gold Practice, "Model-Based Testing", https://www.goldpractices.com/practices/mbt/

[161] Stylus Studio Web Service Tester, http://www.stylusstudio.com/ws_tester.html

[162] Sun Java WSDP Registry Server, http://java.sun.com/webservices/jwsdp/index.jsp

[163] Systinet, "Systinet Policy Manager," http://www.systinet.com/products/spm, 2005.

[164] A. Tarhini, H. Fouchal, N. Mansour, Regression Testing Web Services-based Applications, International Conference on Computer Systems and Applications, 2006, pp.163-170.

[165] Abbas Tarhini, Hacène Fouchal, Nashat Mansour, "A Simple Approach for Testing Web Service Based Applications", IICS 2005, LNCS 3908, pp. 134–146, 2006

[166] Towards OpenGrid Services Architecture. http://www.globus.org/ogsa/

[167] W. T. Tsai, R. Paul, Y. Wang, C. Fan, and D. Wang, "Extending WSDL to Facilitate Web Services Testing," In Proceedings of HASE 2002, pp. 171-172, 2002.

[168] W.T. Tsai, R. J. Paul, W. Song and Z. Cao: Coyote: "An XML-Based Framework for Web Services Testing". Proc. of IEEE HASE 2002, pp. 173-176.

[169] W. T. Tsai, R. Paul, Z. Cao, L. Yu, A. Saimi, and B. Xiao (2003), "Verification of Web Services Using an Enhanced UDDI Server", Proc. of IEEE WORDS, pp. 131-138.

[170] W.T. Tsai, R Paul, L Yu, A Saimi, Z Cao, "Scenario-Based Web Service Testing with Distributed Agents," IEICE Transaction on Information and System, 2003, Vol. E86-D, No. 10, Page(s): 2130-2144.

[171] W. T. Tsai, D. Zhang, Y. Chen, H. Huang, R. Paul, N. Liao, "A Software Reliability Model for Web Services" 8th IASTED International Conference on Software Engineering and Applications, Cambridge, MA, November 2004, pp. 144 - 149.

[172] W. T. Tsai, Y. Chen, Z. Cao, X. Bai, H. Huang, and Paul, "Testing Web Services Using Progressive Group Testing", Advanced Conference on Content Computing, Zhenjiang,

November, 2004, pp. 314-322.

[173] W.T. Tsai, Y. Chen, R. Paul N. Liao, and H. Huang, , "Cooperative and Group Testing in Verification of Dynamic Composite Web Services", in Workshop on Quality Assurance and Testing of Web-Based Applications, in conjunction with Proc. of IEEE COMPSAC, September, 2004, pp. 170-173.

[174] W. T. Tsai, "Service-Oriented System Engineering: A New Paradigm", IEEE International Workshop on Service-Oriented System Engineering (SOSE), Beijing October 2005, pp. 3 - 8.

[175] W. T. Tsai, X. Wei, and Y. Chen, "A Robust Testing Framework for Verifying Web Services by Completeness and Consistency Analysis", IEEE International Workshop on Service-Oriented System Engineering (SOSE), Beijing October 2005, pp.151-158.

[176] W. T. Tsai, X. Wei, Y. Chen, B. Xiao, R. Paul, and H. Huang, "Developing and Assuring Trustworthy Web Services", Proc. of the 7th International Symposium on Autonomous Decentralized Systems (ISADS), 2005, pp.43-50.

[177] W. T. Tsai, X. Wei, Y. Chen, R. Paul and B. Xiao, "Swiss Cheese Test Case Generation for Web Service Testing", IEICE Transactions on Information and Systems 2005 E88-D(12):2691-2698.

[178] W.T Tsai, X. Bai, Y. Chen, X. Zhou, "Web Service Group Testing with Windowing Mechanisms," IEEE International Workshop on Service-Oriented System Engineering (SOSE), Beijing October 2005, 213-218.

[179] W.T. Tsai, Dawei Zhang, Raymond A. Paul, Yinong Chen: Stochastic Voting Algorithms for Web Services Group Testing. QSIC 2005: 99-108, 2005

[180] W.T. Tsai, R. Paul, B. Xiao, Z. Cao, Y. Chen, PSML-S: a process specification and modeling language for service oriented computing. In: The 9th IASTED international conference on software engineering and applications (SEA), Phoenix, pp. 160–167, 2005.

[181] W.T. Tsai, Y. Chen, D. Zhang, H. Huang, "Voting Multi-Dimensional Data with Deviations for Web Services under Group Testing," Proc. of the 4th International Workshop on Assurance in Distributed Systems and Networks (ADSN), in conjunction with ICDCS-25, June 2005, pp. 65 - 71.

[182] W.T. Tsai, Y. Chen, R. Paul, H. Huang, X. Zhou, X. Wei, Adaptive Testing, Oracle Generation, and Test Script Ranking for Web Services," 29th IEEE Annual International Computer Software and Applications Conference (COMPSAC), Edinburgh, July 2005, pp.101-106.

[183] W. T. Tsai, , B. Xiao, et al. 2006. Consumer-centric service-oriented architecture: A new approach. In proceedings of IEEE 2006 International Workshop on Collaborative Computing, Integration, and Assurance (WCCIA), April, pp. 175-180.

[184] W. T. Tsai, B. Xiao, Q. Huang, Y. Chen, and R. Paul, "SOA Collaboration Modeling, Analysis, and Simulation in PSML-C", to appear in The Second IEEE International Symposium on Service-Oriented Applications, Integration and Collaboration

(SOAIC'06), October 2006.

[185] W. T. Tsai, Q. Huang, B. Xiao, Y. Chen, "Verification Framework for Dynamic Collaborative Services in Service-Oriented Architecture", 6th International Conference on Quality Software, Oct. 2006, pp. 313 - 320.

[186] W. T. Tsai, Yinong Chen, Ray Paul, Xinyu Zhou, and Chun Fan, "Simulation Verification and Validation by Dynamic Policy Specification and Enforcement," Simulation: Transactions of The Society for Modeling and Simulation International, May 1 2006, Volume 82, No. 5, pp. 295-310

[187] W. T. Tsai, Xinyu Zhou, Xiao Wei, A Policy Enforcement Framework for Verification and Control of Service Collaboration, Information Systems and E-Business Management, Springer, Sep, 2007.

[188] W. T. Tsai, Zhibin Cao, Xiao Wei, Ray Paul, Qian Huang, Xin Sun, Modeling and Simulation in Service-Oriented Software Development, SIMULATION, Vol. 83, No. 1, pp. 7-32, 2007.

[189] W.T. Tsai, Xinyu Zhou, Raymond A. Paul, Yinong Chen, Xiaoying Bai, A Coverage Relationship Model for Test Case Selection and Ranking for Multi-version Software, 10th IEEE High Assurance Systems Engineering Symposium (HASE'07), pp. 105-112, 2007.

[190] W.T. Tsai, Xinyu Zhou, SOA Simulation and Verification by Event-driven Policy Enforcement, to appear on 41th Annual Simulation Symposium, 2008.

[191] UDDI Version 3 Specification, available at http://uddi.org/pubs/uddi_v3.htm

[192] A. Uszok, J. M. Bradshaw, M. Johnson, R. Jeffers, A. Tate, J. Dalton, and S. Aitken, "KAoS policy management for semantic Web services," IEEE Intelligent Systems, vol. 19, pp. 32-41, 2004.

[193] C. Walton, Model Checking Multi-Agent Web Services, In Proceedings of the 2004 Spring Symposium on Semantic Web Services, Stanford, CA, USA, March, 2004.

[194] Web 2.0, Wikipedia, http://en.wikipedia.org/wiki/Web_2

[195] Web Services Description Language (WSDL) 1.1, http://www.w3.org/TR/wsdl

[196] WebInject, http://www.webinject.org/

[197] WEBSTRAR , http://asusrl.eas.asu.edu/webstrar/

[198] J. A. Whittaker and M. G. Thomason. A Markov Chain Model for Statistical Software Testing. IEEE Transactions on Software Engineering, 20(10):812-824, 1994.

[199] Wikipedia, "SOA Lifecycle", available at http://en.wikipedia.org/wiki/SOA_Lifecycle

[200] WSCA1.0, Web Services Conceptual Architecture, IBM Software Group, May 2001.

[201] WS-Policy, Web Services Policy 1.2 - Framework W3C Member Submission 25 April

2006, available at http://www.w3.org/Submission/2006/06/

[202] WS-PolicyConstraints, "XACML-Based Web Services Policy Constraint Language (WS-PolicyConstraints)", October 2005, available at http://research.sun.com/projects/xacml/.

[203] WSUnit, https://wsunit.dev.java.net/

[204] XACML-Based Web Services Policy Constraint Language (WS-PolicyConstraints), October 2005, available at http://research.sun.com/projects/xacml/

[205] Bingnan Xiao, W. T. Tsai, Qian Huang, Yinong Chen, Ray Paul, SOA collaboration modeling, analysis, and simulation in PSML-C. The proceedings of the 2nd IEEE International Symposium on Service-Oriented Applications, Integration and Collaboration (SOAIC 06), Shanghai, Oct.

[206] Pulei Xiong, Robert L. Probert, Bernard Stepien, An Efficient Formal Testing Approach for Web Service with TTCN-3 , In Proceedings of the 13th International Conference on Software,Telecommunications and Computer Networks (SoftCOM 2005), Split, Croatia, 2005.

[207] XMethods, SOAPBuilders Interoperability Lab, http://www.xmethods.net/ilab/.

[208] Xmlpsy, http://webservices.smlpsy.com/

[209] XMSF SAIC Web-Enabled RTI. 2003. http://www.movesinstitute.org/xmsf/projects/WebRTI/XmsfSaicWebEnabledRtiDecem ber2003.pdf (Accessed: 27 February 2007).

[210] W. Xu, "Generating Test Cases for Web Services Using Data Perturbation", Proc. of the Workshop on Testing, Analysis and Verification of Web Services, Boston, MA, July 2004, pp.144-149

[211] Wuzhi Xu; Offutt, J.; Juan Luo; Testing Web services by XML perturbation, 16th IEEE International Symposium on Software Reliability Engineering (ISSRE 2005), Nov. 2005.

[212] J. Yang and M. P. Papazoglou, "Web Component: A Substrate for Web Service- Reuse and Composition", Proc. of the 14th International Conference on Advanced Information Systems Engineering (CAiSE02), Toronto, Lecture Notes in Computer Science, Vol. 2348, pp 21-36. pp.21-36, Springer, 2002

[213] X. Yi and K.J. Kochut, "A CP-nets-based Design and Verification Framework for Web Services Composition", Proceedings of the IEEE International Conference on Web Services, March, 2004.

[214] Y. Yuan, Z. Li, and W. Sun. A graph-search based approach to bpel4ws test generation. In Proceedings of the International Conference on Software Engineering Advances (ICSEA 2006), page 14. IEEE Computer Society, 2006.

[215] Yongyan Zheng, Jiong Zhou, P. Krause, A model checking based test case generation framework for Web services, 4th International Conference on Information Technology

New Generations, 2007.

[216] X. Zhou, W. T. Tsai, X. Wei, Y. Chen, B. Xiao, Pi4SOA: A Policy Infrastructure for Verification and Control of Service Collaboration, The IEEE International Conference on e-Business Engineering (ICEBE'06), pp. 307-314, 2006

[217] H. Zhu, A Framework for Service-Oriented Testing of Web Services, 30th Annual International Computer Software and Applications Conference, 2006.

Wissenschaftlicher Buchverlag bietet

kostenfreie

Publikation

von

wissenschaftlichen Arbeiten

Diplomarbeiten, Magisterarbeiten, Master und Bachelor Theses
sowie Dissertationen, Habilitationen und wissenschaftliche Monographien

Sie verfügen über eine wissenschaftliche Abschlußarbeit zu aktuellen oder zeitlosen
Fragestellungen, die hohen inhaltlichen und formalen Ansprüchen genügt,
und haben **Interesse an einer honorarvergüteten Publikation**?

Dann senden Sie bitte erste Informationen über Ihre Arbeit per Email
an info@vdm-verlag.de. Unser Außenlektorat meldet sich umgehend bei Ihnen.

VDM Verlag Dr. Müller Aktiengesellschaft & Co. KG
Dudweiler Landstraße 125a
D - 66123 Saarbrücken

www.vdm-verlag.de

www.ingramcontent.com/pod-product-compliance
Lightning Source LLC
LaVergne TN
LVHW022309060326
832902LV00020B/3363